THE
QUESTION
BOOK

CONTRIBUTORS

Robert C. Andringa, Ph.D., Denver, Colorado
Bill Armstrong, Denver, Colorado
Stephen Arterburn, Laguna Beach, California
Jerry Ballard, Lit.D., Wheaton, Illinois
Anne Batty, San Clemente, California
Daniel Batty, Dana Point, California
Allan H. Beeber, Ph.D., Orlando, Florida
Denny Bellesi, Laguna Niguel, California
Bobb Biehl, Laguna Niguel, California
Nathan Birky, Indianapolis, Indiana
Dwight E. Bowers, Bristol, Indiana
Norman Bridges, Ph.D., Mishawaka, Indiana
Sue Cappelen, Bakersfield, California
George Caywood, Los Angeles, California
Paul A. Cedar, D.Min., Minneapolis, Minnesota
Juan Carlos Cobo, M.D., F.A.C.S., Laguna Niguel, California
Brian Cox, Santa Barbara, California
Scott J. Crabtree, Esq., Trabuco Canyon, California
Thomas L. Delahooke, CLU, ChFC, Pasadena, California
Steve Douglass, Orlando, Florida
John Erwin, Edina, Minnesota
Paul Eshleman, Laguna Niguel, California
Terry Fleck, Carmel, Indiana
Eric Floreen, White Rock, British Columbia, Canada
Kathleen Goble, Scottsdale, Arizona
Richard A. Goebel, DVM, Bristol, Indiana
Dave Golden, Bad Kreuznach, Germany
George R. "Chip" Grange II, Esq., McLean, Virginia
Ed Gruman, Monrovia, California
Don Guyer, South Laguna, California
David M. Harmon, Lubbock, Texas
Bruce S. Herwig, Esq., San Bernardino, California
Craig Holiday, San Juan Capistrano, California
John Charles Jackson, Austin, Texas
Bruce R. Johnson, Charlotte, North Carolina
Hal Jones, Honolulu, Hawaii
Douglas G. Kay, Fairfax, Virginia
Bob Kelly, Colorado Springs, Colorado
Joe Kimbel, Laguna Hills, California
Chuck Klein, San Diego, California
Dick Koeth, Irvine, California
Anne E. Lehman, Milwaukee, Wisconsin
Paul Lewis, San Diego, California
Lindy Lindelius, Costa Mesa, California
Ronald S. Loshin, San Leandro, California

Gordon D. Loux, L.H.D., Colorado Springs, Colorado
Jerry "Chip" MacGregor, Ph.D., Langley, British Columbia, Canada
Randall R. McCathren, Nashville, Tennessee
Susan P. McGann, Esq., South Laguna, California
Sue McMillin, Fairfax, Virginia
Greg McPherson, Leavenworth, Washington
Stanley H. Martin, Lubbock, Texas
John B. Mumford, Fairfax, Virginia
Maynard Munger, Walnut Creek, California
Lloyd Murray, St. Louis, Missouri
Roma Murray, St. Louis, Missouri
William L. Needham, Tallahassee, Florida
Joseph A. O'Connor, Jr., Laguna Hills, California
Archie Parrish, D.Min., Atlanta, Georgia
Bob Peters, Colorado Springs, Colorado
Duane Pederson, Hollywood, California
Terry B. Picklo, Tomball, Texas
Chuck Rathfon, San Juan Capistrano, California
Linda Rathfon, San Juan Capistrano, California
Dave Ray, Royal Oak, Michigan
Joel Robertson, Pharm.D, Saginaw, Michigan
Claude L. Robold, Middletown, Ohio
Norman B. Rohrer, Hume Lake, California
Ellen Roth-Wilson, Dana Point, California
Adele Schrag, Ph.D., Sun City West, Arizona
Douglas Shaw, Ph.D., Dallas, Texas
Cecily Shea, Houston, Texas
Bill Shepherd, Jr., Brunswick, Georgia
Doug Sherman, Little Rock, Arkansas
Donald E. Sloat, Ph.D., Grand Rapids, Michigan
Ray Smith, Des Moines, Iowa
Robert Smullin, San Juan Capistrano, California
John Snyder, Laguna Hills, California
Augustine A. Sodaro, Claremont, California
Brady Sparks, Esq., Dallas, Texas
Gregory L. Sperry, J.D., Brunswick, Georgia
Carole "Cich" Thaxton, Prague, Czechoslovakia
Ed Trenner, Orange, California
Glen T. Urquhart, McLean, Virginia
Dale Walters, Laguna Hills, California
Lewis M. Webb, Irvine, California
Bill White, Ph.D., Pittsburgh, Pennsylvania
Joe White, Ed.D., Branson, Missouri
Bill Wilkie, Ph.D, Grand Rapids, Michigan
Enoch Williams, Redlands, California
Kurt R. Winrich, Lake Forest, California
Steve Woodworth, Seattle, Washington

THE QUESTION BOOK

BOBB BIEHL

OLIVER
NELSON

THOMAS NELSON PUBLISHERS
Nashville

Published in Nashville, Tennessee, by Oliver-Nelson Books, a division of Thomas Nelson, Inc.

The Bible version used in this publication is THE NEW KING JAMES VERSION. Copyright © 1979, 1980, 1982, Thomas Nelson, Inc., Publishers.

Printed in the United States of America.

Library of Congress Cataloging-in-Publication Data

Biehl, Bobb.
    The question book / Bobb Biehl.
        p.   cm.
    ISBN 0-8407-9619-6 (pbk.)
    1. Life skills—United States—Miscellanea.   2. Decision-making—United States—Miscellanea.   I. Title.
HQ2039.U6B53   1993
302.3—dc20   93-12739
                                                                          CIP

1 2 3 4 5 6 — 98 97 96 95 94 93

Contents

Introduction

Why is asking questions such an important part of life?

We simply can't make clear distinctions without the use of questions! No distinctions! No decisions! No action! No wonder questions are such a powerful force. Without questions we would not—could not—take any action!

Ultimately, our ability to ask questions influences some critical areas:

- Communicating effectively
- Making decisions
- Creating visions for the future
- Setting goals
- Influencing people and policies
- Prioritizing
- Taking risks
- Delegating
- Solving problems

No problem in the world has ever been solved without a question or series of questions being asked first. *Learning to ask is a prerequisite to learning to think clearly.* If you are not able to ask questions, you will ultimately make cloudy distinctions, reach uncertain decisions, and take wrong actions.

Most questions seem to fall into one of ten categories. You may want to choose one type in which to specialize over the next few months and then work on another type until you have mastered the art of asking all ten types of questions.

Type of Question	Function	Example	How to Develop
1. Problem solving	Finding an unknown answer or solution.	Would you marry me?	Clearly define the problem, then ask questions around the problem to solve it.
2. Teaching	Teaching someone a new insight or thought.	Can you see advantages in being married?	Clearly understand the process involved. Ask questions to find the next logical steps.

3. Mind stretching	Considering new and creative dimensions of a situation.	What would it really be like to be married?	Artificially change the context of the problem. Create an imaginary context for the situation under consideration.
4. Inner searching	Starting an introspective process.	Why do I want to get married?	Just keep asking why.
5. Logic checking	Keeping from making unnecessary and obvious mistakes.	Is there any reason we shouldn't get married?	Collect questions you can keep on a list to ask yourself before any major decision.
6. Prioritizing	Defining the most important items or steps.	Which of the three girls should I marry?	Choose the most important from the many possibilities.
7. Conversation making	Passing information and passing the time of day.	Did you hear that Tom and Sue got married?	Decide what you want to talk about and begin asking questions to find out information you want to know or share.
8. Researching	Collecting basic data.	Are you married?	Decide what you want to know and what you will do with the information, then ask.
9. Rhetorical questioning	Making a more emphatic point.	How do I love thee? Let me . . .	Take one of your statements. Ask it as a question for oratorical emphasis.
10. Manipulating	Trapping a person into *your* perspective.	What single word describes the process by which a man and a woman are joined together in a church for life?	Ask questions with only one possible answer—yours.

Let me urge you to make asking questions a lifelong hobby. It's as simple as the following steps:

1. Decide to!
2. Mark your trail. Whenever you ask a good question, write it down and then file it in a notebook. Whenever

you hear or are asked a good question, write it down in the same way.

3. Read lots of articles on the subject of interest. You may even choose to write on the subject.

4. Experiment constantly with new questions and combinations of old ones and new ways of asking them.

5. Learn to master the attitude of asking. Be one who seeks to know and help, not one who seeks to coerce and manipulate.

Business

Buy a Business

The decision to buy a business is made by a small percentage of people. It involves negotiating, patience, and skill. You need every bit of knowledge you can acquire for this purpose. This list includes some of the things you need to know.

1. How much is the business really worth?
Use your CPA to determine the value of the business. Businesses are usually valued by a multiple of earnings or sales, which will vary by industry. Your CPA can tell you the guidelines to use in determining the purchase price.

2. Is the business profitable?
The owner should furnish tax returns or audited statements indicating how well the business has done. A lack of willingness to furnish this information is a sign of trouble. Do not accept the response that the business made money, but the owner put cash in his pocket. A minimum of three years' tax returns and financial statements should be required.

3. How can I compare the business to similar ones in the same industry?
To find out how a business compares with others, ask your banker for Robert Morris Associates (RMA) industry standards for the business. The RMA guidelines will tell you what is considered a good profit for that type of business and what operating expenses should be.

4. Do I have adequate capital to purchase the business?
Will the business have funds to operate for six months or a year if it is not profitable? One of the greatest causes of new business failures is lack of working capital. Usually, it will take longer than you think for the business to be profitable.

5. Is the seller in a big hurry?
Don't let the seller set your timetable. A seller in a big hurry

may be hiding information. Take all of the time necessary for due diligence and being satisfied with your purchase.

6. Is the present owner willing to provide financing?
If the owner is willing to provide financing, it is a sign the owner has confidence in the business. Owner financing may make your purchase much easier.

7. What are the contingent liabilities?
There may be long-term lease obligations or employment contracts that you should review before making your decision.

8. Is the business consistent with my code of ethics?
Check to see if the business has any practice or sells any product that would be inconsistent with your personal code of ethics.

9. Does the business provide an adequate return on the investment?
Consider the amount of money you are paying for the business. Will your annual net profit be more than you would receive if your money were in a savings account or invested in rental property?

10. Does it take everything I have to purchase the business?
Picture how you would feel if you lost everything you own. If it takes all that you have to buy the business, is it worth it?

— OTHER QUESTIONS TO CONSIDER —

11. What is the future of the industry?

12. Is the business right for me?

13. What are the qualities of the assets?

14. Am I aware of all debt owed by the business?

15. Will there be debt I am expected to pay after I purchase the business?

16. What is the structure of the customer base?

17. Will the business require the help of family members?

18. How much time will the business require?

19. Does it sound too easy?

20. Is the purchase of the business consistent with my long-term goals?

David M. Harmon is a senior vice president at Lubbock National Bank in Lubbock, Texas. He has served on the faculty of the Southwestern Graduate School of Banking at Southern Methodist University and he frequently speaks to organizations on banking-related issues.

— 2 —

Change Corporate Image

When deciding to make changes in the image of your corporation, you are communicating to your public that you have examined how you appear and it's not the way that you want to be seen. It involves the painful process of corporate self-examination, recognizing a better way and embracing your new image with confidence.

1. What is our current image?
This is the first question to ask before you decide to make any changes. Ask it of yourself as a leader and then of your management team, board, employees, corporate friends, customers (donors), and the end users of your product or service if they are different from your customers (donors).

2. Is our current image what we have historically been?
Once again, ask yourself first, then ask all of those significant people listed in the first question. You will then have an excellent opportunity to familiarize yourself with your corporate roots.

3. **Have there been changes in the marketplace that warrant a reevaluation of our current image?**
   You may not have left your market, but it may have left you. It may have changed its attitudes and preferences and is about to pass you by. In short, have you stayed in touch with what is going on around you? For example, there is renewed interest in the environment. Since it appears to be a major cultural/social change, you should take it into consideration.

4. **If there have been changes in the marketplace, what have we done to adapt?**
   Adaptation is keenly linked to your company's ability to survive and thrive. But adaptation can come only if your level of awareness is high.

5. **What have we done to communicate that we have changed?**
   If you have seen the need for change and adapted, what have you done to signal your public that you have heard them and have responded? It's not enough to adapt. You need to communicate with a view toward updating the perceptions of your public.

6. **How do we want to be seen?**
   You need to determine exactly *how* you want to be perceived. Once you have done that, you should develop strategies to communicate your priority message(s).

7. **What internal steps should we take before we go public?**
   Be certain that your board and management team have all had the opportunity to

   - understand the difference between who you are as a company and who you are in your public's perceptions.
   - sort out the issues surrounding the disparity of reality versus perception.
   - take joint ownership of the problem.
   - commit to correcting the problem.
   - communicate your position to all employees in their area of responsibility.

8. **What mechanisms are available to us for communicating our message?**

Consider the following:

- Press conferences
- Offer of exclusive stories to selected media
- Speeches
- Articles written by management
- New products or services unveiled at trade shows
- Carefully chosen endorsements
- A carefully selected spokesperson

9. **How do we ensure that we maintain the communication of our new message?**
   Develop specific strategies for the communication mechanisms. Be sure to include time lines and frequency of exposure to your public.
   For example, you might place twelve monthly ads in the most widely read trade journal in your market. Feature your new priority message in this ad. Vary the approach but communicate the same message month after month.

10. **How do we ensure that we are communicating what we intend to?**
    Research is beneficial prior to developing a new corporate image, and it can be useful after you have made a change. A third party survey can be helpful.

— OTHER QUESTIONS TO CONSIDER —

11. **Does our current image accurately reflect who we are now?**

12. **Is who we are now what we intended to be?**

13. **How does the public perceive us?**

14. **What is our priority message?**

15. **How can we begin to change the public's perception of us?**

16. **How should we take our message to the public?**

17. **When should we take our message to the public?**

18. **Who should present the message?**

19. Was the message understood and received?
20. Where can I get help with this process?

Douglas Shaw, Ph.D., vice president of the Stratmark Corporation, Dallas, Texas, a strategic planning and direct-response marketing firm, has consulted with over forty not-for-profit organizations through the United States and Canada over the past twelve years. He has helped raise over $100,000,000 for major national health care organizations, relief and development organizations, private schools, colleges, graduate schools, rescue missions, publishers, and overseas missions organizations.

— 3 —

Establish a Telemarketing Service for a Company or an Organization

Telemarketing may be an effective tool to increase the sales, services, or promotion of a business. However, too many people view telemarketing as a magical tool. A number of tough questions must be objectively addressed before moving ahead with a telemarketing/teleservicing strategy.

1. **What has been done before within your type of industry?**
   Hunches and intuition may be correct, but you must check your hypotheses against historical facts. Do the research necessary to learn who and what has been done before in applying telemarketing concepts to your particular industry. Look for success stories *and* failures; you can learn from both.

2. What is the product or service you are selling?

If you are selling products or services, you are describing telemarketing. However, if you are part of a nonprofit group offering a free service, it would fall into a category I term *teleservicing*.

3. What would success look like?

What measurements would spell success (short-, medium-, and long-term) to you and to the company leaders? In a for-profit organization, profitability/sales may be key. In a nonprofit organization, success may be measured much differently. Perhaps the number of people using the service or involved in fulfilling the goals of the organization is key. Visualize success and put some numbers to it.

4. Should it be outbound or inbound telemarketing/servicing?

With outbound telemarketing/servicing, you use lists of possible customers and aggressively prospect. With inbound telemarketing/servicing, you rely on different types of publicity and/or public relations to motivate interested people to call you. Costs may vary widely depending on the approach chosen. Both inbound and outbound telemarketing strategies have their pros and cons, and a growing number of books are available on the subject.

5. Should you use an 800 number or a toll number?

The cost for toll-free 800 numbers continues to drop. However, it can still be a major expenditure depending on the length of the phone calls and time of day. Because of a limited budget or a desire to filter out those who are not very interested in your product/service, you may want to use a regular toll number. Often you can ask the phone company for digits whose corresponding letters spell the name of your company or service (or some suitable acrostic).

6. What are potential problems?

Balance is the key. Don't spend too much time attempting to figure out all the problems you may encounter. It is far better to launch a small experiment using your best hunches coupled with research than to sit for days thinking of all possible contingencies. However, as problems arise, often the best solutions will come from your employees.

7. How do you know when something has failed?

Measurable goals are critical. Failure can actually be a blessing if you learn from the mistakes. Experimentation on a small scale is critical with each new development of a telemarketing/servicing strategy. Objective analysis of the failure may lead you to conclude that further effort is futile or that refinement may be necessary to turn the experiment into a success.

8. How do you determine who is your best audience?

Many telemarketing ventures fail because the leaders neglect to analyze the audience. Audience research must include questions that ascertain if there is a true *felt* need for the product/service, which segments of the general population are most interested, what are the best media and messages to communicate with these particular segments, and so on.

9. Are you meeting real or felt needs?

This area is tricky. With some products, you may be dealing with real needs, such as a piece of machinery that will increase production, yet costs less to operate than previous models. With other products, you may be dealing with felt needs, such as people wanting to project an image of success with the clothes they wear. With others, people may need guidance to accomplish something deeply felt, such as learning how to minister to other people in the community when trained workers are not available.

10. Do you have a program enabling you to continually survey your audience?

You must set up a continual program of surveying your target audience(s). Not only do you want to make sure that you are using the best medium to motivate them to use your service, but you also want to know if their real/felt needs are changing. If they are, you need to make the necessary changes quickly. Also, you want to know if your telemarketing representatives are doing a good job over the phone.

— OTHER QUESTIONS TO CONSIDER —

11. What is the attitude of the leaders within the company to the idea?

12. What quick wins are possible?
13. How determined are you to see success?
14. What are your strengths and weaknesses?
15. What should your short-, medium-, and long-term goals look like?
16. What type of personnel is necessary?
17. What are your plans for growth?
18. Have you planned to run experiments with each new strategy?
19. Is your audience sufficiently segmented?
20. What training needs to be done with your phone representatives?

Allan H. Beeber, Ph.D., is the designer and director of Student LINC. This innovative teleservice concept within the Campus Ministry of Campus Crusade for Christ, Orlando, Florida, is resource-intensive rather than staff-intensive. Over the past five years the strategy has resulted in growth from 1 to over 162 campus ministries directed by just thirteen staff members from a central location. Dr. Beeber has consulted with numerous ministries in the U.S. as well as overseas on how to employ the LINC concepts to accelerate their growth, have greater impact, and work more efficiently.

— 4 —

Form a Business Partnership

A man once said, "The happiest day of my life was when I purchased my motor home. The second happiest day of my life was when I sold it." Many former partners feel the same way. Considering whether to form a partnership is a critical decision. The following twenty questions may help you as you make your decision.

1. Do I need a partner?

Is it absolutely necessary that you have a partner? If you can go it alone, you will find the road much smoother. You will enjoy the freedoms that a partnership cannot allow.

2. Have I considered a corporation?

In a corporation you can own controlling interest by owning 51 percent. You can still have other investors. In a general partnership there is no absolute authority. Decisions are by consensus.

3. What kind of buy-sell agreement will the partnership have?

A rigid buy-sell agreement can work for you or against you. It may be best to leave some room for negotiation at the time a partner wants out. You may find yourself paying too much to a departing partner or selling too cheap when you want out.

4. Who will be authorized to borrow money?

You may authorize one or both partners to sign to borrow money. If you authorize one partner to sign for the debt, both partners remain liable for the debt.

5. Will I have exposure to other liabilities?

In a partnership, your partner may create liabilities for which you will be responsible.

6. Should I be a limited partner?

Limited partnerships are the least desirable. Limited partners have no control. The Internal Revenue Service looks very carefully at limited partnerships.

7. Should I be a silent partner?

A partner who provides investment capital but is not involved in the business on a daily basis is headed for trouble. You must be on the job to protect your investment.

8. What type of partnership agreement should I have?

Have an attorney draw the partnership agreement. Before

you do, look at a few model agreements from successful partnerships.

9. What if my partner has financial problems?
A partner with financial difficulties could cause difficulty for the partnership. If your partner has assigned his or her interest to a creditor, the creditor could become your partner.

10. Why should I consider forming a partnership?
A partner can add stability to your income stream, expand your customer base, and provide coverage for you when you need time off.

— OTHER QUESTIONS TO CONSIDER —

11. Will the partnership have debt?

12. What if my partner becomes lazy?

13. What are the chances the partnership will last?

14. What type of accounting should the partnership have?

15. What kind of partner should I have?

16. What if my partner dies?

17. What if my partner is disabled?

18. What if my partner quits?

19. Can I trust my partner to take care of my family in the event of my death?

20. How will the lender view the partnership?

David M. Harmon is a senior vice president at Lubbock National Bank in Lubbock, Texas. He has served on the faculty of the Southwestern Graduate School of Banking at Southern Methodist University, and he frequently speaks to organizations on banking-related issues.

Hire a Marketing, Public Relations, or Fund-Raising Agency

As organizations grow, they face the necessity of hiring outside help to support the marketing function. Even companies that already use advertising or public relations agencies are routinely faced with the question of whether to change agencies. The following questions will help anyone facing a decision about outside marketing, fund-raising, or public relations support.

1. **Has the agency reviewed your business and made a presentation?**
   It is customary for an agency to make a formal presentation, including its new ideas for your business. The more specific the ideas, the better able you will be to decide if the agency seems creative and able to understand your needs.

2. **What does the agency feel it can do for you?**
   Ask for projections of *measurable* results.

3. **What services does the agency offer?**
   You may at first be interested only in advertising, but a full-service agency could later help you with public relations, strategic planning, or other support.

4. **Who is selling you?**
   The more senior the agency person, the more the agency wants your business. If the leaders sent a junior staffer, watch out. Your business is not important to them.

5. **Who would work on your account?**
   Senior people are important. If new people are involved or

they are not yet hired, you are taking a big risk. They have no track record at the agency.

6. **Do you like the people?**
   You'll be working closely with them. Life is too short to work with people you don't like.

7. **How often will they visit your offices?**
   You want them to get involved in your business, but you don't want to pay for excessive meetings. Once or twice a month is enough.

8. **Do the agency representatives have other experience of immediate benefit to you?**
   One of the biggest benefits of an agency is that it has experience with multiple clients. Look for an agency that has experience with your target market or a similar product or cause. You'll get more for your money.

9. **How does the agency charge?**
   Most charge a fixed fee, a commission, or both.

10. **How will you review performance?**
    Work out the review process in advance, and do it on a regular basis. Quarterly reviews are essential at first because both sides will be working out bugs. An agency should never be surprised at being fired.

— OTHER QUESTIONS TO CONSIDER —

11. **What do you really need?**
12. **What agencies are available?**
13. **Have you interviewed two or more agencies?**
14. **In what areas does the agency excel?**
15. **How does the agency present itself?**
16. **How successful have the agency's clients been?**
17. **Is the agency growing?**
18. **What new accounts has it acquired recently?**
19. **What accounts has it lost in the last year?**
20. **Who on your staff will manage the agency?**

Steve Woodworth is a partner in the Thomas Group, a Dallas-based company specializing in implementing change in large companies to improve competitiveness. Before joining the Thomas Group, he spent twelve years with World Vision, the Christian relief and development organization; he served there as vice president for marketing. He resides in Seattle, Washington.

— 6 —

Market a Product or Service

Marketing a product or service is an exciting and re-warding process. The purpose of marketing is to connect those who have specific needs with the organizations that have the right answer to those needs. Successful marketing begins with needs, not a product or service. If there is not a sizable, pressing need for the product or service, even a brilliant marketing plan can fail. But if there is a vast unsatisfied need for your product or service, often a medio-cre marketing program can be successful.

1. **Who needs your product or service? Why?**
   Few products or services appeal to everyone. Identify the specific types of people or organizations that should be the most excited about what you have to offer. Why do they have this need? Are enough of these people out there? What have you learned from current customers? The more you understand the real needs you are meeting, the more suc-cessful you will be.

2. **Are people confused about your product or service?**
   If people are confused about a product or service, they will

make poor decisions or no decision. How can you simplify the process and help people make wise choices? Look at the words and images you are using, and eliminate anything that is confusing or overly complicated.

3. **How much time will you invest in marketing planning?**
Time is your most limited resource. The time you invest in marketing *planning* is critical. In today's era of rapid change and swift competitive response to good ideas, planning must be constant. Have a dynamic marketing plan that is updated often. Check your assumptions based on real-world feedback. Get out of your building and mingle in the marketplace. Develop good street-smarts.

4. **How many dollars will you invest in marketing?**
If you have a fixed budget for marketing, you'll lose. Marketing is an agent of change. Marketing will accelerate either success or failure. Your marketing budget will require some fixed costs, but your total budget should be built on a variable formula. A percentage-of-revenue formula is usually the easiest. If sales go up, the budget goes up. If sales go down, the budget goes down. Keep in mind that it always takes more to launch a new company or new product. Extra front-end investment is required. Adjust your budget at least quarterly.

5. **What can you do to increase awareness of your product or service with your target audience?**
Before you can increase sales, you have to increase awareness with the target audience. It's hard to gain new customers if they don't know who you are, what you have to offer, what the value is for the time/dollars they have to spend, and so on. Do you know your current awareness level? If not, consider some market research to sample current awareness levels. You can then go back and measure your awareness months later and find out what marketing has done to change your awareness. What are your ideas for increasing your awareness within your budget and time limits?

6. **What is the most effective way to build awareness for your product or service?**

Out of all the ideas you listed in response to question five, what single idea appears to be the most effective? Select a cost-effective and message-effective idea. Some options may be inexpensive, but the message they deliver may not be right (e.g., promotion of a new church on matchbook covers isn't a good idea). You won't have enough money to do all you want to do, so put money in the area that will do the most good. Repetition is vital. Avoid putting a large share of money into one-shot approaches (it is better to run three small space ads than only one large space ad).

7. **How can you increase appreciation of what you have to offer?**

People will be investing time as well as money with you. Whether they buy once or repeat again is based on their perceived trade-off of time and money versus the benefits they receive. If they don't perceive enough benefits, they will look elsewhere. Since perception wins out over reality, be sure you are communicating the value of your product or service as clearly as possible.

8. **What is your central message?**

If a customer will give you a half hour, keep an open mind, and eliminate all distractions, you may have a good chance to sell something. The problem is, you won't have this much time. In many cases you have only a few seconds to get a customer's attention and build interest in finding out more. You need the strongest possible core message to turn disinterest into active interest. Develop several alternatives for your central message, and test them on your target audience. When you find one that works, *repeat, repeat, repeat it,* even though you may be bored with it. Your customers and prospects don't live and breathe your product or service like you do. If you have something significant to offer, make sure it is communicated in a significant way.

9. **What shortcuts could weaken your marketing?**

Flashy marketing programs often get center stage, but some of the most successful programs receive hardly any notice. Being flashy is not a substitute for covering all the bases. If you take a shortcut or leave out an important step, you are inviting disaster. Develop a countdown checklist before launching a new program. Many of the questions here should be on the checklist. Avoid getting carried away with the potential sizzle while the meat of your program decays.

10. Will success spoil you?
It's ironic that many organizations fail after they have become huge successes. What happened? Usually, the organization gets overconfident and loses the drive and determination that got it to the top. A major sign of impending decline is foolish tinkering with the formula that got it there. To stay successful, stay in tune with the market. When others see your success, they are already working on ways to capitalize on what you have done. Be open to needed change, but stick to your knitting as much as possible.

— OTHER QUESTIONS TO CONSIDER —

11. What are the five most important benefits you offer?

12. What is the greatest benefit you offer?

13. What are the current alternatives?

14. What do people dislike about the alternatives?

15. What is your mission?

16. What are your three most important marketing goals you would like to accomplish within three years?

17. What are the three greatest obstacles to success?

18. How can you overcome the obstacles you listed?

19. What can you do to make your product or service more available to your target audience?

20. Who is on your marketing team?

Dick Koeth has a diverse background in marketing and communications and currently is the president of Koeth & Associates, Inc., a marketing consulting firm in Irvine, California. His experience includes work for Campbell Soup Co., Pepsi, Bristol-Myers, Alcoa, Lipton, Pet, Inc., Times Mirror Cable Television, and many others. He has also helped nonprofit organizations communicate their causes more effectively.

Sell a Business

Selling a business can be an opportunity or a disappointment. The more knowledge you have, the better prepared you will be to get the most for your business. These twenty questions may help you decide if you really want to be a seller.

1. Will I enjoy working for someone else?
Selling your business increases the possibility you will need to work for someone else. You should weigh the pros and cons of how you will feel about this outcome.

2. Will selling the business improve my financial situation?
If you sell the business, will you have less debt to worry about? Does meeting a monthly or weekly payroll cause you stress?

3. Should I provide financing?
Providing financing may have some tax advantages for you. Only provide financing if you are receiving a down payment of 30 percent or more. Keep in mind that if you provide financing, there is a 50 percent chance you may have to take the business back.

4. What are the tax implications for me?
Have your CPA provide different scenarios of your potential tax liability. Be aware of the capital gains taxes you may owe.

5. Should I list the business with a broker?
If you list the business with a broker, visit with other clients the person has represented. See if they were satisfied. Make sure the broker has a good track record and is not out to make a fast buck. Compare the broker's fee with that of other brokers.

6. What is a reasonable selling time?

One year would be a normal and reasonable marketing period. If you are in a hurry, you will not get the best price. It is not unusual for a good business to take two years or longer to sell.

7. How should I market the business?

In most cases, you will want to be discreet in letting others know the business is for sale. This is one reason for using a broker. You may advertise through trade publications or blind newspaper ads.

8. Will I be employed by the business?

It is not unusual for the business owner to work in the business under the new owner. Are you interested in continuing as an employee?

9. Do I want an employment contract?

If you plan to stay after the sale, you may want a contract for a specific period of time. It will protect you in the event of a dispute or early termination.

10. Am I willing to sign a noncompete agreement?

The buyer will want you to sign an agreement not to compete in the same business. It may limit your options in future business ventures.

— OTHER QUESTIONS TO CONSIDER —

11. What will I accomplish by selling my business?

12. What is my business worth?

13. Should I represent myself?

14. What does the future hold for my business?

15. Am I willing to subordinate my debt?

16. What about my employees?

17. Is the buyer paying for goodwill?

18. Will I be protected from the buyer's mistakes?

19. Am I satisfied with the character of the buyer?

20. How will I invest my money?

David M. Harmon is a senior vice president at Lubbock National Bank in Lubbock, Texas. He has served on the faculty of the Southwestern Graduate School of Banking at Southern Methodist University, and he frequently speaks to organizations on banking-related issues.

— 8 —

Start a Business

The decision to start a business has probably crossed everyone's mind at one time or another. In my opinion there is no more complicated and humbling a decision in life. A person should go through many considerations before embarking on such a venture. If someone asked my opinion about whether or not to go into business, these are the twenty questions I would ask.

1. **Have you thought about the possibility of the venture failing?**
   Fifty percent of start-ups fail the first year; 50 percent of the remaining ones fail before the end of the second year. That's 75 percent in two years, and seventeen out of eighteen don't make it eight years. With odds like that, you should give at least a little thought to the venture failing.

2. **In your estimation, what will be the biggest problem in running a business?**
   People. Any other answer is wrong.

3. **Do you tire easily? How do you handle stress?**
   Running a business takes loads of energy day in and day out, 365 days a year, and you have to cope with tons of stress.

4. How easily do you make decisions?

Running a business means making decisions, many decisions. If you have a hard time with a few small ones, you will certainly have much trouble with many.

5. Have you ever been told that you should run your own business?

My experience is that truly successful businesspeople have been told by others early in their careers that they should eventually own a business. Not mom or dad but someone who knows and can recognize the special mix of ingredients indicating business success.

6. Do you have a background as a leader?

To succeed in your business, you must be a people person, a team player who doesn't care who gets the credit. In fact, you must gain some sort of satisfaction in others' accomplishments. A lot of people from public corporations don't fully grasp the fact that when you own a business, you will be working with the same people the rest of your career. You must be able to lead.

7. Are you planning to have partners?

I'm 100 percent against having partners who do not share the same beliefs, and if possible, try to avoid having partners. My experience has been that after about five years, all partners want out and are unhappy until they do get out.

8. If someone would offer you 25 percent more money to work for another firm, would you still want to start your own business?

If the answer is not an emphatic yes!!, don't start your own business.

9. Do you have a business-owner mentor who will share wisdom from time to time?

Running a business is a very complex endeavor. You really don't want to talk to people who guess about how you do it. You want to talk to people who have done it successfully (for at least ten years). Successful business owners are different— not better, but different. If most people would rather be their own boss, why do so few successfully become their own boss? It must mean that successful ones are different, and you want their advice.

10. **What will be your biggest shortcoming in running this business?**
Being able to state your shortcoming shows how prepared and/or how naive you are. You must have a plan for dealing with this shortcoming.

— OTHER QUESTIONS TO CONSIDER —

11. **How is your relationship with your spouse and kids?**

12. **Can you be a good businessperson and retain your integrity?**

13. **What books have you read about starting this or any other business?**

14. **What demographic studies or sources do you have showing the available market?**

15. **Have you tested your abilities with a management testing service so as to understand your strengths and weaknesses?**

16. **Do you have a history of problem solving?**

17. **How have you taken care of your personal finances?**

18. **Have you completed a pro forma five-year income statement, balance sheet, cash flow forecast, and proposed organizational chart?**

19. **Why do you feel you should start your business?**

20. **What specific market niche are you aiming for?**

Dave Ray has been an owner/CEO for over twenty years. His companies, which are based in Michigan and cover a broad base of business expertise, include Dave Ray & Associates, Inc.; George Instrument Company, Inc.; GIC Thermodynamics, Inc.; and Custom Wiring Harnesses, Inc. Dave has a staff of over fifty people and does annual business in excess of $10,000,000.

Turn Around a Financially Troubled Organization

Regrettably, many businesses have been in trouble, and more will be. As a result of various factors, owners and managers eventually realize things aren't going well. Soon payroll and payables become a real burden. Business in general gets worse—employees leave, and vendors place the company on "cash only" terms. Then the owner or manager finds you and asks what should be done. You should ask several basic questions before committing the time and energy required for a turnaround effort.

1. **Should the business or enterprise continue?**
   Some businesses should not continue for many reasons. Perhaps the product or service is obsolete. Or the work force and market have been allowed to degenerate to the point that starting over completely is the best option. Others may have a debt load that excludes profitability or success.

2. **Is the emphasis right?**
   Discover whether or not the company emphasizes the right service or product for which it is best suited. Sometimes companies think their best product is one that is less profitable than another given less emphasis. Look at the company itself. Is the emphasis on making profits or on providing a quality service or product from which a profit will necessarily follow?

3. **Can the company become financially solvent?**
   In a turnaround situation, everyone must pitch in and help.

Are some units or personnel not making the necessary sacrifices for success? Are the necessary financing and vendor pool in place or potentially attainable? Does adequate market potential exist for the product or service?

4. Is the enterprise willing to face the truth?

Do individuals involved recognize that there is trouble and that help and change are necessary? If a principal thinks everything is okay, yet the employees are ready to walk, no amount of additional resources or help will resolve the real issues. The need must be seen and backed by a desire for positive change.

5. What is the commitment level to a turnaround?

Most people are committed to making whatever they are doing successful. However, some people are the proverbial "nine-to-fivers" who will never do more than that. The football game or whatever else may be more fun and may take precedence. Make sure a commitment to work long hours and to sacrifice is there to make what needs to happen, happen.

6. Is there a will to turn around and stay that way—to always espouse good business principles?

A long-term commitment to the vision of the company must be present. The reasons that caused the problem in the first place must be permanently changed. For example, if an owner has a life-style the business cannot support and bleeds the company to death with personal draws, the practice must be modified permanently for the long-term health of the business.

7. Does the organizational structure reflect the necessary framework for the enterprise to be successful, or are changes needed?

In some cases, something as simple as the way a company is organized defies logic and success as well. A structural change may be necessary. Make sure that this is a possibility within the organization.

8. What are the business relations with the local community, banking, accounting, and legal services?

Good relationships are absolutely essential to the success of a business. If there are broken relationships or burned bridges, repair them where possible. New relationships must be formed if reconciliations are unattainable.

9. **Are adequate outside resources available and affordable for a maximum recovery period?**
The banking or financial backing, personnel, raw materials—the host of things necessary for a successful enterprise must be available or acquirable for the duration of the projected recovery period and beyond. The physical plant and/or buildings along with machinery and equipment must be adequate or acquirable through purchase or relocation.

10. **What are the marketplace dynamics of the organization?**
Most organizations have similar or competing enterprises in the marketplace. What is the position of the subject? How does the product or service compare to others? Is it a high-quality product or service? Is there a positive track record in some area of the enterprise that can be enhanced or built upon? Determine the marketplace dynamics and decide if there is a foundation or business base that warrants the amount of energy required for a turnaround.

— OTHER QUESTIONS TO CONSIDER —

11. **Is merging an option?**
12. **Is there integrity?**
13. **Are the leaders committed to a turnaround or to personal gain?**
14. **Is there a spirit of cooperation and flexibility?**
15. **Are the administrators and employees competent?**
16. **Is there sufficient existing personnel for a turnaround management team?**
17. **Is the company prepared to formulate and implement a long-term plan and strategy for success?**
18. **Is the information for decision making available?**

19. Are the visible images right?

20. Are employees open to needed changes?

Nathan Birky is the publisher of Wesley Press, Indianapolis, Indiana. In addition to starting two successful businesses in the construction and recreational vehicle industries, he has led a turnaround in publishing. Under his supervision, red ink has turned to black, and printing and catalog orders are now completed and shipped in days instead of weeks. New customers are satisfied, and old customers are returning.

— 10 —

Work with a Commercial Artist

Searching for, selecting, and working with a commercial artist or design firm can be confusing and frustrating. How and where do you begin? What should you expect? Unlike buying a product that is uniformly manufactured en masse like a car, refrigerator, or lawn mower, each project brought to a commercial artist is unique. The following twenty questions will help you in the process of choosing and working with the right commercial artist.

1. **What should I consider when starting to look for a commercial artist?**
   You must first understand exactly what you want before you begin. You also need a clear-cut time line, due date, and an idea of how much money you have to spend.

2. How do I find the best commercial artist for my project?
Ask yourself if you know anyone who could recommend an artist or a design firm to you. Also, if you've seen a logo you like, received in the mail a brochure or catalog that's attractive, or just been impressed by someone's business card, call the person or the company on the phone and ask about who designed it. You may also want to ask about the cost on that project.

3. Does the artist have a portfolio of work I can review?
A portfolio more than anything else will give you a good idea if this artist is the right one for your project or not. Look at style and range of projects to see if your likes and dislikes would be compatible.

4. What kind of clients does this commercial artist or design firm have?
Are they all giant corporations with a giant budget for each project? Are all of the clients in one field, or is there a great variety? Using the artist's past and present clients as a measure, see if you feel you would fit with them.

5. What is this commercial artist's experience?
Find out if the artist specializes in graphics, illustration, or concept work. Can the person deliver specific elements of the project or every part of it?

6. Do the artist and I communicate well with each other?
Are you clear? Explain yourself and your thoughts clearly to see if the artist understands. Do you feel that you connect? Does the artist take notes or write ideas as you speak?

7. Does the artist place a greater value on the work than the goals of your project?
You want the artist's opinions and impressions, but you must find someone who realizes you are the boss. The artist must not place the value of the work or even personal opinion over the ultimate goal or end of your project.

8. Is this an isolated project, or will I work on a series of them?
Determine if this is a one-time project or if you want to work

together to come up with a plan or series of projects. Ask yourself if you could see yourself working long-term with this commercial artist or firm.

9. **How many revisions and changes are included in the artist's price?**
   What is the exact number of rough designs you'll see? Find out if you can see a second set. Ask if you can make one, two, or three sets of changes on the final art boards or work. If more than first-agreed-upon changes are needed, how much will they cost?

10. **If my project involves printing of any kind, who will handle that?**
    Decide if the artist will do it all from start to finish or just provide you with camera-ready artwork to take to the printer. If the artist takes it to a printer for you, you might want to find out how the person is marking up the print cost.

— OTHER QUESTIONS TO CONSIDER —

11. **How busy is this artist's schedule or work load?**

12. **Do the artist's style and strengths suit the goals of my project?**

13. **What is my first impression of the artist?**

14. **What is the cost of the project?**

15. **What is the breakdown of the quote?**

16. **What is the payment schedule?**

17. **Have I established a specific time line and due date on this project?**

18. **How involved will I be in each step of the project?**

19. **When my project goes to a printer, can I do a press check (review it before quantity printing begins)?**

20. **Who owns the rights to the logo/character/slogan that was paid for?**

Lindy Lindelius is the founding partner of Design Asylum, a Costa Mesa, California, based screenprint and graphics firm. Clients that have come to Design Asylum for the unique and creative approach to design and graphics include Disney, Masterplanning Group International, Mattel Toys, and Carl's Jr. Restaurant chain.

Career

Become an Attorney

In our highly litigious society it's not surprising that so many young people decide to become attorneys. Contrary to a common misconception that attorneys primarily litigate, many attorneys never step foot in a court of law and have no desire to do so. Before deciding to become an attorney, you should focus not only on the daily responsibilities of an attorney but also on your personality. Do you have the inner strengths to deal with the constant conflicts between society's often misguided interpretation of the law and the constitutional premise upon which all laws are based?

1. **What are your perceptions of an attorney?**
   The focus of your desire to become an attorney should be based not on society's or television's image and purported life-style that an attorney leads but on the deep-rooted desire to serve society. You must believe that you can and will make a difference. Venturing into the legal profession believing anything less will likely prove discouraging.

2. **What motivates you to become an attorney?**
   Your motivation in becoming an attorney should be focused on the protection of the rights and freedoms of society and not on personal conceptions of wealth and status. The pursuit of material goals, though they may be achievable, can lead only to consternation and frustration.

3. **Are you willing to accept the responsibilities associated with the practice of law?**
   The legal practice is founded on the premise that an organized society can exist only through the fair and responsible application of the law. An attorney not only enjoys the ultimate power but carries the ultimate responsibility for personal actions.

4. Do you have the unbiased objectivity required to effectively counsel the public in the law?

You need the ability to objectively discern both sides of a particular situation. This ability, which is not prevalent in most people, is critical to the legal adversarial process. An understanding of this principle is essential to the successful practice of law.

5. Do you enjoy expressive writing?

Attorneys do an extensive amount of writing. You must enjoy and be proficient in expressive writing. Although it represents only one of two primary forms of expression, it represents the most common form of communication in the legal community. Even a litigating attorney communicates to the court more through written briefs than oratory.

6. Are you analytical?

Ferreting out the factors required to make legal determinations requires certain analytical abilities. This trait can be a positive as well as a negative. A balance is essential because of time constraints often placed on an attorney.

7. Are there any present limitations in your family or your professional or personal life that could interfere with your goal of becoming an attorney?

Most aspiring attorneys proceed directly from undergraduate studies into law school. Although that is the preferred course of action, it, too, can be affected by external forces such as family needs. That is not to say that law students must cut themselves off from society. If you are aware of an impending matter that will require a material part of your attention, you may be prudent to schedule your admission into law school around it if at all possible.

8. Are you willing to withstand the pressures of the Socratic form of teaching?

In most law school courses you will interact with your professor often. Basically, the premise of the Socratic form of teaching is learning through your mistakes. There should be no doubt that good law professors will find even the most undetectable weakness in your class preparation and capitalize on it. This is no place for ego, and your success will directly depend on how well you handle the pressure.

9. **What form of practice most interests you—private, corporate, or government?**
   These are the primary forms of practice available to attorneys in today's market. The significance of the type of practice you desire primarily affects the law school you select and the level of academic achievement you set for yourself. For better or for worse, many of the most prestigious law firms require as a minimum that you graduate from a prestigious law school. Thus, you should consider this fact if you seek this form of practice.

10. **Which state do you want to practice in?**
    Every state in the United States has different licensing requirements for the practice of law. All are surmountable, but you would be well-advised to attend law school in the state you are most likely to practice in initially. Once you complete five continuous years of practice, you can petition to other states to be licensed there or if necessary take their bar exam.

— OTHER QUESTIONS TO CONSIDER —

11. **Do you possess the strength and morals necessary to advise people when such advice may not be consistent with their objectives?**

12. **Are you considering becoming an attorney because of pressures from your family?**

13. **Are you comfortable with public speaking?**

14. **Do you have the self-discipline required to endure law school?**

15. **Are you willing to devote three to four years of your life after undergraduate studies to law school?**

16. **What undergraduate studies have you pursued or are you planning to pursue?**

17. **What area of legal specialization interests you the most?**

18. **What law schools are you considering?**

19. **How are you planning on paying for the costs of law school?**

20. **Are you willing to sacrifice in personal ways for law school?**

Scott J. Crabtree, Esq., attorney for an independent oil and gas company in southern California, began his career with the U.S. Department of Treasury in Houston, Texas. His practice encompasses a variety of legal issues, including tax, securities, oil and gas and employment law, and corporate and transactional matters.

— 12 —

Change Career Path

Making a major career change is emotionally challenging since it affects your personal and professional lives. There are benefits to be gained and certainly losses to be avoided. As Peter Drucker once said, "When the facts are clear, the answers jump right out." These twenty questions are designed to guide you through a process bringing clarity to critical career issues.

1. **What is your long-term or mid-term career goal?**
   Take time right now and write down your mid-term and/or long-term career goals, as best you see them today. What are you trying to accomplish with this move? Will this career change enhance skill development and experience? Will this career change move you toward your long-term and/or mid-term career goals?

2. **What phase or life cycle of business do you find most enjoyable?**
Every industry, product, and company has a unique life cycle. From past experience and temperament, which life cycle do you enjoy most? Do you enjoy the design phase, the development and expansion phase, the administration and management of a mature market, or a turnaround situation? Seek an industry and a company that complement these styles.

3. **How will this career change affect you?**
Are you and your family in balance? If not, what can you do? Would waiting and staying focused on the basics be best for you and your family? Consider the following areas: marriage and family; social; friends; physical; personal career development; and spiritual. Think in terms of one to three years and also in terms of five to ten years.

4. **What is the corporate culture like?**
Are there open, honest communications and a team spirit, or is the company a political beast? Is it a tightly managed family-run business or a privately held autocratic firm? Take time to know and understand the corporate culture and how you and your personality will fit in.

5. **What assumptions are you making about your present work situation and this new opportunity?**
Check out each assumption for truth and accuracy with your spouse and a friend who is "in the know." Is the market and/or product maturing rapidly with a lot of government regulations, or is it a new industry that is emerging with almost unlimited gross margin potential?

6. **How are the interpersonal relationships with the key people you'll interface with?**
Realize that 85 percent of job changes are due to poor working relationships, not a lack of skills and qualifications. If you would not feel comfortable having your colleagues be with your family, take a hard second look.

7. **What do you fear about this potential opportunity?**
Make an exhaustive list and share it with a few close friends and your spouse.

8. **What skills will you need to develop or sharpen?**
   What are your developmental needs, and how will they be addressed? How will you sharpen up these new skills, and how much time will it take? Share these facts with your potential employers in an open and frank conversation.

9. **What does your new employer expect you to do exceptionally well?**
   Really understand in what and where your employer expects you to shine. Maybe you need exceptional selling skills and diligence for paperwork and administrative details.

10. **Who are the major players in the industry or business?**
    Identify companies and consumers. Get firsthand information from the key companies and consumers. You'll have two advantages: (1) you'll establish your network within the industry, and (2) you'll get the inside track of the positives and negatives of the product and/or company.

— OTHER QUESTIONS TO CONSIDER —

11. **What are your major strengths?**

12. **Are you willing to make a lateral move?**

13. **Is anything holding you back in your professional life?**

14. **Why are you considering changing your present work situation?**

15. **What doors would this new position open or close for you?**

16. **What are you risking in making this move?**

17. **What would your three closest friends say about this move?**

18. **Is your spouse involved in the interviewing process?**

19. **What is your spouse saying about the career change?**

20. **Do you have peace of mind about this decision?**

Robert Smullin has been involved in the high-tech medical industry for the past eleven years in sales, sales management, and marketing. During this time he has made four strategic career moves. Leveraging experience, newly acquired skills, and even failure, he continues to contribute to his profession and is recognized as a top performer. He has helped pioneer the equipment used for innovative surgical procedures for ophthalmic surgery, and he has worked with such companies as Cooper Vision Surgical Systems, Allergan, and Storz Surgical.

— 13 —

Choose a Career

Choosing a career is the most significant investment of your life and time that you will make. The selection of a career field obviously will determine what you will be doing during this time, what kind of life-style you will enjoy, and your level of fulfillment. However, few will select a career field and stay with it for their entire adult lives. The average person graduating from college today will have four separate careers and several jobs with each career. As a result, your criteria for career selection will be very important to you. Choose wisely! Here are some questions to ask that may help.

1. **What contribution would I like to make to others?**
   No amount of money will offset a career that is not fulfilling. You will be most fulfilled when you know you are in a career that makes a contribution to society and you know your efforts are important to that contribution.

2. **Do I have the proper training to make that contribution?**
   Find out the education and training needed to be an asset to the career field you are considering. In a time of rapid technological change, continuing education will likely be significant to you.

3. **Am I prepared to pay the price the career will demand of me?**

This question is not simple. You must ask yourself what kind of time and emotional energy will be required in light of your commitment to nonwork responsibilities.

4. What is the work environment that allows me to do my best?

Do you like working inside or outside? Do you like a fast pace or a slower, more steady routine? Do you like change or predictability?

5. Where will I be in this job in ten years?

Picture your position, your income, and your responsibility ten years from now. Would you be content with what you envision?

6. Will a person I respect in the career be willing to talk to me about it?

Look for someone with gray hair in the career or company you are interested in. The person can provide a wealth of wisdom about what you would be expected to do and what the career might hold for you. Find out the good and the bad. Every job has both.

7. What would the ideal boss look like?

Do you need structure, or do you need lots of freedom? Can you work with a boss who is fairly autocratic, or do you need a more participative style of leadership from your supervisor? Should you be on your own?

8. What are the ethical challenges I will face?

To find this out, you need to talk to an ethical person in the prospective career field. The more you can find out ahead of time, the better you can prepare yourself to keep your integrity.

9. What is the reputation of the company I am interested in?

Go to the library and get help in researching articles and information about the company. Find out its reputation among the critics.

10. What is the market for the product the company offers?

Some products have a short-lived life span. Some high-tech companies have products that can become obsolescent in a few years. Your future is tied to the company, so know something about its future.

— OTHER QUESTIONS TO CONSIDER —

11. Do I need to have increasing levels of responsibility to be happy?

12. What kind of people will I be working with?

13. What would an average day look like in this career?

14. What kind of nonwork life would I have?

15. How much travel would I be comfortable with?

16. Am I open to moving around the country?

17. What are the annual sales of the company over the last few years?

18. In what ways will my job challenge me?

19. What weaknesses could hinder me in this job?

20. What strengths would make me an asset to this company and career?

Doug Sherman is the founder and president of Career Impact Ministries, Little Rock, Arkansas. He is the author of five books (over 150,000 copies in print), including *Your Work Matters to God* and *Keeping Your Head Up When Your Job's Got You Down*. Doug is a nationally recognized speaker. Over the last decade, hundreds of thousands of business people have benefited from his practical solutions to work challenges.

Enter the Military

All five branches of our military (army, navy, air force, marines, and Coast Guard) recruit through advertising that promises a challenging and exciting environment with unlimited opportunities for personal growth. Every year thousands of young men and women accept the challenge to be all they can be. Unfortunately, some find out too late that the timing was not right or they were not cut out for the military. The following questions can assist you in making the decision about whether to enter military service.

1. What do I expect to get out of military service?

Military ads and recruiters focus on fast action, challenge, travel, self-discipline, personal development, and educational funds for college. With personal effort you will build self-confidence, experience the thrill of success, and develop a deep understanding of teamwork. But there is more. Military service is often a gateway to future plans. How does military service fit into your plans?

2. What will the military require of me?

Talk with men and women who have served in the military. Most will give you a fair assessment of what you can expect. Don't rely just on a recruiter for your information. In fact, the best recruiters will encourage you to ask around and get a variety of views and opinions.

3. How well do I accept authority?

Everyone struggles with authority. However, the most successful people in the world learn how to live under authority and to exercise authority. Despite all your good intentions, you will not grow and excel in the military if you distrust and rebel against authority.

4. Am I willing to pay the price?

There is no free lunch. You will live in an authoritarian, demanding environment. Sometimes you will have great leaders. Other times you will have to endure and persevere through poor leadership. And make no mistake about it, the military trains and exists for war.

5. Have I talked to significant people in my life about entry into the military?

If you are married, your spouse must be involved in this decision because it directly affects his or her life. In fact, military life requires a commitment from the spouse, too. Young single adults should be at least willing to consider parents' observations. If you are entering the military to get away from home, remember that geographical distance does not provide emotional separation or heal family wounds.

6. What do I believe about killing human beings?

Somewhere in the sorting-out process you need to address this question. Many try to ignore the issue. However, basic training in all branches of the service teaches you the skills necessary to take another person's life.

7. Am I prepared to let someone else intimately run my life for awhile?

This may sound like the question on authority, but it has a different twist. Throughout basic training, the drill sergeant will tell you what to do and when to do it. You will be told when to get up, what to wear, how to wear it, when to eat, and when to go to sleep. The only control you will have is in your choice of attitude and how well you accomplish what you are told to do. It does get better, but even generals receive and must obey orders.

8. Do I like physical exercise?

If you truly dislike to exercise, forget the military. Even after basic, the army and marines require daily physical exercise, often early in the morning. On the positive side, the military provides free physical training facilities that will rival some of the most expensive health clubs. Additionally, you will have the opportunity to enjoy a wide variety of intramural sports to include worldwide, interservice competition.

9. **How well do I deal with boredom?**
Everyday military life is not quite like the recruiting ads. There are short periods of exciting action and demanding challenges. But they are interrupted by long periods of routine, repetitious work, and training that can become very boring.

10. **Am I willing to be a team player?**
Some people are natural loners who do best working for themselves. Military service is a team effort that requires interdependence. Working with and helping others are absolute necessities. You will be unhappy in the military if you work well only by yourself and feel uncomfortable in a life-style requiring close coordination, interdependence, and supervision.

— OTHER QUESTIONS TO CONSIDER —

11. **What do I want to do with my life?**

12. **Am I willing to commit myself for the number of years required on the contract?**

13. **Are my spouse and I prepared for short and long separations?**

14. **Is my spouse prepared to move away from home?**

15. **Have I prayed about this major decision?**

16. **What kind of spiritual support will my home church provide me?**

17. **Can I serve in the military and serve the Lord at the same time?**

18. **Can I tolerate unpleasant weather and outdoor conditions?**

19. **Women should ask, "Am I prepared to live in a male-oriented and -dominated environment?"**

20. **Have I read the fine print in the enlistment contract?**

Dave Golden is currently the division chaplain of the First Armored Division, Bad Kreuznach, Germany, where he is responsible for the pastoral supervision of thirty-one chaplains. A Vietnam veteran with more than twenty-one years in the army chaplaincy, he spent seventeen years in direct ministry with soldiers and their families. He is now serving his third tour in Germany.

— 15 —

Invest in a Multilevel Marketing Business

Income diversification is truly a necessity in the times in which we live. Multilevel marketing has become for many a viable means to diversify and create additional residual income. However, looking for and choosing the right company, one you can depend on long-term, can present challenges. One of those challenges, for instance, can be that multilevel marketing is perceived as an illegal pyramid. It is important to note the difference between the illegal pyramid structure and the legal multilevel business. Illegal pyramids typically allow headhunter fees for signing up (recruiting) distributors; multilevel marketing does not. Illegal pyramids allow one to buy in at certain levels bypassing others who perhaps could not invest as much capital; multilevel marketing allows advancement only through achievement. Perhaps most important to note, however, is that illegal pyramids will not last—state and federal regulators will shut them down. Watch for the longevity of the multilevel business. If the business you're considering has been in business for more than a decade and has been stamped with approval by appropriate agencies, it is proba-

bly okay. The following list of twenty questions will prepare you to evaluate the opportunities that are available today.

1. **Does the company boast of being a ground-floor opportunity?**
   Be leery of this statement. In multilevel marketing, you should be interested in a long-term business. If you cannot make the same opportunity statements five years from now as you can make today concerning the potential for growth, what you are doing is short-term, not long-term.

2. **Who owns the company?**
   You need to study and investigate the owners of the company, their track record, their integrity in business dealings, and their reputation in the business world. You must exercise due diligence in this area. Be on the alert for owners who are on their third or fourth multilevel company.

3. **What is your original investment to get started, and what is that money for?**
   A serious problem in multilevel marketing is front-loading: you are required in the beginning to buy a large amount of product to inventory. This is usually done because a company is undercapitalized and needs immediate cash for growth. Be sure that the product reaches the hands of consumers—there must be customers to be a legal business.

4. **Are you being offered a bonus just for signing up another distributor?**
   It is illegal according to the regulators to pay or receive a sign-up bonus or a headhunter fee. Money is to be made on the movement of product.

5. **Is the entry level the same for all who get started?**
   In a legal multilevel marketing business, everyone starts at the same place. You can't buy in according to a dollar amount, and you should be able to pass or become more successful than your sponsor dependent only upon your effort, not upon the amount of your financial investment. Otherwise you could possibly be dealing with an illegal pyramid structure.

6. **Is the company run by a board of corporate owners as well as a group of successful distributors?**

   Many companies fail to create accountability between the distributor force (sales force) and corporate management. Without this, promises are made and not kept. Communication breaks down, morale becomes low, and soon it becomes an attitude of us against them. Distributors need to feel as though they have a voice in the direction of the company.

7. **Are the income statements being made those of the people who are making the income?**

   Be on the alert for statements of large amounts of dollars made rapidly. New companies boast of making five- and six-figure incomes per month after a short time in business. Legal multilevels take time, even years, to build. Also, the regulators frown on anyone who quotes the incomes of others for credibility.

8. **Do you have a training program that can be duplicated by all types of people?**

   Many people feel that building a multilevel marketing business takes a certain type of person. You must find one that has a proven record of success, with the opportunity to hear from many of the people whose success has come from a system that works—not because of certain personalities.

9. **What happens to the downline if a distributor you sponsor quits?**

   Some companies choose to take the downline of the distributor who quits, therefore invalidating any reason to work in depth under your personal sponsorship. Make sure that in the event of a distributor leaving the business, the group will move up to you, not to the company.

10. **What will happen to your network when you die?**

    Multilevel marketing appeals to so many people because of the residual income. They can work hard for a period of time and enjoy not only a good income but an even greater commodity, time. These people don't want to work hard for a number of years to lose all they have worked for when they are gone. Get the company's printed material on what will happen to your business when you are gone. Get legal advice about the material, and make sure you understand it.

— OTHER QUESTIONS TO CONSIDER —

11. **Does the company have a track record, or is it a start-up company?**

12. **What is the company's financial condition?**

13. **Does the company meet all Federal Trade Commission guidelines and regulators' guidelines for this type of business?**

14. **What is the product line?**

15. **Is the product approved by all necessary regulators?**

16. **What is the company policy concerning buybacks for customers who are dissatisfied or distributors who quit?**

17. **Can you sponsor a distributor out of state or out of the country?**

18. **Does the system have a support team of successful people who are willing to get involved in your success?**

19. **Does this system function only locally?**

20. **Is there a limit to the size of your business or to the income potential?**

Craig Holiday is founder and owner of Holiday Consulting International, San Juan Capistrano, California, with his wife, Carole. They have been involved in multilevel marketing, associated with a $3.1 billion company as one of their top producers, for over twelve years. Craig and Carole established International Networking Association for the purpose of teaching and training the technique of multilevel marketing.

16

Work with Inner-City Residents

It is my experience in my years at Union Rescue Mission that an increasing number of people find joy and purpose in serving inner-city residents. If you are considering joining an organization designed to help others, these questions may guide your decision.

1. **Do you feel called to this career?**
   A clear call corroborated by circumstances in your life can sustain you in the tough times. Without a call, you can be driven out by trial. With a call, you are obligated to stay until called away.

2. **Would a decision to work with this organization be responsible?**
   Have other people for whom you are responsible been given a voice in this decision? Have you really heard their concerns?

3. **Is this a just organization?**
   Do the staff treat the clientele with love and respect? Do they work to promote a balance in ethnic groups, between races, and in men and women in terms of numbers and authority of staff?

4. **Does the organization have financial integrity?**
   Ask to see financial statements. Ask an accountant to interpret them for you if you need help.

5. **What standard of maintenance do you see in the facilities?**
   Poor maintenance may be the best that can be done in some situations. It may also represent a lack of administrative ability or careless attitude.

6. **Are you comfortable with the stated purpose of the organization?**
   If the organization does not have a statement of purpose, it may not know what God has called it to do.

7. **What are the goals of the organization?**
   Do the goals promise fulfillment of the statement of purpose in a way that satisfies you?

8. **As you interact with employees, do you get a sense that the organization empowers its people?**
   Ask if the organization pays for ongoing training. Do employees have adequate equipment with which to work?

9. **Do your gifts match this job?**
   People are happiest when they work in jobs that line up well with their gifts.

10. **Are you called?**
    The first question deserves to be repeated and answered. Sometimes a person is called into a very negative work situation. If that's the case, decide with the weaknesses of the organization in full view.

— OTHER QUESTIONS TO CONSIDER —

11. **Is this decision cheerfully made?**

12. **Are you aware of your motives in wanting to help others?**

13. **Do you believe that helping others will make you happy?**

14. **How does the organization "feel" when you're there?**

15. **Are clear measurable objectives in place?**

16. **Is there evidence that the salary structure rewards good performance?**

17. **Are you qualified for the job offered?**

18. **If you work in marketing or administration, are those departments second-class citizens?**

19. **Are you comfortable with your direct supervisor?**

20. **Are you comfortable with the level of service provided?**

George Caywood is president of Union Rescue Mission in Los Angeles, California. As president and CEO, he is a visionary offering innovative approaches to solving problems of chronic homelessness. He is one of the nation's leading experts on the subject of homelessness and its related conditions. He is a consultant to missions across the nation and the author of the book *Escaping Materialism*.

Construction

17

Build a Church

It's a sad fact that multiplied millions of dollars have been spent needlessly because people who did not have a proper knowledge of church buildings went ahead with building programs. I hope that these questions will help some persons preparing to build!

1. **Have you thought of the advantage of bringing in an outside consultant?**
   The few bucks it will cost may save much more in the years to come. Remember, you have ideas, but some of them may be very biased, and you need to look at all the options that a man or woman of experience can bring.

2. **What will happen if you don't do a thing?**
   The cost of laissez-faire is something no one doing the Master's business can afford. Yield not to *that* temptation! God has a real reward for those who believe Him and move ahead.

3. **Could you purchase an existing building instead of building from scratch?**
   Purchasing an existing structure often costs less than building a new one and often has the advantage of plenty of parking. A building does *not* have to have stained glass or an elaborate tower to be a church building. *Much* can be done to make an interior pleasant, livable, and worshipful. After all, the church is not the building—it's people!

4. **Are you and yours aware of the "80 percent of full" rule?**
   People will *not* continue to attend where they feel hemmed in or where they get claustrophobic. When any area or room in your building becomes 80 percent (or more) full consistently, look out! *Do* something!

5. Have you considered the "form follows function" rule?

Frank Lloyd Wright was pretty smart! There *are* ways that you can design a building to follow the necessary functions it must have. So many church buildings of the past were profuse with great columns, stained glass windows, buttresses, vaulted ceilings, and so on whose main purpose was to be awesome. We cannot afford such luxury these days.

6. Do you really need an architect?

There are good ones and bad ones. In some states you may get by without hiring someone registered with the American Institute of Architects. Check out the person's work. Talk to those who have used him. Let him know your expectations concerning costs. If he rebels . . . says it can't be done . . . *maybe* you need to look elsewhere. But do give the person some freedom of design. Supply the facts. Be as specific as you can about function. Let the architect do your designing.

7. Have you really counted the cost?

Wherever possible these days, I advise getting firm bids from contractors. Don't get caught as some have with unexpected costs that all but wiped them out. It's not necessary. Check with your lender. See whether more money may be available in case, or go for bonds from your church family. But count the cost!

8. Have you thought of starting sister churches as an alternative?

I believe that this is truly a missionary enterprise. Many large churches draw from their family of believers from long distances. In some cases it is much better to go to the people than have them come to you.

9. How about building an all-purpose or first-unit church?

Usually, this structure includes a large simple room temporarily used for sanctuary, fellowship hall, and youth activities room, besides limited foyer, offices, and classrooms. The people will have to cope with continuous shifting of chairs and tables. But the idea is often worthwhile.

10. Have you seriously considered the available field of contractors?

Contractors can be a bane or blessing. *Be sure* to check out several of them.

— OTHER QUESTIONS TO CONSIDER —

11. Have you really thought about your total needs?
12. Do you have a good building committee?
13. Would having multiple services solve your problem?
14. Do you have enough land for future growth?
15. In your location, do you have both visibility and accessibility?
16. Could you possibly enlarge and remodel instead of building new?
17. Do you have a plan to motivate your people?
18. Are you building with future expansion in mind?
19. Are you willing to suffer with volunteer help as a way to save money?
20. Is the task of building a church too great for the congregation?

Joe Kimbel has been for fifty years an ordained minister. Also a church designer and space consultant, he lives in Leisure World at Laguna Hills, California. Joe was once called a "trilevel preacher" (pastor... art instructor...church designer). He was once described as a "man with a pastor's heart...and a draftsman's hand." He designed two hundred churches individually but was involved in hundreds more "repetitive churches." He has consulted with four hundred to five hundred churches in the U.S. and Canada.

18

Build a House

When you are considering building a house, you first must determine if you can afford to build the house you want or if you are willing to build the house you can afford. Go to your lending institution to find out what you qualify for. When you meet with your builder, be ready to make sacrifices to still achieve your dream house for the price you can afford. With an open mind you are now ready to start.

Address all of these questions before you decide to build because they will affect the price. Never assume anything is included in the bid if it is not listed. And be sure it is all in writing, not verbal. You and your builder can work together with less problems when everything is spelled out ahead of time. It is your house. You are paying for it.

1. How do I select the property?

Location and access are very important factors. Consider them carefully. Does the property have trees? Is that important to you? How is the lay of the land? How would the style of home you are planning to build look on this property? What are the amenities (i.e., septic or sewer, well or public water supply, etc.)?

2. How big a house do I want or can I afford?

You should build the smallest house you can fit everything into. Wasted space in halls and extra rooms will add to your building costs, utility bills, and taxes. Decide on the rooms you want and how big you need them, then shoot for that square footage.

3. What frame materials should I request?

Most builders use fir or pine studs. Fir studs are better, and I recommend them. However, using pine studs will be cheaper, and they are still considered sound construction.

Rafters and joists can be either No. 2 or No. 3 grade lumber, and your decking can be plywood. Your subfloor can be two-by-six-inch center match tongue and groove, or you can cut cost by using three-quarter-inch plywood.

4. What about roof materials?

Your roof can be finished with composition or wood shingles of various weights, or you can choose from tile or slate-type materials. Some metal roof materials such as tin can be very attractive on some houses. This choice will be somewhat dictated by the building codes or deed restrictions of your area and by the design of your house. The price range varies according to quality. Get the best you can afford.

5. Are there many choices of exterior finish?

Once again you will have to check first with your building code or deed restrictions. Some areas require over 50 percent brick. Some of the other materials you might want to consider, depending on your elevation, are stone, stucco, rough cedar siding, masonite or composition siding, or log. These can be very helpful in setting the style of your house.

6. Do I have many options in plumbing?

Some people like their copper pipes in the slab while others like them in the walls. The codes or the area of the country you live in may dictate this choice. As far as fixtures, you can choose from four-inch spread to eight-inch spread and chrome to polished brass to enamel in your faucets. The toilets can be round, elongated, water saver, or standard. Your kitchen sink can be single, double, or triple, stainless steel or enamel. All of these options depend on your taste and your budget.

7. How much air conditioning or heat do I need?

Most air conditioning companies now use a computer program to determine the tonnage needed in a home. They input the square footage, setting (trees, facing south, etc.), and type of insulation and windows to determine this figure. Your choice of electric or gas will depend on your location and accessibility to either. In different areas one is less expensive than the other. The heat pump and the hot water recovery system have been greatly improved in the past few years. You should check with your utility company to see if it offers a rebate for using any energy-saving items.

8. Is more insulation always better?

At some point, the return of savings on your utility bills is not as great as the cost of the insulation. At some point, more insulation is no more effective than less. In the Houston climate I use R-13 to R-19 in the walls and R-30 in the ceilings. Your utility company can give you a good opinion on what you need.

9. Will I need to select many items?

You will need to decide on countertops—Formica, Corian, or tile—for the kitchen and utility area. The bathroom counters have the same choices along with cultured marble. Most homeowners use the cultured marble in the baths so they can also use it in their tub and shower surround for a complete look. Tile is also used in the bath frequently as well as a flooring. You can use carpet, vinyl, wood flooring, or pavers (stone, brick, or tile). Wallpaper is another item to be selected, usually from an allowance. All of these items should be spelled out in your bid or an allowance given for them.

10. What are some specialty items I should consider?

One item I tend to include for a lot of homeowners is an intercom system. These systems are available with tape decks and radios. They are now able to tie in with a security system and computerized thermostat setting. Some systems are well worth the cost. A few of the other smaller items are vacuum systems and built-in trim items like ironing boards.

— OTHER QUESTIONS TO CONSIDER —

11. What design do I want?

12. What type of foundation is best?

13. What type of windows do I want?

14. What should I look for in the electrical systems and fixtures?

15. **What can I do with interior trim?**
16. **Are there differences in paint?**
17. **How should I finish my interior walls?**
18. **What finishing hardware do I need to select?**
19. **What appliances are usually included?**
20. **Who finishes the outside work—me or the builder?**

Terry B. Picklo and his wife, Terry Ann, are the owners of Country Builders Inc., which has been building in the Houston, Texas, area since 1981. Country Builders Inc. specializes in custom homes and builds an average of ten to twelve contract homes a year in the $100,000 to $350,000 price range. In addition, their business includes remodeling jobs.

— 19 —

Design and Construct a Custom Building

Most people have only one opportunity to build a significant project in a lifetime. Regardless if it is your dream home, corporate headquarters, or church complex, architecture is a multifarious art, which must accommodate technical, cultural, economical, and psychological demands. Award-winning architecture is an artistic, intrinsic response to these demands. Answering the following questions will lead you in the right direction as you plan your project.

1. **What steps should I take to determine whether or not to build?**

Analyze the problem. Try to discover the opportunities! Throwing space around is not always the solution. Answer these questions: What are the economic consequences of building at this time? Can present space be better utilized? Will a new building help my life or business in a way that other measures can't? The beginning of proper architectural design is a proper understanding of the issues.

2. **What kind of architect-client relationship will produce the best architecture?**
   I believe that both a strong client and a strong architect combine to make excellent architecture. The honest evaluation of and mutual respect for each other's ideas is essential for a good project. (Sort of like marriage!)

3. **How do I select the right architect for the job?**
   Firms can be broadly categorized as one of three types: strong idea, strong service, or strong delivery firms. Most firms strive to be all these things but generally flourish in one area. When you interview architects, try to gain an understanding of where they see themselves in this spectrum and select a firm most compatible with your goals. Personally visit the works and clients of firms being considered to evaluate their capabilities.

4. **How do I establish a budget for my building project?**
   Consider the big picture to arrive at a construction budget. Include applicable issues such as land cost, site improvements, administrative costs (such as city inspection fees), professional fees, and furnishings. Be sure to build in a contingency fund—it is always needed. Allow the architect to help you develop this information.

5. **What things should I communicate to the architect to produce the best product?**
   Communicate your priorities. An architect is specially trained to deal with many conflicting issues at once but needs to prioritize to design discerningly. Also, communicate your goals, applicable facts, and most efficient spatial relationships. Communicate broad concepts that would guide the architect's solution without dictating it. (For exam-

ple: "The building/space should be expandable." Not: "Put a flat roof on the building so I can add on later.")

6. **Is it necessary for a licensed architect to do this work?**
   Local and/or state building regulations will stipulate under what circumstances professionals are required. The benefits of using an architect on your project can go far beyond fulfilling the law. Life safety, life cycle costs, environmental economics, not to mention imagination, creativity, and appropriate aesthetics—all are part of the services of an architect.

7. **Is it necessary to have contracts?**
   A formal contract is important for all parties involved (owner/architect and owner/contractor). Standard AIA contracts have been developed by legal professionals, which the architect will initiate. They have been specially developed over years of use to protect the interests of each party.

8. **What are the most common mistakes made in designing and building a project?**
   Different localities have unique sets of design issues. Discover what they are by asking professionals in the area, those who have recently built, and suppliers who have had callbacks on materials. Typical to all regions will be issues such as not allowing enough contingency in the budget, not planning enough storage space, and designing for initial costs rather than long-term costs.

9. **When is the best time to build?**
   As you know, time is money. If the planning of the project is complete for a "fair weather" beginning, that is ideal. Getting out of the ground is the phase typically most vulnerable to inclement weather. Having a building enclosed by the time bad weather arrives permits construction workers to maintain progress.

10. **Who will I work with if I hire an architectural firm?**
    Architectural firms are often built around the personality and skills of one of the partners. You may eventually work more closely with a project architect within the firm. Be

sure to understand who will be the proposed project team and what their responsibilities will be.

— *OTHER QUESTIONS TO CONSIDER* —

11. **What is program development?**
12. **What is a schematic design?**
13. **How important is design development?**
14. **What construction documents are involved?**
15. **How do contractors bid and negotiate?**
16. **Who is responsible for observing actual construction and checking compliance in all areas?**
17. **When should I select the site I want to build on?**
18. **Do I need an architect as well as an interior designer?**
19. **Should I choose a specialist for the particular building type I need?**
20. **How can I build and still be environmentally sensitive?**

John Charles Jackson (American Institute of Architects [AIA]) has programmed and designed projects of a great variety from simple tight-budget projects to multimillion-dollar complexes, winning awards at the local and state levels. He has worked for and/or studied under two of the most highly celebrated architects in America, E. Fay Jones and Charles W. Moore. He resides in Austin, Texas.

— 20 —

Remodel Any Building

People tend to love old buildings! Regardless if it is their generous ceilings, detailing, or mature landscaping, the fact remains that these buildings seem to play our memories like an old record. Some buildings are historically significant; others do not seem to be now but may be seventy-five years from now. These questions are designed to help you determine whether or not to remodel and, if so, what precautions to take.

1. **What are the advantages of remodeling versus new construction?**
   Often remodeling is less expensive and less time-consuming. The quality of the location is known. The appearance of instant stability can be an advantage in some situations. If character of the older building interests you, constructing it from ground up is difficult to achieve on the same budget with the same materials.

2. **What qualities should I look for in a structure if I want to purchase and then remodel?**
   Older buildings often have hidden faults. A thorough inspection would be in order. The building should be compatible with your space needs and functional needs, but don't expect a perfect match! Look for room to grow.

3. **What is involved in establishing a budget for remodeling?**
   Consider the big picture to arrive at a construction budget. Include applicable issues such as demolition costs, site improvements, administrative costs (such as city inspection fees), professional fees, and furnishings. Also consider the cost of temporary facilities if they are required. Be sure to build in a contingency fund—it is always needed. Allow the architect to help you develop this information.

4. **What specialists will I need in remodeling a building?**
   That depends on the type of facility and your intentions for remodeling. If the structure is historically significant, you would be wise to choose an architect with experience in this area. He is trained to know when to recommend other consultants, such as a paint analyst, if necessary. Many craftspeople in restoration work are experts in their own right and can recommend solutions to issues.

5. **How should I treat a structure that has the potential to be historically significant?**
Do your homework first. Visit with your local preservation office and get recommendations. If removal of any architectural items is necessary, remove them without damage if possible and store in a safe dry place for future generations to restore. Often the exterior is significant and caution should be used, whereas the interior can be adapted.

6. **Can the needs of my family or business be met by this existing facility?**
Older buildings were not designed for today's cultural standards. Kitchens were places of utility, not socializing. Moving walls sometimes requires structural modifications. Electrical needs have changed significantly and sometimes require extensive modifications.

7. **Where is the most strategic place to spend my money if I'm on a limited budget?**
Painting is a quick, relatively inexpensive improvement. Lighting also makes a noticeable difference if the building's system is outdated. Even the smells of new materials give you the psychological lift of being in a new place.

8. **Am I purchasing a liability if I buy this building?**
Make sure you are not buying a liability. Or if you are, that you have budgeted for the improvements. Asbestos removal is very expensive. Make sure the roofing is in good condition. Poor roofing condition is a good indication that something below is also deteriorated.

9. **Should I expect to save money remodeling as compared to starting new?**
Not necessarily. Don't forget you are paying to take things out before you can begin to put them back in. Some restoration work is extremely time-consuming and costly. However, consider that you will have little foundation work to do and that the building is already "in the dry" for working in inclement weather.

10. **What are the disadvantages of remodeling?**
Since the space may have originally been designed for other purposes, a retrofit is sometimes less than ideal. It may be

difficult to get natural light to occupants or to make furnishings fit properly with the space. If the building is not in a new part of town, some people may be reluctant to imagine themselves working or doing business "down there." New construction can be properly planned by the architect to satisfy more of your particular needs, but I expect more and more people will reutilize existing buildings in the future.

— OTHER QUESTIONS TO CONSIDER —

11. What process for architectural services should I anticipate in remodeling a facility?

12. What are some common mistakes in remodeling a building that I should be careful to avoid?

13. How would I add on to this building if I needed to expand?

14. Is this structure in an area of town that is likely to retain its property value?

15. Why do I like this building and want to stay here?

16. What are the things that are difficult to change about this building?

17. Does this facility have adequate site amenities for my needs, such as parking, infrastructure, visibility, and accessibility?

18. What building codes must I meet?

19. How will remodeling affect my current operations?

20. Can the contractor schedule disruptive work for off-hours?

John Charles Jackson (American Institute of Architects [AIA]) has years of experience as an architect in giving new life to old buildings. He has resided in a home on the National Register of Historic Structures for eleven years. He functioned as lead designer in an award-winning preservation and adaptive reuse firm and has worked for and/or studied under the AIA's most recent gold medalists—E. Fay Jones and Charles W. Moore. He resides in Austin, Texas.

Education

Apply for a
College Scholarship

Paying for a college education is a concern for many families. Financial aid information is often confusing and its language unfamiliar. The following list of twenty questions will give you a perspective on your college goals and the means to attain them.

1. Do I want to go to college?
Every high-school graduate should ask this question. College is not for everyone. Your high-school grades and your SAT/ACT test scores are helpful predictors of your potential for success in college. Most important, however, is your determination. Students with modest ability who are willing to work hard can be successful in college. College is not the only opportunity for success—the armed forces, the business world, and proprietary schools are other acceptable choices. But in our modern world, having a college degree is becoming more and more important for success.

2. Do I want to go to a private or public college?
The choice between a public or private college can be significant. It is no longer simply a choice between prestige or price. Some public institutions, such as the University of Michigan, are very prestigious, and some private institutions, such as College of the Ozarks, are tuition-free. Generally speaking, however, public institutions are significantly less expensive in their charges for tuition. Community colleges are the least expensive institutions of higher education. They are generally close to home and have low tuition.

Private colleges are more likely to provide what we think of as the "college experience." Smaller colleges tend to offer more opportunities for faculty/student interaction, personal attention, participation in college activities, and lifelong friendships. In some instances the most prestigious private colleges may also provide entry into the business world at a much higher level than would be likely from associations and friendships developed at public institutions.

3. Should I visit any colleges?

By all means! Visiting colleges is by far the best way to learn about your choices. Visit several, but don't visit so many that they become a blur in your mind. Talk to the current students. If they are happy, the chances are, you will be, too. Don't be overly impressed with buildings. The people and the programs are the important ingredients in a great college experience.

4. Should I pay full price?

Maybe! If your heart is set on a particular institution and if there is a great demand for places in that institution, you may have to pay full price. However, even the most selective institutions provide financial aid for students with financial need. If you are willing to choose among more than one or two institutions, you will likely find a college that will give you a substantial discount (financial aid).

5. Should I use a scholarship service?

Probably not! If you are seriously considering three or four colleges, you are better off talking to their representatives directly about financial aid. They can be much more specific about the assistance they can provide. Scholarship services can be helpful if you wish to survey a large number of possibilities. However, they are expensive, and most of the information is available from either your high-school counselor or your college financial aid adviser.

6. What is a financial aid package?

A financial aid package is the combination of scholarship, grant, loan money, and work opportunity that a college might offer you.

Financial Package for Jim Student

$1,500	Federal Grant (Pell)
500	State Grant
1,000	Academic Scholarship
6,000	Student Loan
1,200	Work Study: 10 hours per week, $4.00 per hour for 30 weeks

$10,200

7. What is the difference between a loan, a grant, and a scholarship?

A _loan_ is money you must pay back. Most college loans are at reduced interest rates and defer repayment until the student graduates or leaves school. _Grant_ money is gift money; it does not have to be repaid. Eligibility for government grant money is based on family income. _Scholarship_ money is gift money. Originally, scholarship money was for academic success. Today, however, scholarships may also be awarded for music, athletics, drama, and so on. Many colleges use the terms _grant_ and _scholarship_ interchangeably. Work study is generally campus employment whereby students perform services in return for wages.

8. Can I qualify for a federal grant?

Federal grants are awarded on the basis of a formula that includes family size, assets, liabilities, number of students in college, and income reported on last year's tax form. Generally, families with incomes in excess of $30,000 cannot qualify for federal grants. These formulas change from year to year, and families should not assume they do not qualify. Talk to the Financial Aid Office at the college, and fill out the Family Financial Statement (FFS) available from your high-school counselor.

9. How can I compare colleges on price?

The printed costs in the college catalog are not necessarily the prices you will be asked to pay. Your costs are the difference in _gift aid_ and the total costs. In the following example, each college provides a nice financial package for Jim Student. _College A_ offers a good package, depending heavily on loans. *College B* offers the largest financial aid package, but its costs are also the highest. *College C* offers the best financial aid package because the direct family costs are the lowest. (Note that the federal grant money will be the same for all three colleges.)

	College A	College B	College C
Federal Grant	$ 1,500	$ 1,500	$ 1,500
State Grant	500	500	500
Scholarship	500	2,500	2,000
Student Loans	6,500	6,000	5,000
Work Study	1,200	1,000	1,000
Total Aid	$10,200	$11,500	$10,000
Room, Board, Tuition	13,200	15,000	12,200
Family (Out of Pocket)	$ 3,000	$ 3,500	$ 2,200

10. How can I compare colleges on quality?

This question is the most difficult one to answer. College quality is generally based on four things: wealth, facilities, reputation, and professors. College wealth is determined by the amount of endowment it enjoys. Endowment is money set aside in an investment account. Only the income from the endowment may be used to support the college budget. Facilities include college campus and buildings and the equipment in the classrooms and laboratories. Reputation is the view others have about the college; it is the information reported in annual surveys of colleges by national news magazines. Professors actually deliver the academic experience to the students.

Make sure the college is accredited. Talk to students who are in your area of study about the professors. Make sure the college has adequate financial resources so that it can continue. You don't want to be the alumnus of a college that has gone out of business.

— OTHER QUESTIONS TO CONSIDER —

11. Do I want a Christian college?

12. Should I go to my denominational college?

13. Should I go to a college out of state?

14. What part of the country should I apply for?

15. Does this scholarship continue each year?

16. Can I take this scholarship to another school?

17. Does this scholarship require work or participation?

18. Does this scholarship demand an essay?

19. Does this scholarship demand a minimum GPA?

20. Is a large scholarship at an expensive institution better than a smaller scholarship at a less-expensive institution?

Norman Bridges is the president of Bethel College in Mishawaka, Indiana. He has twenty-five years of experience in higher education in both the public and the private sectors. He has an M.A. and a Ph.D. from the University of Michigan.

— 22 —

Attend College as an Older Adult

When deciding to attend college as an adult, you are making a life-style change that will radically alter your perception of life as well as others' perceptions of you. Therefore, carefully considering several factors will help you clarify your decision to further your education.

1. Has attending college always been a dream, and is now the time to fulfill that dream?

Some mature students had to delay entering college because of marriage, illness in the family, or immediate financial needs, but now the time has come. These students are so excited about having a chance to achieve this goal that their eagerness is infectious within the college classroom. One student helped her husband finish college; she had four children, all in school now; and she is thrilled that it is her turn now. She takes only two courses a semester, but she's an enthusiastic and interested student.

2. Are you in a dead-end job and you want to change that life?
One motivator to attend college is a desire to do more on the job, to rise above the present position. Sometimes experience isn't enough to rise to the next rung of the ladder. Advanced training in your career area is necessary, and the only way to achieve it is to go to college.

Some jobs have no positions with which to rise; therefore, you have to go out on your own, find a new goal, and return to college. You must be ready to balance job, school, and personal life to achieve this higher goal.

Your dead-end job may not allow you to earn enough money to do more than survive. Education will not always make you rich beyond your wildest dreams, but it at least puts you in a better position to realize more financially rewarding circumstances. Consequently, with a more satisfying job that pays better, your future can be brighter. Therefore, your motivation to go to college is very high.

3. Are you the only one in your family to go to college?
If this is a self-motivator, it is a worthy goal. You will be proud that you have gone farther than anyone else in your family, and your family will be pleased that you have achieved this goal. You have a built-in cheering section with the internal voices of your ancestors and the external voices of your family.

4. Do you enjoy learning for learning's sake?
Some people just have a zest for learning, and so college is an excellent place to put that desire to good use by pursuing a degree. Some courses in college allow you to survey a variety of topics while others require a focus in one area.

Whichever seems to be your desire, put this opportunity to work for you so that in your quest for knowledge, you will earn a degree, added respect, and maybe even a new job.

5. **Is attending college going to give you a second chance at life?**
   College is an excellent place to be because it doesn't look at your past life-style to see if you will succeed. You don't need a resume to get into college. All you need is a high-school diploma or a GED and a desire to complete a program. You are able to prove yourself once you get into the institution.

6. **Are you willing to learn that procrastination deters your goals whereas hard work rewards you with success?**
   Some people have been procrastinators all of their lives. Once they enter college, they become doers because they are working toward a definable goal.

7. **Do you feel as if age is a deterrent to learning or returning to college?**
   More and more people are returning to college as older students. My classes are peopled with students who range in age from eighteen to sixty-seven. Even my mother returned to college at age forty to finish the degree she began at age eighteen. Many colleges have specific departments set aside for older people. Learning is a lifelong pursuit.

   Many colleges have refresher programs for students who have been out of school a long time. These courses prepare older students in areas of study skills, mathematics, and academic support. The colleges recognize the special needs and provide for them with academic support centers.

8. **Should you attend college full-time or part-time?**
   If you go to school full-time, you may have to quit your job with benefits, rely on financial aids or loans and work only part-time. Some students find this a very difficult situation because of financial obligations.

   The next option is to attend college on a part-time basis. You take longer to finish, but you may get the best of two worlds. Usually, the older student has a family to consider; consequently, part-time is the answer. Many colleges have entire courses that can be taken at night and on weekends to accommodate part-time students. Some employers allow employees flexible time to take day classes.

Check out these options. If one college doesn't offer the options, seek out a college that will. Usually, colleges and employers have many creative ways to provide for the nontraditional student.

9. How do you pay for this education?

One way, of course, is to have the money in the bank and to use your savings. You may not have that kind of money available, however.

Another way is to borrow the money and gradually pay it back after you are out of college. Many student loans are available at low interest through your college, bank, or other financial institution. These financial aid packages are usually outlined through the college's financial aid office; contact that office to see what is available.

Grants in aid are also available. Once again the financial aid office can supply information.

Scholarships, fellowships, and internships come in many forms. College counselors can help; the financial aid office, churches, unions, local organizations, national organizations, and many other sources offer information on scholarships. Sometimes the search turns into a puzzle, but in the long run, it could pay big dividends.

10. Will this education help you become a better and more fulfilled person?

If you can answer yes, you should go to school. You should follow several steps.

First, take a career inventory to identify your interests and abilities. *Second*, seek support from your family, friends, and a mentor. *Third*, explore the best college program for you. *Fourth*, check out the financial package you need. *Fifth*, enroll in a course of study.

Then, you'll have to study and work hard. Become acquainted with your professors so that you can use their expertise to the best of your ability. And enjoy your new life because, in the long run, your hard work will pay off in many different ways.

— OTHER QUESTIONS TO CONSIDER —

11. What personal influences are pushing you to go to school?

12. What external influences are pushing you to go to school?

13. Is attending college a requirement to achieve your long-term goals?

14. Have you come to the realization that you are the only person who can change your circumstances?

15. Are you ready to influence your children's lives as well as your own?

16. Do your role models have positions that you would like to have, and do these positions require a college education?

17. Do you have a support group to encourage you in this new life?

18. If you enter college underprepared, are you willing to take the extra courses to catch up and to repeat courses in which you do not make the grade?

19. Are you ready to have a new respect from others and a new self-confidence?

20. Do you feel that because you have a General Equivalency Diploma (GED), your chance of college success is slim?

Anne E. Lehman is an instructor at Milwaukee Area Technical College, Milwaukee, Wisconsin. She has been teaching high school through college for twenty-seven years. As a reading specialist, a writing professor, and an instructor in developmental education, she has been directly involved with adults who have decided to return to college.

23

Choose a College or University

About half of America's high-school graduates pursue formal education in community colleges, four-year colleges and universities, or other vocational schools. The federal government recognizes over ten thousand institutions for which students may seek financial aid. Making the right choice is a critical decision. Can you make a list of "must have" and "must not have" features of the school you desire to attend? Then ask whether it is possible to finance a school that you describe. Many helpful books are available.

1. How determined am I to complete a four-year degree program?
Some vocational schools offer programs that are difficult to transfer for credit recognized by four-year schools. Approximately half of those who start postsecondary education actually complete a baccalaureate degree.

2. Do I prefer a large school or a small one?
You have choices all the way from one hundred to fifty thousand or more students on one campus. You should feel at home in whatever campus environment you choose.

3. Can I afford to attend a private college?
Because public institutions get taxpayer support, they are less expensive for in-state students and, generally, even for students from other states. Private colleges must, of necessity, charge more—up to $20,000 per year at some. Private "proprietary" schools are more expensive than community colleges, but it often takes less time to complete a course of study.

4. Is the school accredited?
Several regional and specialized accrediting organizations give their seal of approval to institutions of all types. You should choose one that is accredited.

5. Does the school itself offer additional student financial aid?
Some schools, particularly private colleges, have their own aid programs. Eligibility may be tied to financial need or academic record or other criteria.

6. What is the academic level of students who already attend a school?
Most schools report the SAT or ACT scores of entering freshmen. It helps you determine how academically competitive the school will be.

7. What are my housing options?
Schools may require some students to live on campus. Others depend on local rental apartments. Where you live is a big part of what you get out of college and how much it will cost.

8. What is the availability of ROTC, cooperative education, and study abroad?
These special programs can be as significant to learning as the course offerings in that they broaden your learning and career options.

9. What academic departments are considered outstanding?
Especially if you are thinking of graduate school, the quality of your department major may make a difference in graduate school acceptance, financial aid, or good job offers upon graduation.

10. What help does the school provide in placing graduates in jobs?
Some schools pride themselves on their placement rates, feeling it is important to help find good jobs for their students. That strengthens their alumni support and builds harmonious relationships with various employing organizations.

— OTHER QUESTIONS TO CONSIDER —

11. What is my primary career goal or interest?
12. What values do I want reflected in the school I attend?
13. What location or school environment fits my needs?
14. What extracurricular programs do I desire at my school?
15. Is the school recognized by the federal government as one at which students can receive federal student assistance?
16. How long does it take for most students to complete the program?
17. What kind of academic advising can I expect?
18. Is the campus a safe environment?
19. What special services or facilities are important to me?
20. What is the mix of students—on-campus and off-campus living, age range, distribution of majors, involvement in fraternities and sororities?

Robert C. Andringa, Ph.D., is president of CEO Services Group in Denver, Colorado. His clients include over sixty chief executives and several boards of international, national, and regional organizations. Bob has spoken to at least four hundred organizations and trained over twenty thousand people. In 1980, the Education Commission of the States called Bob to become its third executive director. For five years Bob served the nation's governors, legislators, and state boards of education. He has served on several governing boards including the International School of Law, Trinity College, Ucross Foundation, Institute for Educational Leadership, the Christian Coalition of Youth Initiatives, Princeps Partners, Inc., and the Christian Management Association.

24

Educate at Home

Home-school, like politics, elicits strong reactions. Some people think that everyone should home-school. Some think every child should attend a Christian school. And others think that every child should be in a public school. Ask yourself the following questions before you decide.

1. **Do I have a realistic picture of home-schooling?**
   Misconception 1: There is a home-school type. More than one million families are teaching their own children. There's a wide diversity of personalities, educational backgrounds, religious preferences, and abilities. The majority are middle-class parents with some college education. Only a minority have had teacher training.

   Misconception 2: It's not legal. Each state determines what demonstrates school attendance—attendance records, samples of schoolwork, superintendent supervision, and/or testing.

   Misconception 3: Home-school kids receive an inferior education. The National Home Education Research Institute shows higher scores in academics, social skills, and self-confidence.

   Misconception 4: Kids need school for social reasons. Kids with more family contact than peer contact get along better socially.

2. **What are my goals for our children?**
   First, decide what you want. For example, you want your children to

   - have godly character.
   - be fully equipped for life (academics, thinking skills, practical living, character).
   - love learning.

As parents we have the responsibility to decide what is best for our kids.

3. Do my spouse and I agree?
If you and your spouse disagree on major goals for your children, don't home-school. First, get some counseling to learn how best to work together as a team. For your children's sake, have a solid game plan, whether you home-school or not.

4. Would home-school best meet our goals and needs?
Maybe home-school isn't the best option now. List the benefits, for example:

- Practicing godly character
- Learning at individual pace
- Motivating each child according to personal bent
- Having practical living experiences
- Building problem-solving skills
- Focusing on family
- Enjoying free time for special interests

5. What about the children's social needs?
At-home children develop better social skills because they are not limited to a classroom of one age group, they have greater freedom to travel and meet people, they have more time with family, and they can choose specific friends and social groups (e.g., youth group, sports, clubs, other home-schooling families). Teach your kids respect for everyone, no matter the age, limitations, or interests.

6. How do I choose curriculum?
You can choose standard textbooks and workbooks designed for classroom use or at-home unit studies where all subjects are related to a theme (e.g., airplanes—learning the history of flight, doing science experiments about air and flight, reading biographies such as *The Wright Brothers*, writing about how an airplane works, drawing airplanes, taking a trip to an airport). Choose a curriculum that meets your family's needs.

7. If I home-schooled, what would be my strengths?
Do you sew? Do you do woodwork? Can you write well? Are

you a good organizer? Can you care for a baby? Can you read aloud? Can you learn new things? Can you play an instrument? Don't underestimate what you already have going for you.

8. **If I home-schooled, what would be my weaknesses?**

   Are you disorganized? Does math scare you? Is your spelling atrocious? Don't fret. You will learn along with your children, *and* help is available. Keep your eyes and ears open to tutors, lessons, and other parents that can supplement your teaching.

9. **What helps are available for home-schoolers?**

   The National Center for Home Education, P.O. Box 125, Paeonian Springs, VA 22129 (Tel: 703-882-4770; Fax: 703-882-3628) is a good place to start. Subscribe to *The Teaching Home* magazine, 12311 Brazee, Portland, OR 97230. Get to know your state and local home-school support groups.

10. **How long should I home-school?**

    Take it one year at a time. You can home-school for one year or through high school. Don't worry about your children entering school. Most children fit in well after a few weeks of transition. In fact, they tend to be more enthusiastic and better students.

— OTHER QUESTIONS TO CONSIDER —

11. **Should everyone home-school?**
12. **Can I picture myself home-schooling?**
13. **How well do I know my kids?**
14. **What are the legal requirements in our state?**
15. **What if our kids are different ages?**
16. **What training do I need?**
17. **Can I home-school with another family?**
18. **Can I afford to home-school?**
19. **How can I teach my kids and still have a life?**
20. **Is home-schooling really worth it?**

Carole "Cich" Thaxton, professional counselor and author, has home-schooled for ten years. She is coauthor of the renowned KONOS Curriculum, which has revolutionized home education. She and her family currently reside in Prague, Czechoslovakia.

— 25 —

Enroll Your Preschooler

Deciding where and what program in which to enroll a preschool-age child is one of the more important decisions in the child's life. Not only will it have a profound effect on the child, but it will also have an effect on the family. Investigate thoroughly and choose wisely.

1. **What type of program best fits the individual needs of the child and the family?**
   Programs range from drop-in and part-time care in a family day-care home to the full-time care offered in a child-care center. Half-day and full-day programs meet two, three, and five days a week across the nation. There are church-affiliated preschools, college campus preschools, government-funded programs, and private programs, each offering something special for the child. Analyze your particular situation to find the perfect early childhood program for your child.

2. **What are the costs involved in the prospective program, and how often is there an increase?**
   Typically, several costs are involved. Annual registration fees or enrollment fees for separate programs are charged.

Tuition is calculated weekly or monthly and occasionally on an annual basis. Tuition payment is set by this schedule.

3. Is the program open during the summer, or does it operate on a nine- or ten-month school year?
Try to match your needs as closely as possible. If year-round care is a priority, a nine-month program could cause chaos for you and your child. Think ahead.

4. What are the staff's qualifications and training?
Minimal requirements are set and regulated separately by each state regarding child-care centers. Find out what they are, and make sure the prospective center uses them as a guide. Remember that these are minimal requirements and, therefore, may not create the optimal program. Individuals with college classes and training in child development and early childhood education are more knowledgeable about growth and development.

5. What are the child/teacher ratios in the center?
Most states regulate this area by establishing the maximum amount of children that one teacher can care for at a given time. One association has established recommendations of no more than eight two- and three-year-old children with one adult and no more than ten four- and five-year-old children with one adult.

6. What is the policy regarding discipline?
Early childhood programs vary to a small degree in this area. Some simply redirect the child's behavior into more constructive areas, while others use a time-out method. The latter involves a child sitting and thinking about his actions and how they affected someone else. This is rather advanced thinking for a three-year-old. Positive reinforcement methods are always more successful than negative. *Absolutely no physical punishment should be allowed.*

7. Has a volunteer parent program been established?
This type of program can range from occasional cookie baking to a scheduled daily, weekly, or monthly arrangement at the school. When a volunteer program is established, more networking and communication occur between the parents,

the staff, and the child, which ultimately benefits the child. Many high-quality early childhood programs provide this opportunity for meaningful parental involvement.

8. Does the center follow an open-door policy?

Are the parents allowed to visit the classroom unannounced at any time? The intention of this policy is to dispel any doubts in the parents' minds about what occurs in the rooms between the teachers and the children. It does not apply to visitors, only to the parents whose children are enrolled in the program.

9. Are the classrooms organized with a variety of learning centers?

The learning centers or areas within a classroom do not always have to be the same, but certain basics should be provided. Young children need to develop fine motor skills. Are there small manipulatives available? Is there a pretend area that will foster imaginative play and social-emotional development? Is there a quiet area with quality children's books? Is there a science area with plants or other natural objects? Are art and sensory materials provided so that a child's creativity and uniqueness can develop? Is there an ample supply of blocks to promote cooperative play and the beginnings of math and geometry? Are any music opportunities provided?

10. Do the teachers develop daily plans to foster growth in all the areas of a child's development?

The ideal is to provide a balanced curriculum so that all areas of a child's growth and development are fostered. The teacher becomes the facilitator and creates an environment in which the child explores, discovers, and masters the materials and activities provided. The medium of play becomes the most valuable tool with which the teacher can provide the meaningful experiences that lead to learning. This all takes deliberate planning on the teacher's part.

— OTHER QUESTIONS TO CONSIDER —

11. What are the hours of the program or the center?

12. When is registration for the program?

13. How long have the staff members been with the program or center?

14. Is there a parent handbook available, and is it distributed to the parents?

15. Are healthy, nutritious snacks served?

16. Are the facilities clean, safe, and in good repair?

17. Is the outdoor equipment conducive to the development of gross motor skills?

18. Are ample educational toys and equipment accessible to the children?

19. Are any enrichment classes or programs offered?

20. Are field trips encouraged, and if so, what mode of transportation is used?

Ellen Roth-Wilson is a preschool director currently associated with a church-related program. She is a credentialed teacher with an extensive background in psychology and early childhood education. During her ten years of experience in the field, she has directed for-profit and nonprofit programs, private and church-sponsored programs, and an on-site child-care center for employees.

— 26 —

Go to College

Dreams often are the first indication of genuine interest and giftedness. High-school students will spend incredible amounts of time and energy on their dreams. Smart parents piggyback on a student's dreams. The college-bound deci-

sion process should really begin in the middle of the freshman year, and end in the middle of the senior year. The following questions will help parents identify their student's dreams and interests.

1. **What are you good at that is also fun?**
   Interests emerge around strengths that can later lead to careers. Do not challenge the student's perceptions. Just accept the view of reality.

2. **What do you dream about doing in your wildest dreams?**
   Dreams in an area of interest and strength often become realities. It takes at least three years to make a dream into a reality.

3. **How can we help you make your dream into a reality?**
   The student needs to be the primary person implementing. However, time and experience are limited. You can help.

4. **Do you know what a mentor is?**
   A mentor is a nonrelative who receives nothing except personal satisfaction from the relationship with the student. Mentors at this age are generally teachers who choose the student. Go beyond that.

5. **What does *distinctive* mean?**
   Distinctive means "doing the out-of-the ordinary well." *Excellence* means "doing the ordinary exceptionally well."

6. **What could be your distinctive contribution to our family?**
   Help the student find one contribution that no one else is doing presently. Make a list of six possibilities.

7. **Could we turn it into a project?**
   It should last two to three years. It does not have to relate directly to college or work. It could be a life project.

8. **What role could your mentor play in this distinctive project?**
   The student needs someone other than parents to discuss ideas with. The mentor will encourage the student to go beyond normal abilities.

9. **If we cannot pay for your college education, would you still go to college?**

Most students' first reaction is, "NO! How could I go?" Students assume you will pay. You will feel guilty if you cannot pay for college. There are alternatives, however.

10. **Can you work part-time, go to college, and get a degree in five years?**
The typical student has never talked to college graduates who financed their own education. Find one and encourage your student to interview the individual. A student who works fifteen hours part-time, all summer, and earns $8 per hour can pay for almost all of a college education over five years at a public institution. Most college students today take five years to complete a degree.

— OTHER QUESTIONS TO CONSIDER —

11. **How do you learn best?**

12. **Do you have a mentor?**

13. **What kind of person would you choose for a mentor?**

14. **How could we approach that person to help you?**

15. **Do you ever dream about going to a particular college?**

16. **Have you ever thought about visiting a college next summer?**

17. **Why don't you pick two colleges and plan a trip with your two best friends?**

18. **If you had a skill that earned you $8 to $10 per hour, what would you select?**

19. **How can we organize a program for you to get that skill in case we cannot pay for your college education?**

20. **How much debt are you willing to accumulate to get a college degree?**

Bill Wilkie, Ph.D., is a former college professor and administrator at Michigan State University, program director at the Kellogg Foundation, executive vice president of Multifastener Corporation, and president of the Rockmont College in Colorado. In 1989 at Grand Rapids City

High School, Dr. Wilkie began developing materials for academically oriented high-school students. He is the author of *The College Bound Student: A Parents' Guide.*

— 27 —

Improve Grades

At least twelve years of our lives are spent as full-time students. Few of us, however, have ever been taught how to be good students. The following twenty questions are designed to motivate and equip students to learn quicker and better, to perform better on tests and homework and in class, and to have some time left to enjoy life. Students spend so much time, effort, and money on their education that it makes sense for them to invest a little of the same resources to become good at it.

1. **What are the most important things I can do to improve my grades?**
   Attend class faithfully and sit in one of the first three rows! This advice probably isn't what you expected, but statistics indicate the greatest correlation between taking these actions and receiving good grades.

2. **When I am in class, is there some strategy I can employ to learn the most?**
   Yes, this acrostic will help you listen and think aggressively in class:
   *S*can. Stay awake and pay attention.
   *A*sk. Ask yourself how each concept presented fits and whether it is important enough to write down.

Focus. If the concept is central (important), think about it more. (See the next question for what to think about.)

Explore. Ask (or at least write down) questions.

3. What are particular kinds of information to focus on?

You should focus on four kinds of information (facts):

Causes. When you hear the word *problem*, ask, What causes this?

Objectives. When you observe an activity, ask, What is the objective?

Patterns. Ask, How does this concept link or group with others I've learned in this class?

Eighty-twenties. A rule of life is that 80 percent of benefit generally comes from 20 percent of activity. When you see or hear a list of items, ask, Which is the top priority?

4. What are some good questions to ask?

Clarifying. What does this mean?

Applying. How does this work?

Trying. How does this fit with what else we are learning?

5. How can I think of the big ideas I need for my theme papers?

Load. Two weeks ahead of the due date, have several times of reading and thinking and talking about the topic.

Relax. In between, don't worry about the topic.

Capture. Expect and write down immediately ideas that come to you on the topic during the two weeks. More than likely one (or even several) of those ideas will provide you with the approach for your paper.

6. What are some tricks to memorizing material for exams?

Ridiculize. Picture the fact in an extreme and memorable fashion (e.g., the *Sherman* Antitrust Act can be pictured by one hundred huge *Sherman* tanks moving toward and shooting at a fortresslike bank and *trust* company vault).

Associate. Link your pictures of related concepts (e.g., the Clayton Antitrust Act can be pictured and associated with the Sherman Act by imagining *tons* of *clay* pouring out of the tanks' guns and burying the vault).

7. What are some ideas to help me make better decisions?

Tough decisions often benefit by being charted:

- List alternative choices across the top of the chart.
- In a column on the left, list specific objectives or benefits you hope to achieve.
- Write in the chart how well each alternative satisfies each objective.
- Compare the columns under each alternative to see which seems best overall.

8. What are some ways I can prepare for exams?

First, review the text and your class notes and talk to your classmates (and teacher), looking for what is most likely to be on the exam.

Second, distill the course content down to the most essential concepts and memorize them.

Third, practice thinking about and applying these key concepts in typical problem situations presented in the class and text.

9. What are some tips for top performance *during* an exam?

Show what you know! A test is simply a device to convey to the teacher what you know and how you can apply the course material. On essay exams write out as much of your reasoning as possible. Partial credit is possible even if you don't get the totally "right" answer. On true/false and multiple choice exams, go through the entire exam answering the questions you know before going back and thinking about the questions you are unsure of.

10. When choosing the assignments to do first, do I pick the one that contributes the most to my overall grade?

The two key words in prioritizing are *importance* and *urgency*. In the homework context, *importance* refers to how much the assignment contributes to your overall grade; *urgency* refers to how soon it must be turned in.

Although you normally will do urgent, next-day assignments first, sometimes you may need to do a little less on an *un*important, urgent assignment so you can put some quality time into a 50 percent-of-your-grade assignment not due for a few days yet.

— OTHER QUESTIONS TO CONSIDER —

11. Is getting better grades important to me?

12. Do I speak with conviction to improve my impact as I present my views in class?

13. Do I write down the boundaries of a problem to help me get unstuck when I'm bogged down?

14. Do my friends and I discuss our topics before we write our papers?

15. Have I started keeping a calendar of assignments that I review daily?

16. Where can I get more help to improve my grades?

17. Have I determined the best time and place for *me* to study?

18. As I consider my choice of college or major, am I paying attention to my strengths and career desires as guides in the decision?

19. Do I try to ask my teachers only relevant questions?

20. Have I thought of ways to deal with the sometimes extreme pressure of homework, tests, and relationships?

Steve Douglass is the executive vice president of Campus Crusade for Christ. He majored in electrical engineering at the Massachusetts Institute of Technology and received his Master of Business Administration from Harvard, graduating in the top 2 percent of his class. He has spoken live and through video to tens of thousands of college students on how to get better grades and have more fun. His book by that title has more than 100,000 copies in print.

Employer and Employee Relations

Evaluate a Staff Member

The subject of reviewing and evaluating personnel is vital to every successful organization. You need to create a pattern of thinking that enables you to limit errors bringing tragedy into organizational or personal life. The desire is to provide a win-win position. Review and evaluation sessions are a time for encouragement, correction, and team building. Bear these questions in mind during these sessions.

1. **Is the initial job description still applicable?**
   Have both the organization and the person involved been operating under mutually agreed assumptions? Are these assumptions the best ones for the organization and personnel?

2. **What other personnel should be consulted before making a final evaluation of this person's performance?**
   There is wisdom in the midst of counselors. Do other people have broader experience, greater perspective, and more objectivity than you have?

3. **How can I help this person win?**
   Should this person be under your tutelage for further growth and advancement? Have you done all you can for this person?

4. **Is it my position to help this person win?**
   You do not want to circumvent the authority of any staff members working with the person in question.

5. **Is there a personality or a performance problem?**
   You want to discover if the person is having difficulty in any area. You want to discover if you have properly documented performance records.

6. **What would I look for in the ideal person for this position?**
   You want to gain a clear picture of what is actually needed

to fulfill the expectations of this position. You must determine if your expectations are realistic.

7. **How has this person performed in regard to agreed-upon goals?**
   You want to track the performance of personnel in regard to their target goals during a specified period.

8. **What is the long-term outlook personally and organizationally for this individual in our organization?**
   You must see beyond today. A long-term look may help you discover the best use of personnel in the organization.

9. **Do we need to continue this position within our organization?**
   Can the organization do without this position? Often streamlining organizational personnel will bring greater efficiency.

10. **What process should I use in carrying out my decision?**
    You must do this task professionally, ethically, and compassionately. As you develop the process, you want to be balanced in all of these areas.

— OTHER QUESTIONS TO CONSIDER —

11. **What were the appealing characteristics I saw in this person when hired?**

12. **How have the initial positive characteristics changed?**

13. **What possible mistakes did I make in the hiring process?**

14. **Were there any misrepresentations in what was initially perceived of this person?**

15. **Can we use this person in any other position within the organization?**

16. **Is this person happy in our organization?**

17. **Would additional training for the person enhance performance?**

18. **As I view the organization as a whole, in what way is this person valuable to its operation?**

19. Should I consider dismissal or transfer of this person?

20. Am I pleased with this person's performance?

Claude L. Robold has served as a senior pastor for twenty years, administering multiple staff ministries. As a consultant to national and international ministries, he has assisted in setting policies and procedures for securing staff personnel. He has served on national boards of denominational ministries developing policies and direction for ministry agencies. As chairman of the board of a health care agency, he provides leadership for hiring staff for the management of nursing care facilities. He is the founder and senior pastor of New Covenant Church in Middletown, Ohio.

— 29 —

Hire a Staff Member

It is said the easiest time to fire a staff member is before you hire the person. That is good advice. It becomes a much more painful and complicated process to dismiss a staff member once on the payroll. You can save yourself, your organization, and unqualified applicants time and trouble by asking yourself the following questions before you decide to hire someone.

1. **Specifically, what do I need to accomplish?**
   Go beyond the standard job description of tasks and responsibilities. Write in one or two sentences what you need to accomplish. This statement will help you define the type of person you need.

2. **What characteristics and personal abilities should this staff member possess?**

Identify traits needed to be successful in this position. Do you need a quiet or outgoing personality, someone steady or innovative, a follower or catalyst?

3. **What skills and experience are needed to do this job?**
List essential requirements—computer literate, verbally adept, executive experience, supervisor capabilities. The more specific you are, the better understanding you will have of the person you need to hire.

4. **In addition to salary and benefits, what costs will I incur in filling this position?**
Count up all the costs—furniture, equipment, computer, relocation, training, program budget, subscriptions, travel, office space, and so on.

5. **How will I enable this person to be successful?**
Hiring a person will not necessarily accomplish the task. People need to be empowered. Are you willing to provide information, delegate authority, extend relationships, and allocate funds?

6. **Is someone already in the organization who could do this job?**
Don't overlook a qualified person within your organization who is familiar with the structure and is tested and proven. You save time in the orientation portion of the training curve. Offering new opportunities is a good motivational tool.

7. **What do others think of the candidate?**
Involve others in the decision. They also have to live with the final decision and would appreciate being consulted.

8. **How compatible is this person's value system with the organization's philosophy and culture?**
Build your organization with people who will be loyal and believe in what you do.

9. **How compatible is this person's career focus with the direction of the organization and the need faced?**
As long as both parties are contributing to each other's goals, you will have a long-term relationship. Make sure your ultimate goals are the same.

10. **How would my best friend view this person if they met?**
    Evaluate the person through the eyes of a friend whose opinion you respect. You will gain a more realistic perspective.

— OTHER QUESTIONS TO CONSIDER —

11. **Will hiring this person affect any other staff member's responsibilities?**
12. **Is the person needed primarily to design, develop, or manage in this position?**
13. **Who would be perfect for this position?**
14. **Is this the right time to hire a person?**
15. **Who else should meet this person?**
16. **What was my first impression?**
17. **What is the person's role preference?**
18. **Would I enjoy working with this person?**
19. **Who could give me a candid evaluation of this person?**
20. **Do I have any reason to think that in six months I may face some difficulty with this person?**

Bruce R. Johnson is director of operations of Leighton Ford Ministries (LFM), Charlotte, North Carolina. LFM is focused on developing a new generation of leaders worldwide. Bruce oversees the day-to-day operations of LFM and takes time to consult with young leaders who are just developing their organizations. He has interviewed hundreds, hired dozens, and fired a few.

30

Terminate an Employee

I approached this task from the standpoint of the plaintiff's attorney, as if a terminated employee came to me wondering if there was "a case" against the employer. Because each employment relationship has so many different variables, it is virtually impossible to address all of the questions you should answer before ending an employment relationship. Above all, be fair, consistent, and thorough. Become familiar with local labor laws. Seek legal counsel if you are uncertain.

1. **Has the employee been given adequate training and orientation to perform well in the assignment?**
   An employee cannot be expected to pick up necessary information on a haphazard basis. Review your training and orientation procedures if this complaint is voiced in an exit interview.

2. **Is there adequate documentation to support the termination decision?**
   Document, document, document. You may be required to provide all records to an attorney for review. How does that make you feel . . . confident or queasy?

3. **Was the employee given enough time to correct a performance problem?**
   Experts agree on a period of about twenty-one days to create new habits or change old behavior. Certainly that doesn't suggest someone guilty of theft should be given three weeks to stop.

4. **Does the punishment fit the crime?**
   You're asking for trouble if you terminate an employee who hasn't been confronted and is unaware of the performance

problem. Consider a final warning, detailing the consequences of continued poor performance.

5. **Are performance reviews conducted on a regular basis with feedback to the employee?**
An employee who is unaware of a performance problem cannot be expected to correct it. Performance reviews must include open, honest feedback aimed at correcting behavior and rewarding performance.

6. **Is the person a long-term employee?**
Consider the employee relations impact. A termination here may create more ill feelings on the part of the remaining staff than it's worth. Look for other options if at all possible.

7. **Has the employee been recognized recently for performance or productivity achievements?**
Having recently granted a merit increase to an employee you're now considering releasing for poor performance is ludicrous.

8. **Has the employee (or dependents) incurred a large medical expense recently under the company's health plan?**
This situation would certainly raise a great deal of suspicion that the company is attempting to cut its losses. It may be coincidental, but be prepared if you're challenged.

9. **Has the employee recently filed legal claim against the company (e.g., OSHA or Workers' Compensation)?**
Be careful. It's difficult to defend against what appears to be a clear case of retaliation on the part of the employer—whether it is or not.

10. **Is the employee approaching retirement age or some tenure-related benefit?**
Without adequate documentation, you would be hard-pressed to prove that the employee was being released other than for the reason of avoiding paying those benefits.

— OTHER QUESTIONS TO CONSIDER —

11. **Can you specifically identify job responsibilities that were not performed or below standards?**

12. Could you transfer the employee to a different position within the company where the person might be effective?

13. Does the employee's work history suggest termination is called for?

14. Historically, have employees with the same or similar problems been handled the same way?

15. Have you documented the employee's unwillingness to respond to corrective action?

16. Is the discharge particularly abrupt?

17. Would the termination oppose any written organizational policies or procedures?

18. Have you followed the company's disciplinary procedures?

19. Is the employee popular within the company, with vendors, or with the community?

20. Is the employee a protected minority member?

Bob Peters is the director of Human Resources for Focus on the Family, an evangelical nonprofit organization with a staff of approximately eight hundred, headquartered in Colorado Springs, Colorado. The organization has ministered to families around the world.

Fund-Raising

31

Ask a Foundation or Donor for a Major Gift

If you have succeeded in getting an appointment with a key person capable of considering a major gift, be prepared to take full advantage of the opportunity by being ready to quickly and convincingly communicate the why behind your request. If you are not able to answer the majority of these questions, you are not yet prepared to ask.

1. **Are there any specific reasons that would disqualify you from receiving a grant from this donor?**
   Because they are regularly approached by so many people for funding, many donors—especially foundations—have specific guidelines defining their giving priorities to screen out funding requests they do not even want to consider. Have you researched their guidelines and current giving opportunities? If you do not currently qualify, what can you do or adjust to qualify?

2. **How do you know that the proposed solution to the need will work?**
   Document the qualifications and the expertise of the person proposing the solution. Case histories of this person dealing with the actual problem are crucial.

3. **What distinguishes this proposed solution from other ones?**
   Explain what else has already been tried and why it worked or why it did not work. Be assured that your prospect has already received numerous requests, even for projects that may seem similar to yours.

4. **Other than funding, what is the greatest obstacle that would prevent you from implementing the proposed solution?**

Sometimes factors that are completely out of your control can affect a project. Anticipating them can help you prepare for contingencies. They could include changes in governments, changes in the law, natural or other disasters.

5. **How will you know if and when the proposed solution is successful?**
List the objects of this effort, and explain the criteria that will be used to objectively measure the success—or failure—of the proposed solution. If you don't know where the finish line is, how will you know when you get there?

6. **What are the strategic dates involved?**
Sometimes a day saved can make or break an entire project. Define the strategic dates into which you are locked (i.e., start dates, completion dates, windows of opportunity, applications deadlines, etc.), then place these dates on a time line for tracking purposes. Use a pert chart for one-time activities and a process chart for ongoing activities.

7. **How much will it cost to implement the proposed solution?**
Define the funding needed to actually accomplish your stated objectives. Do not pad the figures with things not really needed, but include everything to do the job right. State who determined the cost, how they determined the cost, and what qualified them to determine the cost.

8. **Does the proposed solution require long-term funding?**
People don't want to get involved in a bottomless pit that will demand their continued funding to keep the initial funding from being wasted. If this project needs long-term funding, demonstrate how you plan to ensure funding for the project in future years. If the project can become self-funding, explain the steps that are being taken to see that this occurs.

9. **Will your involvement in implementing the proposed solution carry the full approval and support of your board, executive leadership, staff, and current donors?**
It is difficult to undertake a project without the proper support of your staff, leaders, and donors. If they are not currently excited about the project—and you are sure that

you should proceed—determine why they are not behind the project and what you must do to win them over.

10. **How will the completion of this project accelerate progress toward your organization's stated purpose?**
Explain how your purpose, objectives, and goals are reflected in the project's goals. Show that this project or program "fits" your organization like a glove and that it is natural for you to be doing it. You need to show that you are proceeding according to your purpose and not following a false trail.

— OTHER QUESTIONS TO CONSIDER —

11. **Do you currently have a relationship with this donor?**

12. **What is the specific problem your organization intends to address?**

13. **What are the circumstances that led up to, influenced, or caused this need?**

14. **What is your proposed solution to the need?**

15. **What qualifies your organization to implement the proposed solution?**

16. **Who are the strategic staff members necessary to manage the implementation and to monitor the progress of the proposed solution?**

17. **Who else's help or cooperation will be needed to ensure the success of the proposed solution?**

18. **How will you fund the implementation of the proposed solution?**

19. **How will you assure the investor that the money is being used wisely and has a valid return on the investment?**

20. **What immediate benefits and what long-range benefits will be realized when this project is completed?**

Bill Shepherd, Jr., is a development consultant with fifteen years of "hands on" experience. He has been involved with several million dollars of foundation and donor funding. As well as serving with two Christian organizations for seventeen years, he has consulted with numerous other nonprofit organizations in all aspects of foundation and donor development.

— 32 —

Raise Money for an Organization

As we consult with people, we find the most common roadblock to growth and development is lack of funds. Every organization needs capital. Yet most people hate the thought of being responsible to raise it. Generating dollars is a process, like any other process, that needs to be carefully designed and managed. Whether you are asked to raise $100 for your local Cub Scout troop or $1 million for a hospital, the following process will prove invaluable.

1. **What am I willing to give to this cause or project?**
   Asking people to part with their hard-earned dollars is a tough task. You must believe in the project and be willing to give of your own time, talent, and treasure before you can ask anyone else to participate. You don't have to fund it all, but you must be willing to set the example to others.

2. **How much money is needed?**
   That's the key question. Is this a one-time event or an ongoing need? Figure out how much is needed and set a goal. Most people prefer knowing an exact amount rather than giving to an open fund. That's why even general fund organizations like Feed the Children break down their costs

to read: "$17 a month will feed and clothe Armando." This information will also help when you ask people to put you "over the top" or give "the last $500."

3. **Who is our audience?**
Is this a local community need or a national concern? Can you identify the people who have the greatest interest in your project? You'll find it more profitable than trying to tell everybody and hoping the right ones get involved.

4. **How can we best communicate with them?**
The closer you are to people, the more likely they are to contribute. So the best way to ask someone for money is face-to-face. The next best way is by phone, then by letter, then by advertising. You have to decide how you can reach that target audience.

5. **How much will we ask them to give?**
You'll find you are much better off asking for a specific amount than for a donation. People who want to contribute prefer direction so that they aren't embarrassed by giving too much or too little. You can determine a suggested amount, or you can tailor an amount for each donor based on the ability to give. Try to maximize your work—it is much less work to ask one person for $100 than to ask twenty people for $5! Take a look at your goal and determine how many people need to give what amounts of money.

6. **What exactly do we suggest to the potential donors?**
Ask for a specific amount to be given for a period of time, usually two or three years. Remind them of your reasons for being involved. Above all, tell them of the benefit they will receive if they donate! I believe people really want to know what they'll get out of giving.

7. **Do we have any seed money?**
Raising money is easier if you have some money to start with. It can pay for printing costs, phone calls, and mailings. If you are starting with nothing, you might consider borrowing (usually from someone already involved), asking local businesses to donate their services, or just asking friends to begin the grass-roots work with you.

8. Do we have anything to sell or swap?

For a one-time project there are dozens of sales ideas: bake sales, car washes, auctions, garage sales, jog-a-thons, tours, Christmas bazaars, and so on. You'll find a plethora of ideas in any fund-raising book. You can also do a group project, such as clean a park or help a department store do inventory, or you can swap a service (cleaning) for a service (printing). They can be big winners or big losers, but they can happen only once per year and will probably work only three years.

9. Are there foundations, grants, or corporations that will give us money or gifts-in-kind?

Ninety-three percent of charitable donations come from individuals, so only work on this idea if the project is sizable, the foundation or corporation has some clear interest in the project, and someone really knows what she is doing. Grants are most often given for building projects. Gifts-in-kind (e.g., a local business donates a typewriter at cost, then receives a tax write-off for the full retail value) are legal and not as difficult to set up.

10. What do we do after we have raised the money?

Celebrate! Too many organizations ask for your money, then never tell you the results of your gift. Give your donors a special "thank you." Tell them what happened as a result of their donation, and they'll be ready to contribute the next time there is a need.

— OTHER QUESTIONS TO CONSIDER —

11. Do people know what we are doing?

12. Do they know why we are doing it?

13. How often will we ask them to give?

14. Can we ask one person to fund the whole thing?

15. Who are our key people?

16. Can each of them ask a group to be involved?

17. Can each of those people ask friends to give money?

18. Are there people supporting us who have clout?

19. Do we have large numbers of people supporting us?

20. Are we keeping accurate records?

Jerry "Chip" MacGregor, Ph.D., is associate vice president of Trinity Western University in Langley, British Columbia, Canada. He also does consulting through Masterplanning Group International, specializing in speaking/presentation assistance, nonprofit masterplanning, and development work.

Eric Floreen has fifteen years of experience in development with Christian organizations, and he is president of International Christian Development Association of White Rock, British Columbia, Canada.

Give-and-Take

Begin Negotiations

Negotiation facilitates the exchange of something of value and sometimes can create additional value for both sides. Even more successful negotiations result in triple-win possibilities. A triple win will occur when both sides of the negotiation and the larger community benefit. Consider these questions before you begin negotiations.

1. How can everyone win?
A negotiation is conducted between two parties to exchange and sometimes to create additional value to both sides. You negotiate to get a raise or buy an automobile or a piece of real estate. A successful negotiation results in a win for both sides and often for a larger community. For instance, a young couple with children might negotiate a creatively structured purchase of a home from a recent widow using mechanisms such as shared equity. The widow would be relieved of a mortgage and a too large house; she also would receive some cash and half the future appreciation. The young couple would get the space they need and a lower mortgage payment; the neighborhood would be revitalized with children and a family better able to maintain a house and yard. Both parties and the community would win—this would be a triple win.

2. What are the essential issues, principles, or goals vital to an agreement?
What are the absolute goals that your side needs to have at the end of the negotiation? If these deal killers are unclear or doubtful, reexamine your needs and goals and redefine them, or simply stop. Although the triple win is always the ideal goal to sincerely pursue, you must be prepared to walk away from the transaction if your absolute (minimum) needs or goals are unachievable. The widow, for example, could

not accept a note or shared equity arrangement from a financially irresponsible couple; it would not meet her absolute minimum need for financial security. This need must be defined and used as a screening criterion very early to avoid frustration.

3. **Who has what at stake?**
   Determine what is important to the organization on the other side of the table and to the individual who is negotiating. Personal feelings and face-saving sometimes cloud decisions. Some decisions are made by individuals who are acting out of personal, emotional needs and not in the best interest of their organizations. The best negotiators make their point and still make the other side feel good about the process—as well as the substance of winning their absolute needs.

4. **What or where are the triple-win opportunities?**
   Negotiation is an art. A perfectly orchestrated negotiation will allow you to achieve all of your absolute goals while enabling the other side to be part of the real fun of creating a victory for three stakeholders.

   Prior to the start of negotiations, determine how the outcome of the negotiations can truly have a positive impact for both sides of the negotiation as well as the larger community. Where and how can value be created?

5. **How can I address personal needs, goals, or issues of those I negotiate with?**
   Casual conversations before the negotiations begin and during breaks allow you to make friends with members of the other side. Casual conversations can help determine the absolute goals for the other side and what they have at stake. They can also reduce the initial tension that occurs during negotiations.

6. **What are the costs in business, human, and/or organizational terms of success?**
   Occasionally, negotiations can achieve the absolute goals, but only at such a cost in terms of the business creativity that success isn't worth it. Some successful mergers and acquisitions have left dead or wounded companies, individuals, or

communities. Growth and change often do not occur without stress; yet we must strive for the wisdom to know when and where to correctly apply the power to negotiate change. Industries, like people, go through an inevitable life cycle of birth, rapid growth, maturing, and decline. Some must aggregate to survive. But some stay healthy and best serve the community staying small, locally responsive, and flexible. Wisdom asks, "Should we acquire or combine with this company just because we can, and it appears _for now_ to meet everyone's absolute goals?"

7. Is success worth the costs?
You need to determine whether you will win the battle and lose the war. For instance, will you win all of your points but then end up in an antagonistic relationship in all future dealings with the other side? Very few relationships are one-time events. Will your future relationships with other members of the business community be damaged by your efforts in these negotiations?

8. What are the risks to me? To my organization? To the larger communities?
Of failure to reach agreement on essential principles, goals, or items? Essential or absolute goals have to be obtained, or the negotiations have been fruitless. These are the deal killers. Know what they are, and be prepared to do whatever is necessary to get them.

Of failure to reach agreement on additional but nonessential items? How much do my personal career and success depend on winning some nonessential points? What's the risk of causing overall failure or loss of absolute items? Is it probable?

9. How much risk should I take to secure the additional but nonessential goals?
You always want to leave a negotiation with _all_ parties feeling that they have gotten a fair deal. Often continuing to push for nonessential points can create animosity in the negotiations. Risk the negotiations for deal killers but not for nonessential goals.

10. **How will I define, measure, or account for degrees of success on an ongoing basis?**
    Accounting for degrees of success will vary on a case-by-case basis. For me, the first question and the final accounting is, Is this transaction (and our goals and those we perceive for the other side and the larger community) consistent with moral principle and values that have stood the test of millennia by providing wisdom and guidance that work?

— OTHER QUESTIONS TO CONSIDER —

11. **What are the desirable or additional issues, principles, or goals not essential to an agreement?**

12. **Are there personal or emotional issues that conflict with the organization's needs, agenda, and/or position?**

13. **Sitting on the other side of the table, what would I list as concerns, issues, agendas, or needs?**

14. **What are some common goals of both sides?**

15. **Can the mission, enterprise, or process be reorganized to create more convergence of goals?**

16. **How much information can I obtain or divulge?**

17. **Will the goals of all parties stand the test of time?**

18. **What are the time constraints of this negotiation?**

19. **By what criteria will I judge the negotiators' values, character, strength of positions, and desirability of continuing negotiations and/or continuing in future relationships?**

20. **Could we accomplish anything better than the initial or stated goals of these negotiations?**

Glen T. Urquhart is president and founder of Urquhart & Company, which together with its affiliated companies has acted as manager and developer of over $250 million in commercial real estate in the last decade.

34

Seek Reconciliation
in a Conflict

Reconciliation is a complex, painful, and costly process of bringing healing and restoration in the midst of a conflict. Conflicts may range in scope from domestic situations to wars between nations. Persons called to be reconcilers and peacemakers could ask for no greater and noble calling. The following list of twenty questions will help you creatively and knowledgeably approach a situation.

1. **How do you define a *conflict*?**
   A conflict exists when two or more parties perceive that they have mutually incompatible goals. Generally, they will engage in attitudes and behaviors designed to encourage the other party to abandon or modify goals.

2. **How do you define *reconciliation*?**
   There are three distinct faces of reconciliation. The first is to bring together forces that would naturally repel each other. The second is to break down barriers and make a new creation. The third is to change the nature of a relationship (i.e., adversarial to amicable) with another person.

3. **Who are the parties?**
   Who are the chief protagonists in the conflict, and what is their relationship to each other? Conflicts can be bilateral (simple) or multiparty (complex).

4. **What was the threshold of the conflict?**
   Every conflict has a breaking point between nonconflict and conflict. At this point the conflict emerges from a latent stage into a manifest stage.

5. **What was the cause of the conflict?**
   There are generally a complex host of background factors

contributing to the cause of a conflict. They include the needs, values, interests, and goals of the respective parties.

6. What is the desired outcome of the conflict?
Are you satisfied merely with the cessation of hostilities, or is it possible to bring the parties to forgiveness and restoration of a truly amicable relationship? Who will be the winner, and how will *winning* be defined?

7. What attitudes do the parties exhibit toward each other?
Each party in a conflict holds certain stereotypes, beliefs, and images about the other. These are frequently magnified out of proportion when the other party becomes the "enemy."

8. What behavior have the parties exhibited toward each other?
Behavior can span the entire spectrum from violence to rewards. Some behavior is directed toward achieving the goals while other behavior is designed to express anger or relieve stress.

9. What are the relative power and resources of the parties?
Conflicts can be symmetric (equitable power and resources) or asymmetric (inequitable power and resources). This factor may play a significant role in the desire and/or ability of the parties to continue the conflict.

10. What strategies are appropriate to bring reconciliation to the conflict?
The strategy for reconciliation will vary in each situation. However, it needs to address the spiritual and moral dimensions of reconciliation, which include forgiveness, restitution, and justice. It cannot simply be a process of reducing factors to their lowest common denominator.

— OTHER QUESTIONS TO CONSIDER —

11. What is your understanding of human nature?

12. What are the main issues?

13. What previous initiatives have been undertaken to bring reconciliation in the conflict?

14. What roles do other parties play in the conflict?

15. What are the underlying needs, values, interests, and goals behind stated positions?

16. What do the parties fear most about each other?

17. What are the costs to the parties of continuing the conflict?

18. What are the benefits to the parties of continuing the conflict?

19. In what ways has the conflict evolved over time?

20. How do you and the other parties understand your role?

Brian Cox is the senior pastor of Christ the King Episcopal Church in Santa Barbara, California. Over the past seventeen years he has served congregations in southern California and the Washington, D.C., area. In addition, he has spent the last eight years working with political, church, and business leaders in Africa, Asia, Europe, Latin America, and the Middle East. His particular focus has been on the ministry of reconciliation.

Health and Health Care

35

Choose a Nursing Home

Most families face with their parents or other close relatives the ultimate dilemma about professional care when independent living does not provide adequately. This complex decision is usually a process filled with emotion, guilt, and pain. These twenty questions may set the timing and direction of this decision and ease the emotional burden.

1. **Why do I believe the time has come to place my parents in a nursing home?**
   This step for parents is likely a permanent one. Few leave the long-term care system once admission is complete. Recognize that the need for independent living is high in all of us.

2. **Do I have a full understanding of the medical reasons that underlie this decision?**
   Include other members of the family as the parents' physician is carefully consulted. This qualified outside opinion is essential.

3. **Have I addressed my feelings about this decision?**
   There is usually a sense of shame and guilt associated with this type of placement. Improved care and physical environment for parents must prevail.

4. **Have I discussed this decision with my parents and other concerned members of my family?**
   No nursing home can be or replace family. Family members and the nursing home must become partners for care to be effective.

5. **Do I understand that a variety of care levels are available to be matched to the needs of my parents?**
   Congregate care, without nursing, and traditional supervisory care homes, with nursing, licensed and regulated, are available in most communities.

6. **Have I visited several nursing homes that match the level of care required by my parents?**
   As in all services, quality management and sensitive staff training show even to the novice. Tour the home at least twice—once on a weekend. Ask to have a meal. Be aware of odor. Observe grooming of residents. Do staff members speak to the residents?

7. **Have I sought personal, direct contact inside a prospective home?**
   Being able to speak directly to an employee, a nurse, or a resident about care is very important. If a referral is not available to you, ask the administrator for permission for such an interview.

8. **Have I asked the administrator for a copy of the most recent state-conducted biannual inspection report?**
   Regulations require that the survey letter be posted and copies be made available. Reading it will help you evaluate care level, competence, supervision, and training.

9. **Is the operator financially sound?**
   Financial stability is a major problem in the long-term care industry! Financial stress is evident in the industry due to undercapitalization and increased regulatory standards against lagging public revenues. And credit, service, and care are affected. Run a credit report on your choice.

10. **Have I accepted that the most important component and perhaps the hardest to measure is the attitude of the staff in the home toward my parents?**
    This intangible factor determines the quality of your parents' daily life, their ease of adjustment to the home, their response to therapy, and their self-images.

— OTHER QUESTIONS TO CONSIDER —

11. **Have I prayed earnestly about this decision?**

12. **Will the decision further the unity of the family and provide to my parents the required results?**

13. Have I inquired about the financial costs associated with nursing home care?
14. Have I sought information readily available from associations and regulators?
15. Have I prepared a list of tough questions to ask the administrator or admissions staff?
16. Are the physical plant, walls, furnishings, and bedding clean and well maintained?
17. Have I identified and sought out the attending physician for the home?
18. Have I asked admissions the correct financial questions?
19. Have I selected a home located nearest to my parents' physician, other relatives, close friends, and clergy who will most likely visit?
20. Am I prepared to be completely involved when the day arrives for the move to be made?

Maynard Munger is a managing partner of Hayden Manor Associates. He personally owned and/or operated 449 nursing home beds in six long-term care facilities in Arkansas, Kansas, and Texas. Mr. Munger is also owner of Maynard Munger, Realtor, an investment brokerage located in Walnut Creek, California.

— 36 —

Determine Whether Your Child Uses Drugs

The determination about whether a child is using drugs is a difficult task. In today's society the question will be asked by every parent at some time or another. Because of denial, fear, and anger, parents rarely ask themselves or their children the right questions. Each parent should ask the following twenty questions and discuss them before confronting your child.

1. Has my child's behavior changed in recent months?
Drugs will cause behavioral changes when a child begins to use them. The change in behavior is more important than the particular behavior. Each child has an individual personality that makes it difficult for a parent to determine appropriate responses for a particular situation. Recognizing a change requires you to observe your child fairly closely over time. Behavioral change is perhaps the best indicator of a problem.

2. Has my communication with my child decreased?
A child who begins to use drugs becomes defensive, which will usually result in the attempt to avoid conversation. Some children become more withdrawn and avoid any conversation, while others will become busy with outside social activities, thus avoiding conversation and interaction.

3. Does my child have hobbies or activities to participate in if stressed?
Children without hobbies or activities to participate in when they are frustrated or stressed are more vulnerable to addictions. Teenagers frequently use alcohol and drugs to relieve tension and stress.

4. Has my child had recent emotional changes?
Insecurity, fears, or other similar emotions that are not part of your child's normal personality may be indicators of drug usage. Adolescence is a time of emotional turmoil, but rapidly developing changes that are not related to acquiring independence are good indicators of some problem.

5. Has my child begun to show mood swings?
Children using drugs will definitely show mood swings. They may appear calm and cooperative one hour and violent and uncooperative the next hour. Mood swings that are

not precipitated by an outside conflict are signs of impending problems.

6. Does my child have a new set of friends?
Making a change in friends is common for a child using drugs. Perhaps your child will describe the new friends as more interesting or more cool than previous friends.

7. Has my child become overly committed to some activity or sport?
Fear of failure or performance needs and expectations can cause a child to turn to drugs. Athletes may be especially vulnerable to always needing to perform.

8. Has my child lost all enthusiasm for activities or sports?
A child who has enjoyed certain activities or sports and then withdrawn may be involved in the drug culture. The lack of enthusiasm for activities is part of the encompassing addiction to drugs.

9. Has my child's physical appearance changed recently?
Most parents, if they dressed their children, would dress them differently from the way they usually appear. However, a change in dress, hairstyle, and physical appearance over a short period of time is a sign of potential drug problems.

10. Have I provided my child with unconditional love and acceptance?
This is the toughest but most important indicator for drug usage. Kids use drugs because of unmet needs. Needs are taught and validated by their parents. A child who never feels quite good enough or feels a need to change before being accepted by you is at very high risk for using drugs.

— OTHER QUESTIONS TO CONSIDER —

11. Has my child's choice of music changed in recent months?

12. Has my child's attitude changed in recent months?

13. Have my child's values changed?

14. Does my child avoid eye contact with me?

15. Have I observed my child struggling with coordination?
16. Have my child's perceptions changed?
17. Has my child accused me of not caring anymore?
18. Has my child become seriously interested in satanism and the occult?
19. Is my child secure with sexuality?
20. Is my child showing increasing signs of irresponsibility?

Joel Robertson, Pharm.D., is the founder and president of Robertson Neurochemical Institute in Saginaw, Michigan, a corporation specializing in providing books, tapes, and information to people in need of recovery from addictions. He is the author of the Help Yourself Series and Home Recovery Series published by Oliver-Nelson and Thomas Nelson. He has personally treated over eleven thousand persons suffering from addictive disorders.

— 37 —
Enroll in a Health Maintenance Organization (HMO)

With the introduction of managed care, employers are offering employees, and in some regions Medicare is offering retirees, a choice between traditional indemnity coverage and HMOs (Health Maintenance Organizations). Choosing a health plan is an extremely important and very complex decision that you should not enter into lightly. This list of questions has been developed to assist you in the selection process.

1. **If I travel outside the service area of the HMO and I need emergency care, how is it covered?**
   Generally, HMOs contract physicians and hospitals within a specific geographical area. Find out how they will reimburse you or the medical provider that treats you if you are not within the service area.

2. **Is my current physician in the HMO network?**
   Most often an individual physician is not in the HMO network, and you will need to decide whether you are willing to change physicians.

3. **If I am referred to a specialist not contracted by the HMO, am I covered?**
   If your primary physician in the HMO must send you to a specialist for specific care and that specialist is not contracted by the HMO, the services may *not* be covered. It is important to know that the HMO will assume all responsibility for your medical care as long as you follow the HMO guidelines.

4. **If I am required to select a primary-care physician and I am not satisfied, can I switch physicians?**
   Most HMOs require you to select a primary-care physician you will see regarding any problem. If you are not satisfied with this physician, you should be able to change physicians immediately without having to wait until the end of a month or the end of the year.

5. **Has the HMO been in business long enough to earn my trust?**
   Generally, HMOs are regulated by the federal government or a state agency, but like any other business, should they be mismanaged or managed by unscrupulous business operators, they could fail.

6. **If I'm just not happy with the HMO, can I switch back to a less-restrictive health plan whenever I want?**
   Once you select an HMO, you may be locked into that plan

for as long as twelve months until another open enrollment occurs.

7. What happens if I receive a bill from the doctor?

Coverage under an HMO usually requires only a small copayment to your doctor with all other charges being covered by the HMO. Determine if you have any obligation to pay any other bills that the doctor might submit to you.

8. What happens if I have a preexisting condition?

If you have an ongoing illness or take medication on an ongoing basis, you have a preexisting condition. Many plans offer little or no coverage for preexisting conditions. Understand the benefit prior to enrollment.

9. Does the HMO have a conversion option?

If you should leave employment and wish to continue with the HMO on an individual or a family basis, it would be important for that option to be available.

10. Are second opinions covered?

If a physician suggests that you need to undergo surgery or some other significant procedure, you need to have complete freedom to seek advice from other physicians specializing in the same field before you make a decision. If you choose to have a second opinion, the charge for that opinion should be covered by the HMO.

— OTHER QUESTIONS TO CONSIDER —

11. If the HMO physician treats me poorly, how do I solve the problem?

12. Are the HMO physicians in my area overloaded with patients?

13. Can I select more than one primary-care physician for my family?

14. How much will this HMO cost me out of my paycheck?

15. Is there any chance that I might move out of the area in the near future?

16. How much have the rates increased each year over the past three years?
17. Does the HMO offer benefits that are important to me and my family?
18. Where can I get my prescriptions filled?
19. Which hospitals can I use?
20. What are the qualifications of the HMO physicians?

John Snyder is president and founder of Source Employee Benefit Services. His organization assists employers in the selection, design, and implementation of benefit plans including HMO coverage. Over the past fifteen years John has consulted with several hundred companies.

— 38 —

Evaluate Your Drug Usage

For people to sincerely want to know if they are addicted to drugs, they must be open, avoid rationalization and justification of actions, and not blame others. These questions are based on experience with thousands of chemical dependent persons. The term drug *will also refer to alcohol and nicotine since they are forms of drugs.*

1. **Do I use drugs when I feel depressed?**
   The situation in which drugs are used is more important than the quantity or frequency. Using drugs to change the feelings of depression is an indication of addiction.

2. **Do I use drugs to celebrate when good things happen?**
   Using drugs as a part of a celebration is an indication of addiction. To consistently consume alcohol to celebrate a

promotion or something of that nature can lead to addiction.

3. **Has anyone close to me expressed concern that I have a drug problem?**
If someone close to you believes you have a problem, you probably do. Only in rare situations (e.g., the other person believes in abstinence) is an affirmative answer open for debate.

4. **Have I developed a medical condition recently that the doctor has warned me about, but I continue my drug use?**
If your doctor has asked you to stop your drug usage, but you have only decreased it or continued it, you are addicted. A person who isn't addicted wouldn't place the importance of the usage over that of health.

5. **Do I use drugs to unwind?**
Although drug usage appears to be a quick and easy way to unwind, it will eventually cause anxiety. If you use drugs to bring about a calmer feeling, addiction is close if not present.

6. **Have I ever asked myself if I am addicted?**
People who aren't addicted to drugs never ask that question. Those who do are obviously using drugs enough to feel guilty or uncomfortable and are therefore addicted.

7. **Do I feel better when I am using the drugs?**
The high of drugs does feel good, but if you aren't addicted, the guilt and remorse overshadow the temporary good feelings. If you continue to feel better using drugs, you are addicted.

8. **Does it take more of the drug to cause the same effect than it used to?**
Tolerance, the need for more drugs to cause the same effect, is an indication of physical dependency. If tolerance is present, the brain has adapted, and addiction exists.

9. **Do I spend money on drugs when I don't have enough to pay the bills?**
Other than dealing in drugs, the drug business destroys a person's financial security. First, they cost a lot of money;

second, the person is less productive at making money; and third, the drugs can become more important than financial security.

10. **Am I willing to talk to my spouse, parents, or children about my drug usage?**
    If you aren't addicted, you can ask your family about your drug usage with comfort. If they are comfortable and you are comfortable talking about the quantity, frequency, and purpose of use, you are probably not addicted. If you manipulate or require them to agree with your position, you are probably addicted. Your family members know, but they won't tell you if they are afraid of losing your love or acceptance.

— OTHER QUESTIONS TO CONSIDER —

11. **Do I change my plans so I can be around people who can relate to or use drugs with me?**

12. **Have I lost time from school or work because of drug usage?**

13. **Have I been less productive around the house, at school, or at work since I began using drugs?**

14. **If my drugs are prescribed, am I willing to seek counseling to eliminate the usage of the medication?**

15. **If my drugs are prescribed, am I willing to obtain a second opinion to see if there are other options?**

16. **Am I ever confused after using drugs?**

17. **Do I forget periods of time while using drugs?**

18. **Am I having mood swings?**

19. **Do I have a void in my life?**

20. **Do I defend my usage as recreational or optional?**

Joel Robertson, Pharm.D., is the founder and president of Robertson Neurochemical Institute in Saginaw, Michigan, a corporation specializing in providing books, tapes, and information to people in need of recovery from addictions. He is the author of the Help Yourself Series and Home Recovery Series published by Oliver-Nelson and Thomas Nelson. He has personally treated over eleven thousand persons suffering from addictive disorders.

— 39 —

Pick a Vet for Your Pet

Looking for and choosing a veterinary practice can be an exasperating experience, especially if you don't know where and how to begin that selection process. There are numerous kinds of veterinary practices with varying specialties and services. The following questions help you sort out the issues and choose the right veterinary practice for you and your pet.

1. **Should I select a veterinary practice that focuses on the species of pet I own?**
   Generally speaking, the more focused veterinarian has a greater depth of knowledge and experience. For example, a veterinarian who treats only dogs and cats will be able to concentrate on maintaining health and treating disease in just two species. If the veterinarian also treats horses, cattle, birds, "pocket pets," and pygmy goats, the operative knowledge base is dispersed over seven or more species— probably with less depth.

2. **Do all veterinary hospitals offer the same range of services?**
   Certainly not. Some offer outpatient services only. These clinics usually offer routine health maintenance and minor treatment services such as flea control, treatment of eye, ear, and bladder infections, and so on.

Full-service hospital facilities are most common and offer a full range of medical, surgical, and hospitalization services. Full-service hospitals may expand and become a pet center where boarding, grooming, pet foods, and pet supplies are offered under the same roof or as a complex of businesses. Full-service facilities extend in other ways, too, such as providing care by specialists qualified as surgeons, internists, dermatologists, and ophthalmologists, among others.

3. **Can my present veterinarian help me find a reputable veterinarian in a new community when I move?**
   The veterinary profession is quite small. It is surprising how many veterinary colleagues collaborate across the country in sharing continuing education opportunities and solving problems as volunteers for veterinary organizations. Your veterinarian is likely to be acquainted with someone in your new community. Further, directories of organizations such as the American Animal Hospital Association could identify an accredited facility near your new home. Don't hesitate to ask for a referral.

4. **Should I rely on the yellow pages for selection of a veterinarian?**
   Yellow page advertising is useful in that it can help you locate veterinary facilities within easy driving distance. However, specific selection of a veterinarian should not be based merely on the list of services or claims made in paid advertising.

5. **Should I visit the veterinary hospital before making a final decision?**
   Good idea! The visit may be a very obvious exercise to evaluate your potential pet health care provider, or you may choose to be more subtle. Schedule your pet for a nail trim or an exam for a minor digestive upset (or similar minor episode) to evaluate for yourself the facility, the support staff, the doctors, and the range and quality of services.

6. **What kind of treatment should I expect?**
   The receptionist should be pleasant and professional in manner and show interest in you and your pet—both by

phone and in person. The exam-room technician should be gentle and friendly as your pet is weighed and temperature taken. The doctor should be confident, a good listener, thorough, and reassuring. All your questions should be considered and answered in a manner you can understand.

7. What kind of facilities should I expect?

An easily read, professional-looking sign should mark the location. The parking lot should be adequate in size and free of debris. The building entrance should be clearly marked and readily accessible with a pet in arms, on a leash, or in a carrier. The client waiting area should be neat, comfortable, and odor free. Exam rooms should be spotless and well-equipped with examination equipment, scales, and educational materials to help you understand your pet's problem or needs.

Veterinary staff members who are proud of their well-equipped facility will gladly take you on a tour to see their sterile surgery room, X-ray room, laboratory, treatment room, and animal housing areas. Many hospitals have been certified as having met high facility standards set by their state licensing agency or by the American Animal Hospital Association.

8. Should I select a group practice?

Group (multidoctor) practices can offer more hours of doctor availability, which may provide convenience in scheduling appointments. Larger practices may offer a larger staff and more equipment than a solo practice. The large practice may appear less personal to you as a pet owner—a problem that may be minimized by selecting one doctor as your favorite for all routine or planned health care visits.

9. Should I save some money and get my pet's shots at a vaccination clinic?

Although mobile vaccination clinics or other vaccination services provided by some transient arrangement can mean some cost savings, beware of some hazards. Most mobile or transient "shot clinics" do not make provision for emergency care in the event of vaccination reactions, injection abscesses, or other unanticipated side effects. Additionally, a thorough checkup or physical exam is not usually performed, thus a dangerous health threat or advancing disease may escape detection.

10. **What if my pet develops a really unusual problem?**
Your veterinarian may suggest a referral to a specialist, either in private practice or in a university setting, who can provide such services as cataract removal, treatment for glaucoma, reconstructive surgery for abnormal limbs and joints or severe skin injuries due to burns or auto accidents. Allergy testing, cancer treatment, pacemaker implants, endoscopic exam/diagnosis/treatment, and many other procedures offered only to human patients a decade ago are now available for your pet. Progressive private veterinarians in your community may have developed expertise in one or several of these specialized high-tech procedures as well.

— OTHER QUESTIONS TO CONSIDER —

11. **Have I relied on pet owners' recommendations rather than convenience of location to guide me in my decision?**

12. **Have I determined the importance of continuing education to the veterinarian and staff?**

13. **Is the veterinarian interested in topics other than physical health (medicine and surgery), such as behavior problems, pet selection, and so on?**

14. **Does the veterinarian offer services other than medicine and surgery?**

15. **Have I weighed the advantages and disadvantages of a solo practitioner?**

16. **Is the veterinarian reluctant to make a referral to a specialist?**

17. **Is the veterinarian reluctant to allow my seeking a second opinion?**

18. **Does the veterinarian offer house call service?**

19. **How do animal emergency clinics serve my pet?**

20. **Are animal emergency clinics ever open on weekdays?**

Richard A. Goebel, DVM, is principal owner of a four-doctor small animal practice in Mishawaka, Indiana, known as Magrane Animal Hospital. Since 1988 he has served as the director of the Veterinary Teaching Hospital at the School of Veterinary Medicine, Purdue University, West Lafayette, Indiana.

— 40 —
Select a Treatment Center

Someone in your family who needs help from a treatment center is probably not able to make a rational decision. You may be the only person to ensure that the place for treatment is ethical and provides quality care in line with your family's values. Asking the right questions and making the best decision may be the difference between a person beginning a new life of emotional freedom or continuing to be imprisoned by pain.

1. **Is the facility accredited by the Joint Commission on Accreditation of Healthcare Organizations (JCAHO)?**
   Accreditation by this organization means the center is being run in line with quality standards accepted by most hospitals and health care organizations in the country. Without it, there is a good chance that insurance will not cover the cost of treatment and that standards of care may be lacking.

2. **How much does the program cost?**
   Some programs charge an all-inclusive rate, and some charge by the day. Be sure you know the total expected cost. Doctor's charges are separate from the hospital, so ask the staff to break down the charges.

3. **What should I do if my insurance does not cover treatment?**
   If your insurance does not cover treatment at that facility, you have to decide whether you will pay for treatment yourself or choose a facility where insurance will approve payment. Is the treatment important enough to your life to make sacrifices to pay for it personally?

4. **Is the spiritual dimension addressed?**
   The last thing you want to happen is to admit someone into a program that doesn't address the spiritual aspects of problems and solutions. No program should subject a person's faith to attack. Assist the person to find a place where the program incorporates healthy faith into all aspects of treatment.

5. **Does the program provide Twelve-Step groups to patients?**
   Twelve-Step programs, such as Alcoholics Anonymous, are a must if a person is to maintain a long-term recovery. If a facility does not introduce the patient to this type of group, it is robbing the patient of support found throughout the world that is free. A person who starts working with the Twelve-Steps while in treatment seems to accept more responsibility for recovery and becomes less dependent on the therapist over the years.

6. **How is the family involved?**
   Treatment that does not involve the entire family is of little value. Problems do not occur in isolation. They are the result of a sick family system that needs to be changed as a whole and not one member at a time. Without family involvement, all the progress made in the program could be destroyed due to an unhealthy family.

7. **Will my family member get the personal attention required for effective treatment?**
   Some programs will tell you that individual sessions are not important for quality care. Probably, their low staff-to-patient ratios will not allow time for individual sessions. You must find out if the program you are considering offers individual therapy for all patients on an almost-daily basis. If the staff-to-patient ratio is low, the quality of care will be low.

8. Should I see the facility?

No phone call can replace the value of going directly to the facility and seeing firsthand what it looks like and experiencing the feel of the environment. Additionally, when you are encouraging someone to obtain help, the fact that you have been there will mean a lot to the person.

9. Have I considered the wrong amenities in choosing a program?

Some programs will offer horseback riding, pools, golf, and similar options. These things do not make people well, only comfortable. If there are too many diversions from dealing with the problems at hand, treatment can become a waste of time.

10. Is the choice of programs being made by the correct person?

When an adolescent needs treatment, it is better to rely on the judgment of an adult rather than the desires of the adolescent. A person needing treatment has little ability to make rational decisions about the best care. Kids do know which treatment centers have a free flow of their addictive agent. The last person you want choosing the treatment center is the one needing help.

— OTHER QUESTIONS TO CONSIDER —

11. Does my insurance cover the cost of care?

12. Will the facility supply names of people who have been through the program so that I could call them?

13. Do other mental health care professionals who have worked with the treatment team endorse the program?

14. Should I consider inpatient hospital treatment?

15. Is residential treatment more appropriate?

16. Would day treatment work better?

17. Will a halfway house be required?

18. Would outpatient care be preferable?

19. **Does the facility use a team approach?**

20. **When I visited the treatment center, was it well maintained?**

Stephen Arterburn has spent all of his professional life working in and managing treatment centers for addiction and emotional problems. In 1988 he founded New Life Treatment Centers, which operates programs throughout the United States. He holds degrees from Baylor University and the University of North Texas, as well as two honorary doctorate degrees granted by the California Graduate School of Theology and the University of Honolulu.

— 41 —

Set Up a Home Fitness Center

More people in the United States are involved in a regular exercise program than ever before. For a multitude of reasons (convenience, time, cost, etc.), many of these people are setting up a home fitness center. The following list of questions will help you make the right decision regarding your center.

1. **What are my goals for the fitness center?**
   Unfortunately, some people set up a fitness center to impress their neighbors and friends. The equipment that you install should be determined by your goals. Are they aerobic/cardiovascular, rehabilitative, anaerobic/strength building, or a combination?

2. **What is aerobic/cardiovascular exercise?**
   Exercises that concentrate on improving efficiency of the

heart, lungs, and circulatory system are commonly referred to as aerobic/cardiovascular exercises. The exercises that fall into this category are biking, climbing, walking, running, rowing, cross-country skiing, swimming, and so on. These exercises raise the heart rate to a predetermined level and maintain it there for a minimum of twenty minutes.

3. What is rehabilitative exercise?
After an injury operation, physical therapy is required if the individual intends to resume the previous life-style. This therapy can usually be performed at home with the proper equipment.

4. What is anaerobic/strength building exercise?
Exercises that concentrate on improving muscular strength and power are commonly referred to as anaerobic/strength building exercises. Weight lifting (either free weights or machines) is a good example.

5. What types of exercise do I enjoy?
You will have a much better chance of continuing your program if you find an activity that you perhaps have done in the past or that you are quite sure you will enjoy. You may need to do some research at a local health club or fitness store to determine the best type of equipment for you. Today's selectorized machines are quite simple to use and are extremely safe. Free weights may take considerably longer to use, do have some safety considerations, but can be more productive with all these things considered.

6. Should I purchase new or used equipment?
There is nothing wrong with buying used equipment provided that the equipment is a name brand and that you purchase it from someone who will guarantee it. Occasionally, used equipment is available from another individual, but once again make sure that the price is very good and that you are purchasing a name brand.

7. Should I have a physical before I start any fitness program?
Without question, yes. A full physical examination is very important, including a blood scan and stress test.

8. Will fat turn to muscle or muscle turn to fat?
Fat is fat, and muscle is muscle. They do not turn from one

to the other. It is a simple problem. If you eat too much and exercise too little, any calories that you eat beyond your body's requirements will be stored as fat. If you do not use muscles, they will shrink, but they do not change into fat.

9. **Will exercise reverse or slow the normal aging process?**
Although exercise is not in itself a fountain of youth, people of all ages will improve their abilities to function. Exercise will allow you to live your life at its fullest, with more energy, more strength, more enthusiasm, and less stress.

10. **How can I develop exercise discipline?**
People are creatures of habit. Many things that we do during the day are habitual or automatic. Exercising can also become so much a habit that we do it automatically and miss it when we don't. The best way to develop a good habit is to perform that act or action for thirty days consecutively. After that, the habit will be yours.

— OTHER QUESTIONS TO CONSIDER —

11. **Is a home fitness center really for me and/or my family?**

12. **How much can I spend?**

13. **Where do I want to put the equipment?**

14. **Is there a solid warranty on the fitness equipment?**

15. **Can I obtain a preventive maintenance or extended warranty with my equipment?**

16. **Will the fitness store service the equipment?**

17. **Have I determined the reputation of the fitness store?**

18. **Will the dealer service the equipment at my residence or pick it up?**

19. **Will the fitness store take trade-ins on equipment?**

20. **Do I and/or my family need a personal trainer?**

Don Guyer has been in the fitness business since 1961. His experience consists of nine years teaching and coaching in the college ranks and nineteen years as a fitness consultant and owner of United for Fitness.

42

Undergo Major Surgery

The prospect of undergoing major surgery is an anxiety-producing event whose outcome can never be totally predicted. It requires that you put your life in the hands of other people and trust them implicitly. You will have little or no opportunity to contribute to the success of the surgery. However, you can undertake some preparation to improve the likelihood of success and make the process of going through it less anxious. These questions will assist you in preparing to undergo major surgery.

1. What is major surgery?

Major surgery is generally classified as any operation that is hazardous or dangerous. It is appropriate to think of any operation, or procedure, that has the potential to be life threatening or physically incapacitating as major surgery.

2. Are there any alternatives to surgery?

Many medical problems that were traditionally treated with major surgery can be treated with less-invasive procedures today. It is imperative to ask and seek clarification of this issue with your physicians and consultants. Even when addressing cancer, quite often nonsurgical approaches can provide cure rates equivalent to those of surgery. What is important is that you choose a treatment that gives the best likelihood of success and that you feel most comfortable with!

3. Will I need a blood transfusion?

It is good medical practice to avoid transfusions whenever possible, but it's also important to be prepared in case the need arises. Ask your surgeon what the likelihood is of a blood transfusion when the operation is being planned. If a good chance exists that a transfusion may be needed, ask if there is time for you to put your own (autologous) blood aside for potential future use. If there is not enough time for saving your own, ask about relatives or friends that you specify (donor-designated) who could donate blood for your use. If no time exists for either, do not become frantic; Red Cross blood is quite safe now that HIV testing is being performed. Besides, your risk of transfusion hepatitis is greater than acquiring AIDS via blood exchange. Either way, make sure your surgeon understands and shares your feelings regarding the avoidance of blood transfusions whenever possible.

4. How many different bills can I expect?
Have your surgeon clarify as well as possible how many bills you can anticipate. Generally, expect one from the surgeon and possibly from the following entities: assistant surgeon, pathologist, radiologist, clinical laboratory, anesthesiologist, and hospital or surgical center. All these different parties may have dissimilar billing policies, so they will need to be dealt with individually.

5. What if I don't have insurance or funds to pay for the surgery?
Should that be the case, the best place to seek advice is the financial services department of the hospital. They can inform you of the local or state programs for which you may be eligible. Discuss the situation before surgery with your surgeon to confirm if your surgeon is a provider for these programs and, if not, to possibly arrange for a payment plan. Don't forget your family and your church if you must ask for help. You may be surprised by how many people are willing to help you and how many options you have.

6. How do I find a surgeon?
Usually, your family physician refers you to the appropriate surgical specialist (i.e., urologist, general surgeon, thoracic surgeon, etc.). Most physicians refer you to someone they trust and respect; after all, that referral will ultimately reflect on them and their judgment. Sometimes your insurance plan directs you. Also, many hospitals or local medical societies can refer you to a surgeon. Even the yellow pages

of your local telephone directory can provide you with a listing of surgeons if you know the specialty you need for your problem. However, it is crucial that *you* feel comfortable with the surgeon you were referred to or sought out. If you don't feel comfortable, seek someone with whom you will. Be distrustful of any referral that is forced on you despite your uneasiness.

7. Is my surgeon really qualified?

Many persons are led to believe that only board-certified surgeons are truly qualified. That is far from the truth. Many excellent surgeons never sought or gained board certification. I have also encountered surgeons whose judgment and performance are at times questionable and they are board certified. While there are no absolutes, keep in mind that, yes, you are more likely to find good qualified surgeons if they are board certified. You increase that likelihood if they are fellows of their respective colleges. Surgeons are closely scrutinized by their peers prior to being awarded membership in their college. Being a fellow of a professional college implies having achieved a certain level of excellence and being recognized for it by being allowed to add those additional letters after your name and degree: for example, John Smith, M.D., F.A.C.S. (Fellow of the American College of Surgeons).

8. What is a board-certified surgeon?

This person graduates from an accredited medical school and undergoes three to seven (sometimes more) additional years of postgraduate training. Upon satisfactory completion of that postgraduate training and on the recommendation of the departmental chairperson, the individual becomes eligible to sit for the boards. That is often referred to as being board eligible. Then depending upon the rules of the respective board, the person takes and must pass a written examination and sometimes an additional oral certifying examination. (Many boards require only the written exam.) Upon successfully passing, the surgeon is considered board certified. Only twenty-three specialty boards are recognized by the American Board of Medical Specialties, while more than one hundred specialty boards exist in the U.S. Beware of unrecognized specialty boards and surgeons who claim to be certified by them.

9. **Do I have the right anesthesiologist for me, and is the person qualified?**
Choosing an anesthesiologist is no different from choosing a surgeon, so follow the guidelines already given. Quite often there is little chance to choose an anesthesiologist because the person is assigned by the facility where your surgery is being performed. But most facilities attempt to honor requests for specific individuals.

Don't be shy to inquire about the type of anesthesia needed and what choices you might have. The less anesthesia, the lower the anesthetic risk becomes. So, whenever possible, choose local or regional anesthesia over general anesthesia. Discuss these issues freely with your anesthesiologist prior to surgery.

10. **What will my recovery be like, and when can I anticipate going back to work?**
Your surgeon can usually provide you with a fairly accurate idea of what to expect based on experience with previous patients. However, we are all very different and respond distinctively as well. Ask about how much disruption in your normal routine you can expect. If you will be staying in the hospital, clarify the number of days you will spend as an inpatient. Also find out the number of days you can anticipate to be off work. Most major surgeries involve approximately four weeks of disability, and your employer may need to be prenotified to secure your job. Or you may be entitled to state disability benefits, which require review of a form completed by you and your surgeon. An understanding of your limitations during your convalescence can provide you with the opportunity to make advance preparations. After a general anesthetic, you may be advised not to drive for up to a week following surgery.

— OTHER QUESTIONS TO CONSIDER —

11. Is this surgery medically indicated, or is it cosmetic?

12. Do I really understand why I need to undergo major surgery?

13. Do I need a second opinion?

14. Will my insurance company pay for it, or will I be responsible for the entire payment?

15. Will the doctor's office bill my insurance company, or will I be expected to do it?

16. Is the surgeon sensitive to my needs?

17. Do I communicate well with my surgeon?

18. If my surgeon is not a participant in my health plan, have I discussed my financial options with my surgeon?

19. Will the surgery require hospitalization, or will it be done on an outpatient basis?

20. Do I have a choice in hospitals?

Juan Carlos Cobo, M.D., F.A.C.S., is a graduate of the University of California, San Francisco, School of Medicine. He received his surgical training at Harbor-UCLA Medical Center. He is certified by the American Board of Surgery and is a Fellow of the American College of Surgeons. He has been in private practice in South Orange County since 1984.

Home Improvement

43

Decorate Your Home Interior

Have you looked around your home and thought, I really would like my home to have that decorator touch? *Here are a few questions to consider before your venture.*

1. Should I hire a professional?
As in all fields, a professional should be worth the fee. If you have a budget to decorate, set aside a portion to hire a professional or at least consult with a decorator/designer. If you decide not to hire a professional, remember that one mistake in a selection can cost more than the fee.

2. Do I need a decorator or a designer?
If you need architectural changes, hire a designer—a person who has been trained in drafting, perspective, and schematic drawing as well as decorating. If you want to put together colors, textures, themes, and scaled drawing, hire a decorator.

3. What do I look for in a professional?
Integrity is foremost. Be certain the person will not attempt to impose tastes and life-style into your design. Ask how long the person has been in the business, and ask for previous clients' names. There should be no hesitation in referring satisfied clients. Be doubly sure you can work with this person. If you have any doubts, keep looking.

4. How do decorators charge?
Here are a few of the more common methods, but know that this field is full of "creative" people:

- Hourly. Fees range from $35 to $75 per hour. This method is not my favorite because it puts both client and decorator on edge. Some prefer it if the job is limited, but it's very difficult for the client to understand when the decorator started the clock.

- Consultation fee. Both parties agree on a predetermined fee. Decorators who have been in the field for some time will have a good idea of the time and effort required and will be able to quote a fee for their services. Usually, it is to the client's advantage.
- Cost-plus. The decorator will add on a percentage for everything that is sold. However, make clear in advance where the percentage is added: wholesale or retail. If you are paying on top of retail, know the decorator is being paid handsomely.

5. Do I need a contract?

Yes! As best as can be determined, have your professional write out what will be done for what price. If you have a time requirement, include it—knowing in advance it will take longer than expected.

6. Do I need a master plan?

Most people need to execute their goals over an extended period of time. A good decorator will be able to put together colors, textures, fabrics, and wall and window treatments on a color board with current prices so you can execute as the budget allows. Take your time so that you buy right and buy only once.

7. How do I develop a master plan?

Develop a theme, choose a color scheme, balance your textures and patterns, determine furniture needs and scale, and select tones and finishes. Be creative and do not underplay.

Most people are afraid to be bold and make a statement. Thus, when the job is completed, it may lack vigor and personality. Avoid being faddish, either in artwork or in furniture.

8. Should I pick out colors that are "in"?

The decorating world, as the world of fashion, is cyclical. When looking for fabrics and wall textures, you will find manufacturers reflecting the trends. However, my advice is to go to your closet and see the colors you have already selected. Use those colors as a springboard. You should be able to find tones of the hues you prefer and thus be more unique in your decorating.

9. **I like what I have, but it just needs perking up. How do I do it?**

I have worked with some clients through almost two decades—trying not to dispose of what they have. My advice has been that if you have light colors, add dark; if you have dark colors, add light. Rearrange the furniture and accessories. Add a large floral or two with all colors, new and old.

10. **How and where do I buy furniture?**

Look for better-than-average furniture stores. Heed the advice to buy right, buy once. Wait for sales at a reputable *local* dealer. If you have a problem, it's hard to deal with a long-distance relationship. Decide on your needs, stay practical if you have children, and by all means, measure your areas. If you don't know how to do scaled drawings, put masking tape right on your floor using length and width (and don't forget height if you've got windows).

— OTHER QUESTIONS TO CONSIDER —

11. **Have I gotten estimates from three decorating firms?**

12. **What is my budget?**

13. **What are my needs?**

14. **How much involvement do I want?**

15. **Have I chosen quality artwork and other accessories?**

16. **Can I be my own decorator?**

17. **If my spouse and I don't agree, will I be willing to call in a decorator as an arbitrator?**

18. **Have I gotten estimates from upholsterers to help me determine whether to buy a new sofa or reupholster what I have?**

19. **In arranging furniture, have I kept traffic patterns clear?**

20. Do I have referrals from shops and from satisfied clients for resources to help me execute my plan?

Roma Murray has been a decorator for almost twenty years. Although most of her clients are in southern California, she has done homes, business offices, restaurants, model homes, and clubhouses across the country from Aspen to Chicago, New York, and St. Louis, where she now resides. Some of her clients have retained her services through four or five homes.

— 44 —

Landscape Your Property

When you are preparing to landscape a new home or relandscape an existing garden, many aspects that interrelate must be considered. The proper ordering of these conditions will guarantee a successful project flow and completion. Always remember that a landscape is constantly growing and changing; it is never static or stationary in space.

1. What architectural style of garden will best complement my home?
The style of garden architecture should accent that of the house if available; if not, it can enhance a desired theme. Some common examples are Oriental, Mediterranean, English cottage, formal, and historical to your community.

2. What form of garden do I prefer, curvilinear or rectilinear?
The pattern of the elements in your garden enhances the style and controls visual direction: rectilinear (grid patterns and ordered movement) or curvilinear (free form and loose movement).

3. Would a water feature be of benefit?

Water features are a relatively inexpensive way to introduce water into your garden. Not only can they help with noise abatement in a small garden situation, but they also add a pleasing audio aspect.

4. How much hardscape do I need?

The percentage of hardscape to softscape usage can affect budget more than any other aspect; typically, greenery is less expensive than hardscape.

5. Do I want a patio cover or gazebo?

Patio covers and gazebos should be used primarily for needed shade because of their high cost. However, as budget permits, they are effective in enhancing the architectural character of the garden.

6. Which rooms have a southeast exposure?

The rooms with a southeast exposure are the brightest rooms and should be preserved and controlled by shade trees.

7. Do I like deciduous trees?

Deciduous trees are those that drop leaves in the fall. They also give a sense of seasonal color while controlling light and shade in the garden and house.

8. Do any members of the family have plant allergies?

Allergies to flowers, plants, and grasses are very important during the plant material selection.

9. Will growing edible plants be desired?

Growing edible plants can be very satisfying but must be planned for with proper lighting and irrigation. Not every yard is suitable for edible planting.

10. How long do I expect to live in the house?

The length of time you will live in a home affects the initial investment and time required to recoup that cost. Additionally, the size of plant material you select will be determined by the time available for maturity.

— OTHER QUESTIONS TO CONSIDER —

11. Have I established a budget?

12. What is the primary use of my front or back yard?

13. Will I be entertaining in the garden?

14. Do I want a pool or spa?

15. Do I like raised planters?

16. Are there any views I want to preserve?

17. What colors am I most comfortable with?

18. Is actively working in the garden important to me?

19. Do I need a separate play area for the children?

20. Is a dog run necessary?

Chuck and Linda Rathfon have practiced landscape architecture formally for the last ten years, specializing in medium- to large-scale residential projects. They have planned the historical restoration of the gardens at the Forester Mansion in San Juan Capistrano, California, the equestrian and large estate properties of Mr. and Mrs. Jack Flammer of Orange Park Acres, Mr. and Mrs. Dave Reese of San Juan Capistrano, and Mr. and Mrs. Warren Lyons of Laguna Niguel. Chuck also cochairs the Garden Council at the Decorative Arts Study Center in San Juan Capistrano.

Legal
Matters

45

Hire an Attorney

Whether you perceive your legal needs as great or small, hiring an attorney can be just what you need to help set things right in a significant part of your life, or it can be your worst move at the worst possible time. Here are twenty questions you should ask before you decide to hire an attorney.

1. **Is hiring an attorney the right thing to do?**

   What appears on the surface as a legal problem, particularly if it involves conflict resolution, may have its roots far afield from anything legal. Are you seeking reconciliation or vindication? Are your motivations for seeking legal counsel bringing out admirable qualities in you? Is it possible that part of the motivation in seeking a lawyer is greed, revenge, or a desire to evade the law? Are you truly motivated by a desire to see justice and fairness done? It is usually the case that when we are driven to act by wrong motives, we will never be satisfied with the results, win or lose. You need to make sure to forgive and seek what is truly best (even for your adversary), even as you pursue a legal resolution.

2. **What should I do before seeking legal advice?**

   You should seek the advice of family and friends, your pastor, and other trusted advisers. You should have considered (or even pursued) alternative approaches to answering your questions or solving the problem. You should consider the expert assistance available to you at no charge. Your question may be answered by a call to state or local government offices, a private organization, such as the local Chamber of Commerce, or a consumer protection group. If your legal need is conflict resolution, your first step may be to contact a local alternative dispute resolution service, such as the Christian Conciliation Service. Even if these services do not solve your problem, when you contact an attorney, you will have a better idea about what your problem is and what you want to accomplish.

3. What is an attorney's proper role?
Attorneys are most often retained for one of three purposes: (1) document preparation or review (e.g., wills, leases, employment contracts, etc.); (2) transactional analysis (buying or selling a home or business, etc.); or (3) conflict resolution (property damage or personal injury recovery, contract enforcement, divorce settlement, etc.). A general observation is that attorneys are relied on too often to resolve conflict, and not relied on often enough to identify and minimize legal risks in document preparation and transactional analysis. Attorneys can be expensive, but not receiving competent legal counsel beforehand for important legal documents, transactions, and decisions often proves to be much more expensive than solving conflicts or problems after they occur.

4. I have a conflict. Do I need an attorney?
Although an attorney's help for the right problems can be extremely valuable, as a society we go to court far too easily—twelve million civil suits a year are the result of a society drunk with rights and unimpressed with responsibility. Quite often, problems can be settled fairly, at much less cost, if the person with a grievance is willing to go to the other party (either alone or take a friend with a cool head) to work things out privately or to suggest a mediation or arbitration service. Further, your efforts to be understood and to solve your own problems can often be most productive if you are first willing to understand the perspective of the other party. Before you pay for an attorney's time, give serious thought to these alternatives.

5. How do I initiate one of the alternative dispute resolution procedures?
First, contact your local church or the local church of your "adversary" to see if either has a mechanism in place, or is willing to set one up, to resolve such conflicts. If not, contact the Association of Christian Conciliation Services, 406-256-1583, or the Christian Legal Society, 703-642-1070.

6. What if I just need a little legal advice?

If you are starting a new business or entering a new phase of an old endeavor, you may have to report to a new government agency before you begin, fill out and submit a new form or application, or consider new organizational needs to avoid legal problems in the future. Sometimes these are simple matters you can handle on your own. Sometimes, however, you will need an expert's help to set things up as the law requires. If you are unsure of how to proceed and do not know someone who has done it before you with expert help, you would be wise to seek legal advice.

7. I now have a referral; should I call the attorney?

Unless you are in an emergency situation, you may be better off not calling an attorney referral until you have at least two or three prospective attorneys on your list. Then you can compare personalities, experience, availability, and price.

8. What do I say in my initial phone call?

Tell the secretary that you are seeking an attorney for a new legal matter. Generally, you will be put through to the attorney, or in some instances the secretary may be trained to handle the preliminary information. Briefly describe your perceived legal need, and ask for information regarding the attorney's availability, experience with the subject matter, and standard charges. Seek a half-hour-in-person interview whenever possible with at least two prospective attorneys. Ask beforehand what this interview will cost. Many attorneys will provide the initial interview at no cost if they do not end up taking the case.

9. What should I discuss in my first meeting with a prospective attorney?

Discuss availability, expertise, projected fees and costs, and the projected timetable for handling the matter. Money is a very important issue, both to you and to the attorney, and should be discussed fully and forthrightly. When you leave this meeting, you should know exactly how you will be charged and approximate fees and expenses if you proceed.

10. What else should I discuss in the initial interview?

You should get the attorney's initial analysis of the problem, the degree of complexity, and a description of what research, if any, will be required to estimate the fees involved.

— OTHER QUESTIONS TO CONSIDER —

11. **Why do I think I need an attorney?**
12. **Am I willing to give conflict resolution a chance to succeed?**
13. **What sources will I use to find an attorney?**
14. **Do I need a specialist?**
15. **Do I need a Christian attorney?**
16. **Have I determined whether the attorney is known for integrity and wise counsel?**
17. **Do I know the difference between legal fees and expenses?**
18. **Will the attorney take this case on a contingency basis?**
19. **After the initial interview with the attorney, have I called previous clients with similar legal needs?**
20. **Do I have all details of the attorney's representation in writing?**

George R. "Chip" Grange II, Esq., is cofounder of Gammon & Grange, P.C., a Washington, D.C., based law firm with offices in northern Virginia. The firm's attorneys are committed to value-driven service to the nonprofit as well as the business community. Chip and his firm have published numerous articles and conducted nationwide seminars on preventive lawyering and legal risk management. Gammon & Grange, P.C., also specializes in nonprofit law, communications law, preventive law, constitutional law, general corporate representation, and civil litigation.

46

Sign an Auto Lease

Consumer auto leasing can be attractive and very beneficial to many consumers. Offering lower monthly payments and terms that can be matched to your actual intended retention period and use of the vehicle, leasing can free you of the need to trade in or sell your vehicle when you get your next new car. In addition, many manufacturers are offering promotional lease terms that are particularly attractive. But make no mistake about it—a bad lease can be a dreadful experience. Unfortunately, unfamiliar words, lengthy, often confusing contracts, and manipulative sales techniques can make shopping for a lease much more difficult than shopping for a car to purchase. Use the following information and enjoy the benefits of leasing your next car.

1. **What is the capitalized cost of the lease?**

   Capitalized cost is another term for the sales price of the vehicle plus a lease administrative fee. Insist on getting a written capitalized cost, signed by the sales manager or other officer of the seller. Ask for an itemization of any amounts for insurance products or other charges capitalized in the lease. Don't accept the statement that you are just renting or leasing the vehicle and there is no capitalized cost. Don't accept a lease without knowing the capitalized cost. Current federal regulations don't require the lease company to disclose the capitalized cost.

2. **What are my advance payments?**

   Most leases require no down payment and only one monthly payment and a security deposit about equal to one monthly payment in advance. Higher required advance payments should reduce the monthly payment substantially. Making a down payment, termed a *cap cost reduction*, reduces your outstanding obligation and the lease charges you pay and thus your monthly payments. This can be very advantageous if you can afford a down payment.

3. What are the principal types of leases?

Leases are either closed-end, where the end of term value is guaranteed by the leasing company, or open-end, where the customer assumes the responsibility for and risk associated with the end-of-term value of the vehicle. In leasing, the end-of-term value is commonly referred to as the *residual value*. Most consumer leases are closed-end, and most business leases are open-end. There is usually no reason to accept any end-of-term residual value risk in a consumer lease. Guaranteed value is always exclusive of excess mileage, i.e., miles driven in excess of the contracted amount, and excess wear and tear, such as wear and tear caused by failure to service and maintain the vehicle properly.

4. What is the residual value?

The residual value is the expected value of the vehicle at the end of the lease. The higher the residual value, the lower the depreciation payment each month. That offers the obvious advantage of a lower monthly payment. However, a higher residual value also increases the lease charges since the average lease balance over the term is higher. At early termination, a higher residual value results in a higher lease balance and thus a higher early termination obligation and likely deficiency. At the end of the term, a higher residual value increases the purchase option price accordingly, but it also offers the opportunity to bargain with the lessor to purchase the vehicle for an amount less than the residual value.

5. What is the implicit finance rate in the lease?

Technically, there is no interest rate (annual percentage rate, or APR) in a lease because there is no *financing* as defined under federal truth-in-lending laws. However, the lease charges are earned by the lessor against the lease balance, and there is always an implicit finance rate in the lease. The lessor should be able to tell you this implicit rate.

You can approximate the implicit rate by multiplying the average lease charge by twenty-four and dividing by the sum of the capitalized cost and the residual value. Thus, if the average lease charge is $150 per month, the capitalized cost is $20,000, and the residual value is $8,000, the approximate implicit finance rate is (24 × 150) / (20,000 + 8,000) equals 12.86 percent.

6. What are the early termination charges?

Request an explanation of the early termination charges with enough simplicity and examples that you are sure you understand it. Get a written statement of the early termination payoff at the midpoint of the lease you are contemplating. The best early termination formula for the consumer is "level yield" or "actuarial." Any other method most likely results in higher charges. The rule of 78ths or "sum of the digits" method increases the early termination cost by as much as 5 percent of the capitalized cost (i.e., $1,000 on a $20,000 lease). Ask for a comparison of the early termination payoff compared to the level yield payoff at the midpoint of the lease. Early termination costs vary substantially among lessors. If you intend, at the inception of the lease, to terminate early, you have chosen a lease term that's too long for your requirements. Don't try to get lower monthly payments by trading for a lease longer than you expect to keep the car. It may be very costly to terminate early.

7. Do I have a purchase option price at early termination and at lease end?

It is always advantageous to have a purchase option. A fixed price purchase option avoids the possibility of the lessor setting the fair market value above the lease balance. However, some leases have a wholesale value purchase option established at the guidebook price at the end of the lease. You may even be able to purchase the vehicle for less than the residual value at lease end. Regardless of the purchase option in the lease, remember that many lessors do not want the vehicle back and are thus willing to bargain on the sale price.

Find out the average condition wholesale value, which is the most the lessor can expect to get by auctioning the vehicle, and negotiate to purchase the vehicle for that amount, even if it is much less than the residual value or the stated purchase option at lease end.

8. **What is my liability if the lease is terminated early because of a casualty loss of the vehicle?**

If the vehicle is stolen and not recovered or wrecked beyond repair, your lease terminates in most cases. Some lessors agree in the lease not to charge the lessee for this shortfall in the case of a casualty loss. Other lessors offer "gap insurance," a form of credit insurance to cover this risk. The lease should specify the lessor's policy in the event of a casualty loss. Some lessors offer the option of a substitute comparable vehicle in the event of a vehicle wreckage or theft. That can be an attractive option.

9. **Should I buy "gap insurance"?**

As a form of credit insurance, gap insurance can often be purchased to cover the early termination deficiency caused by theft or casualty loss of the vehicle. However, the markup on this product may be very high. On a typical lease, the expected value of the coverage is no more than $100 to $150 in most parts of the country. If gap insurance is priced high, most lessees would be well advised to avoid the product and maintain the cash reserves necessary to pay for any casualty loss or be prepared to negotiate for a substitute vehicle to complete the lease. Alternatively, select a leasing company that provides this protection at a fair price or as a standard feature in its program.

10. **What is the disposition fee?**

Many leases have a disposition fee varying from $150 to $350 to cover the direct costs of preparing a returned vehicle for sale and selling it at auction. These fees are fair but should be included in the lessee's evaluation of the total cost of the lease.

— OTHER QUESTIONS TO CONSIDER —

11. **What is the price to buy the vehicle?**

12. **How much is my monthly payment?**

13. **What is the lease term?**

14. What is the permitted annual mileage, and what are the charges for excess miles?

15. What extra services does the lessor provide?

16. What responsibilities do I have for excess wear and tear, including maintenance of the vehicle?

17. Who establishes wear and tear charges at the end of the lease?

18. Can I move out of state with the vehicle?

19. Apart from excess mileage and excess wear and tear, what is my potential liability at lease end?

20. Is this a good car for me to lease?

Ronald S. Loshin and **Randall R. McCathren** are executive officers of Bank Lease Consultants Inc., San Leandro, California, and Nashville, Tennessee, the nation's premier consulting company in auto lease financing. They are the authors of the definitive industry reference *Automobile Lending and Leasing Manual* and the influential monthly newsletter *Auto Financing Update.*

— 47 —

Sue Someone

It finally happens: you get mad enough to want to sue somebody. It's not just the fact that you were owed money, that you were doing your best to be fair to the other person. You were in the right, and you were still taken advantage of. It's now a matter of principle. Your personal code of ethics has been repeatedly violated. As your initial anger subsides, you grab a cup of coffee and sit pondering your fate. Do you really want to sue someone? Is it worth it? What are the risks?

1. **What's your philosophical bias?**
   This question is critical. Many times people get involved in a lawsuit only to realize in a dark moment that they don't believe in the process. Don't go into litigation if you feel that lawsuits are wrong or that the process is totally corrupt. Your faith in your case, your lawyer, the process, and the rightness of the outcome needs to see you through the valley.

2. **Do you have all the documents; have you read them?**
   Most cases involve documents that clients don't have. Or if they have them, they haven't read them. Put on your thinking cap, find all of the documents involved, read them, develop a chronology, and try to understand the history of your problem. You may stumble on the solution. You will certainly be a better client for a good lawyer.

   An attorney is simply an enhancer, dealing with the facts you present. More often than not, a few months into the process, the lawyer discovers something the client knew from the outset. The sooner you find it, the less it will cost to do so. The more documents you have, the more accurate your assessment will be, and that of your lawyer.

3. **Have you sought the nonlegal counsel of those who are older and wiser?**
   Probably someone in your neck of the woods has had your unique problem two or three hundred times, no matter how unlikely it seems. If your house is being foreclosed upon, find a builder who went through fifty foreclosures. If the water company is sending you a bill you don't owe, find a corporate comptroller who had to deal with a monthly overcharge of $50,000. Ask around, then ask questions.

4. **What are you trying to accomplish?**
   Most uninitiated litigants are in the courthouse because they are angry and feel that suing is the way to alleviate frustration or outrage. Then they wake up and wonder what hit them. This is exactly wrong.

Interview people who have been through the legal process you are thinking about using and the lawyer you are interested in if possible. Ask for client references; find seasoned veterans. Unless you are willing to analyze carefully and make decisions on the basis of the realistic probable value of your case, fairly adjusted by the risk factors, you are headed for trouble.

5. Is it a swearing match?

Is it your word against your opponent's? If so, and this is often the case, you can discount the value of your case by about one-half. If you are not careful, you and your opponent can (and will) play the game of character assassination. Does that sound attractive? Do you have Freon in your veins?

Most juries split a pure swearing match down the middle; they're not going to be less skeptical of you than they are of the other person. Settle the case for a discounted amount and go on about your business.

6. What can you find out about the process, the judge, the other side, and your opponent?

Do your homework. Call around; read the newspapers; look in the local public library or law library. Find out as much as you can about your judge and your opponent. A lawyer who doesn't think this kind of information is important is too inexperienced. Get another lawyer. Try to find one who went to the same law school with the judge, has often tried your kind of case, writes papers on it in the legal periodicals, knows your opponent, knows your opponent's lawyer, has tried cases against both of them, and has won. You'd be amazed at how often that lawyer is out there, and you'll be horrified to meet that person at a dinner party the night after you lose the case.

7. Have you quantified the risks involved in monetary terms?

Probably the most essential assessment you can make of your case is this one. What are the key issues; how likely is it that you will win or lose; what if you lose on this one? Some of this may have to be done by your lawyer or with your lawyer's help, but much of it can be done before you make the decision to sue. Look also at the secondary risks. What will happen to your credit rating if you don't pay the bill? If you sue the only dealership in town, can you get your car serviced? Be as practical as possible.

After the homework and cogitating are done, quantify the case, on a risk-adjusted basis, in a single monetary amount. If the odds are seven of ten on one issue and six of ten on the other one and the case is worth $100, the risk-adjusted value is .6 times .7, or .42 times $100, or $42. If you can settle for a dollar more than that (or even a few dollars less) and can arrange to do it at the outset, *do it*, and don't think about it another instant. Be sure to factor in your attorney's fees, and estimate on the high side. Attorneys are notoriously poor at estimating the cost of litigation.

8. What would the other side settle for?

Ask yourself, What does my opponent want? What will the person pay? What would I pay if I were in the other person's shoes? Your best estimate of what the other side will pay to settle is also your most pessimistic view of the real value of your case. Think hard about taking what might be offered: you might be right.

9. What is a win-win situation?

Is there a way to solve the problem with a business deal, or a settlement, that has something in it for everybody? Often there is. It is hard to discover the true win-win solution to a problem without the active intervention of a trained mediator, lawyer, business counselor, or other disinterested neutral third party because it requires enormous discipline not to "shoot down" the other side's position at every opportunity. Be creative; be open; ask hard questions. Looking for a win-win solution requires a very different slant from trying to win a lawsuit, but the results are generally far more positive.

10. What are the time factors involved?

Litigation usually takes about a year longer than you have to devote to the process, in time and money as well. Focus on the time factors involved. What's the docket situation in your state? What will happen over time if you file suit; what advantages and disadvantages accrue if you do not? Will the construction job on your dream home be hopelessly mired in litigation? If it is left standing there while you litigate with the contractor, what happens to the framing job? Will filing suit against the IRS speed things up or slow them down? Ask professionals for their opinions on the technical issues such as statutes of limitations (how long you can wait to bring suit) and notice provisions, court dockets, trial lengths, and so on.

— OTHER QUESTIONS TO CONSIDER —

11. **What is the nature of the problem?**

12. **What is the other side's position?**

13. **Have you tried listening to the other side's position?**

14. **Can you afford it?**

15. **Is there any alternative?**

16. **Is it worth the trouble?**

17. **What are your strongest points?**

18. **What are your weakest points?**

19. **What does the other side see as your biggest strength?**

20. **What does the other side see as your biggest weakness?**

Brady Sparks, Esq., is a lawyer with over eighteen years of experience. A former felony prosecutor, he has tried approximately 350 civil and criminal jury trials. He has acted as a court-appointed mediator in numerous cases. For more than ten years, his practice has been devoted primarily to civil and commercial litigation and mediation. In 1987, he successfully argued a case involving the federal securities laws in the U.S. Supreme Court. Mr. Sparks practices in Dallas, Texas.

48

Write a Will or Establish a Living Trust

Your plan for the ultimate distribution of what you own requires you to consider writing a will or establishing a living trust. One thing is sure—everyone eventually gives away everything. Your choice is whether you will do it during your life or at death, and whether you will choose the recipient or allow the state to decide for you. If you decide to make the choice, you should think about the answers to the following questions.

1. **What is my estate plan?**
   Have you previously written a will or trust? If so, summarize where it distributes your property interests so that you know your current plan. Then you can determine how you want to change it, if at all. And you will get your mind into the process of writing a more up-to-date plan.

2. **How much (and what) do I own?**
   Make a list of *everything* that you think may possibly be in your estate: real estate, financial accounts, securities held in your name, life insurance you bought or own, retirement funds, personal property, partnership interests, and other items. Even if you have a legal interest in someone else's estate or trust, it may be included in yours. So, write down every possible item of ownership interest, and your lawyer will do a better job.

3. **Who are my heirs and beneficiaries?**
   Once you know what you're going to be giving away, identify people you want to give it to. Only your children? What about grandchildren, other family members, or friends? Also, make an assessment of how much of your estate you

would like to share with each one of your heirs or other beneficiaries.

4. Do I have a taxable estate?

The government allows you to give away up to $600,000 of property (cash or other property interests) and not be subject to an estate or gift tax. If you look at the value of your estate interests and conclude that you're going to give more than $600,000 to noncharitable beneficiaries (your children or other people), or that you and your spouse are going to give over $1.2 million, you have a taxable estate, and more complicated estate planning is in order. This information will help you decide how specialized your lawyer should be in the area of wills and trusts to adequately serve you.

5. What lawyer should I trust?

After weighing the complexity of your estate and your distribution wishes, you should carefully consider the selection of your lawyer. The lawyer's level of expertise in this area should exceed the complexity level of your estate. Do not underbuy! This is an area of law where one thoughtless slip or omission can result in major loss of *your* assets. If your estate is small or uncomplicated and your distribution simple, most lawyers handling other legal matters can draft a simple will to serve your needs. Remember, you're hiring the lawyer (not the other way around) so don't hesitate to interview several.

6. Who are beneficiaries of my insurance policies and retirement plans?

These are often overlooked when people think about the distribution of an estate because insurance proceeds and pension plan proceeds often are distributed directly to beneficiaries listed on the policy or the pension plan years ago. It's good to think about who those beneficiaries are (or who you want them to be) and how their inheritance compares with what other beneficiaries will receive directly from your will or trust.

7. Have I named the executor and/or trustee of my estate?

Your executor manages the distribution of your estate as provided by your will, which is done through the probate court processes. Often a spouse, relative, or friend selected to oversee this process hires an attorney to help. A trustee must be selected for any trust you set up during your life or at death (through your will). Do you want a bank, trust company, family member, or friend to handle this management role?

8. Who determines my incompetency?

With people living longer, more often we encounter unfortunate situations where older persons become incompetent to handle their affairs. Frequently, a court becomes involved in determining who will take over financial and personal management. If you use a living trust or power of attorney, you may state how the determination of your incompetency should be made. You may require certification from your physician, one or two others, plus one or more family members. Carefully think through this answer.

9. Do I want a living will?

This document states the measures a person wishes to be taken in the event of serious illness, such measures as the use of life-sustaining treatment or artificial hydration. Most states recognize the right of a person to forego medical treatment, and the living will is the document used to express this right of the individual who does not wish extraordinary means taken to prolong his or her life. Living wills are simple to do, and your lawyer would do it at the same time that you execute a will or trust.

10. What is my life expectancy?

People more often than not put off writing a will or establishing a trust because they don't expect to die soon. But we all know people who have, and we all know that we don't know when our time is coming. So this is not an excuse to put off the importance of planning, but it can have an effect on whether you use a living trust or a will to draft your plan. Often younger people (perhaps under fifty) do not need a living trust or do not want to be bothered with the property transfer required of such a trust when they are still young and active with their property interests. Discuss this question with your lawyer.

— OTHER QUESTIONS TO CONSIDER —

11. What are my charitable interests?
12. Who should be guardian for my children or me?
13. When do I want to give some, or all, of my estate away?
14. When do I want my children to receive their inheritance?
15. Who will be successor beneficiaries?
16. How do I want to distribute my personal property?
17. Am I expecting any significant inheritances?
18. Are there heirs I definitely want to exclude from the estate?
19. What are the forms of property ownership that I have?
20. What are my debts or other liabilities?

Gregory L. Sperry, J.D., is the vice president and senior counselor of Christian Ministries Foundation. He has personally provided estate planning services and information involving the transfer of over $250,000,000 of assets held by hundreds of families. Christian Ministries Foundation offers planning information and trust and gift distribution services to charitably inclined individuals throughout the United States.

Major Purchases

49

Buy a Car

A dealer's reputation is an overall indicator of how well you should expect to be treated. Driving across town to save a few hundred dollars at the wrong dealership may be a bad investment. Asking yourself the following twenty questions will help you determine how to choose the dealer to do business with.

1. **Should I purchase a new or used vehicle?**
   You can usually buy more car for less money when you purchase used. The downside to a used car purchase is that you may be buying someone else's problems. Buying from a reputable dealer lessens the risks inherent in buying a used car.

2. **Should I purchase American or Japanese or European?**
   There is no right or wrong answer to this question. The Japanese manufacturers have been setting new quality standards for the automobile industry, which has forced many American and European manufacturers to improve. It started with entry level vehicles and has just moved into the luxury field. We are now entering an era where there are numerous examples of automobiles without distinct origin—world cars. This homology is evident with the Japanese-financed manufacturing plants located in the United States and the recent buyout of European manufacturers by domestic manufacturers.

3. **How big is big enough?**
   Today's cars range in size from a two-seat sports car to a twelve-passenger van. The size of your automobile and the body style—two door, four door, station wagon, or van—should be determined by how many passengers you will normally carry and how far.

4. What size engine do I need?

The answer is really based on your expectations of the automobile and how you like to drive. If fuel economy is important, you should pay close attention to the EPA mileage statement listed on the window label. If performance and smoothness are important, a six cylinder or V-8 may be the engine of choice. Additionally, recent engine innovations—multivalve configurations and dual overhead cam design—have increased engine performance without decreasing fuel economy.

5. What options should I consider?

You should customize your car with options that increase your driving pleasure. Automatic transmission, air-conditioning and audio systems certainly fall into this category; a digital dash that can tell you the outside ambient temperature may not.

6. How important is the warranty coverage?

The importance of warranty and the manufacturer who stands behind it increases as the quality of the automobile decreases. Care should be taken when comparing warranty coverage because some manufacturers require a deductible or transfer fee.

7. Should I consider leasing?

Leasing, in many instances, is a viable alternative to purchasing. Leasing offers some interesting benefits such as less down payment, reduced monthly payments, the potential for certain tax benefits, and so on. If you think leasing may be right for you, learn about it prior to your purchase decision.

8. What about the dealer's aftermarket products?

These items, which range from alarm systems to extended warranties, can provide you with value. They are installed at the dealership, and in most instances their cost can be rolled into the total financing of the automobile. You must decide if these options provide a cost-effective value.

9. How important is price?

Price is naturally important, but you need to carefully consider the value you are receiving for your money. The cheapest deal in town is not always the best deal. The best deal considers the price-value relationship rather than just price.

10. **Is the dealer capable of providing me a fair market value for my trade-in?**
A dealer who maintains a well-run used car operation with a good selection of used vehicles is more apt to provide you with fair market value for your trade-in. Dealers who have little or no used-car operation are less likely to provide you full value for your trade. More and more customers today are trading in their cars to the retail automobile dealership. They no longer want the inconvenience and expense of selling their automobiles to strangers.

— OTHER QUESTIONS TO CONSIDER —

11. **How much am I willing to spend?**

12. **What type of transmission do I want?**

13. **Do I want front-wheel drive, rear-wheel drive, or four-wheel drive?**

14. **Which safety items are essential for me?**

15. **What is the shortest time period that I can afford to finance my purchase?**

16. **Is the dealership convenient to my residence or business?**

17. **Does the dealer keep an adequate, well-maintained new car inventory?**

18. **Does the dealer offer convenient service hours?**

19. **How is the dealership ranked on the manufacturer's customer satisfaction index?**

20. **What is the dealership's reputation in the community?**

Lewis M. Webb is president of Webb Automotive Group. The organization's eight dealerships employ more than seven hundred persons. Webb Automotive Group operates exclusively in Los Angeles County and Orange County, California. The Webb Group sells approximately eighteen thousand new and used vehicles per year.

— 50 —

Buy a Major Household Item

Major household items include a broad range of products: kitchen and laundry appliances, electronic audio/ video and security systems, furniture and decorator items, heating and air conditioning systems, exercise and spa equipment, power tools, cleaning equipment, and so on. Since major household items usually require a sizable investment and are to be used for a long period of time, considerations concerning their technology, appearance, durability, serviceability, adaptability, and priority of use are significant.

1. **Do I need this item, or is it a "want"?**
   Essentials for the home should be purchased first and then nonessentials. Determine the importance of the item, and plan its purchase accordingly. As an example, laundry appliances should normally be purchased before an entertainment system.

2. **Is the timing right to purchase this item?**
   Consider your cash resources and requirements. Technology changes rapidly. Often it is better to wait for new models.

3. **Is this item compatible with my home?**
   Determine the size, style, color, quality, and so on that fit

your home. For example, a grand piano may not be as suitable as a smaller model if your home or room is small.

4. **Do I need a professional consultant to help select this item?**
Use a professional if you are unsure of your ability to make a good decision. For example, you may not have an "eye" for interior design. Some companies offer needed services free with the purchase of the item. Be sure you are confident of the integrity and expertise of the company personnel.

5. **What standard of quality should I buy?**
Usually, the least expensive or most expensive items are not the best value. Research carefully to determine the difference between the quality and features of the item. Consider purchasing a used item, a "second," or a slightly damaged item. Consider the frequency of use of the item.

6. **Is there an alternative item that will work as well?**
A portable model may work as well as a built-in or permanently installed model. For example, it may be better to purchase a portable vacuum instead of a built-in one. Consider your life-style. Ask yourself, Will I be living in one location for a long time, or will I move frequently?

7. **Should I pay cash or use financing?**
Pay cash when possible. Avoid financing nonessential items. Borrowing presumes upon the future. If financing is necessary, research its cost, conditions, and terms carefully. Be sure you fully understand your obligations before you commit yourself to financing.

8. **Are there hidden costs related to this item?**
Be sure you know what you are buying. Determine if accessories are included with the item or must be purchased separately. Ask if there are additional charges for delivery, installation, extended warranties, or training.

9. **Are there continuing expenses incurred with the use of this item?**
Determine the operation, maintenance, repair, and insurance cost of the item. Be sure you understand the total cost of ownership of the item over an extended period of time and how long you can expect the item to perform properly.

10. Who repairs the item?
Know if the company repairs the item or if it is repaired by some other company. Some items are required to be returned to the manufacturer for repair. Consider your cost and convenience of the repair policy of the item.

— OTHER QUESTIONS TO CONSIDER —

11. Can I afford to purchase this item?

12. Where do I shop for this item?

13. Am I making an emotional or objective decision?

14. Should I purchase from a local company or a chain?

15. Should I purchase a name brand?

16. Should I purchase, rent, or lease this item?

17. Does the company offer any benefits?

18. Is the item safe to own?

19. Is the item suited for all who may be using it?

20. Do I have intuitive feelings regarding the purchase of the item?

Stanley H. Martin is the president of Hi-Fidelity of Lubbock, Inc., Lubbock, Texas. His company designs, installs, and services home audio/video equipment, car stereo systems, and commercial sound and communications equipment for businesses, churches, and schools. For thirty-one years, Mr. Martin has personally helped hundreds of customers design and select audio/video equipment for their homes.

Buy a Personal or Small Office Computer

This list of questions is aimed solely at the person think-ing through the purchase of a machine for personal or small business usage. These questions are not a prescription that will lead you to purchase precisely the "right" machine. They are, rather, thought joggers. (The list doesn't attempt to speak to networking small computers.) Read all of them before tackling the decisions required to purchase a ma-chine. For purposes of definition, a computer here is con-sidered to include a central processing unit having at least one floppy disk drive, a monitor, and a keyboard.

1. **Will I need compatibility with a computer at the office (or elsewhere)?**
   If you want to pass work back and forth between two loca-tions and readily switch the machine on which the data files are processed, the machines in the two locations should be compatible. Hence, the kind of machine (IBM-compatible/Apple/Amiga) to be considered might be dictated by this single factor.

2. **What software applications do I want to use?**
   The more usual include communications (by modem), word processor, spreadsheet, data base, accounting, desktop manager, personal finance accounting, sales-lead manager, desktop publishing, games, and drawing/art. The software chosen will have certain minimum machine requirements for good performance. This software could, of itself, dictate the kind of machine needed.

3. **Of the most prevalent generic types of personal computers, should I purchase an IBM-compatible, an Apple, or an Amiga?**

The basic operating system of these computers (including the formats of their disks) are different, and compatibility has been slow in coming. If there are questions on this matter, counsel from a trusted person, knowledgeable in computers, should be sought. Each class of machines has its advocates, and each has some advantages and disadvantages. Without knowing what you expect of a computer, it is difficult to address this issue in few words. But the question is a fundamental one, and a choice will be required. In many cases, fortunately, this choice is predetermined by other considerations.

4. **How much machine capacity will suffice for my applications?**
There is little gain in paying for a machine with network-serving capability when you require only reasonable response time for occasionally using a simple spreadsheet or word processor. The machines in the marketplace vary in price from a few hundred dollars to many thousand dollars. The advice of someone (or two or three) disinterested but knowledgeable in personal computers can be a big help. Several questions are implicit in this question about capacity:

- How much Random Access Memory (RAM)?
- How much hard disk capacity?
- How fast a central processor?
- Will I require a math coprocessor?

5. **Do I need growth potential?**
Some computers have a lot of it; others do not. If you anticipate enhancing the machine as more and more use is made of it, does the machine have the framework to support expansion? Computers differ in the number of expansion slots, in the number of serial and parallel ports available for connecting peripheral equipment, and in the capacity of their power supplies to run peripheral equipment.

6. **Do I anticipate adding peripheral equipment?**
It is highly likely that anyone purchasing a computer will be purchasing a printer as well. Other extras commonly added to machines, to increase their usefulness, are a mouse or a

trackball, a modem, a scanner, a CD-ROM disk drive, a tape backup drive, a Bernoulli box, and other electronic paraphernalia too esoteric to mention here.

7. **Do I prefer to work with graphics or words (i.e., a GUI or a "prompt" interface)?**
GUI stands for graphical user interface; it means that the computer presents graphic icons on the screen (monitor) that you can then interact with using a pointing device, such as a mouse. Some people call a GUI a "point and shoot" method of interacting with the computer.

The "prompt" interface, on the other hand, expects you to remember certain basic commands, which must be typed on the keyboard to talk to the computer.

Which is better? Who knows! One tends to be easier; the other tends to be faster. It is a matter of personal preference.

8. **Which size floppy disks do I prefer?**
Floppy disks, the devices used to load programs and data into a computer, come in two standard sizes today: 5-¼ inch and 3-½ inch. Surprisingly, the smaller disks hold more information and are slightly more expensive. This is only a choice if you are buying an IBM-compatible or Amiga since Apple has settled on the 3-½ inch for the various Macintosh computers.

Because so many programs were originally created using 5-¼-inch drives, it is a great convenience to have a computer with a drive of each type. But a choice may be required. Which is better? There is no answer. I prefer to have both for convenience in using various data sources. You must be willing to pay the extra cost for this convenience.

9. **Do I get a reasonable guarantee on the machine?**
The life expectancy of personal computers is measured in years and is really not well known as yet. It is certainly good when compared to automobiles, for example. The parts tending to wear out or require service the quickest are the disk drives, keyboards, and power supplies. These constitute the machine's moving parts.

The reliability of these devices is pretty good. Well-known

brands can be expected to perform reliably for several years, even with daily usage. A computer is an electronic device, in some ways comparable to a TV or VCR in its internal makeup.

10. **After the guarantee period, can I get convenient service and/or repair at reasonable prices?**
The more universal the machine, the easier to find parts and service. The industry is reasonably competitive. Service for all machines can be found but perhaps not with equal convenience. The IBM-compatibles probably have the advantage here.

— OTHER QUESTIONS TO CONSIDER —

11. **Do I need portability?**

12. **How much am I willing to pay for a computer?**

13. **Will I use light-duty or sophisticated applications software?**

14. **How much usage will I give the machine?**

15. **How much physical space can I conveniently allot for the computer?**

16. **Do I want a color monitor (display screen) or a monochrome?**

17. **Does the vendor provide convenient service during the guarantee period?**

18. **What kind of printer will I want?**

19. **Do I need a CD-ROM drive as part of my computer package?**

20. **What will I use for file backup?**

Ed Gruman is the director of the Communications Research Division and the senior marketing analyst for World Vision Inc., Monrovia, California. In 1982 using his personal funds, he purchased the first personal computer in his organization. After demonstrating its wide utility, he guided the purchasing by management of dozens more. Today his organization uses hundreds of such machines. As a hobby, Ed writes data base applications software for small nonprofit businesses.

52

Buy a Recreational Vehicle

When traveling for business or pleasure, you can choose an alternative to going by car and staying in a hotel. A recreational vehicle offers freedom, flexibility, and many of the comforts and conveniences of home. In fact, many owners use their RVs year-round and are considered full-timers. You need to identify and evaluate the types of recreational vehicles available as well as the limitations of each one. Do the evaluation in light of your personal needs and desires. Talk to RV dealers and owners to learn as much as possible before you buy.

1. **How many different types of RVs are available?**
   Here are the two categories of RVs and the classifications within each category:

Towables	*Motorized*
Folding camper trailers	Van campers (Type B)
Travel trailers	Micro-mini-motorhomes (Type C)
Fifth-wheel trailers	Mini-motorhomes (Type C)
Slide-in truck campers	Full-size motorhomes (Type A)

2. **How can I determine what kind of RV is right for me?**
   First, decide if you want to pull or drive an RV. Do you like roughing it, or would you like your RV to be self-contained? Give some thought on how you plan to use it—part-time, weekends, full-time, short or long trips, how many will be traveling with you, and so on.

3. **What does *self-contained* mean?**
   Basically, a self-contained RV is a motorized or towable unit that requires no external hookups to be functional. This RV would be equipped with bathroom, kitchen, sleeping,

plumbing (including holding tanks), and electrical (twelve-volt system, converter or generator) facilities.

4. Should I buy a new or used RV?
Your budget might have a bearing on this answer, but before the decision is made to buy, you might be wise to rent. You would get an idea about the life-style and some of the requirements. You would also be in contact with other experienced RV owners.

5. Do all RVs have the same sleeping and seating accommodations?
No. This is an important factor in selecting the right unit. Determine the maximum sleeping and seating capacity by choosing a floor plan that comfortably meets your needs.

6. What should I know about my tow vehicle before buying a travel trailer or fifth wheel?
Automobiles and trucks have a tow rating, a tongue-load rating, and a gross combined weight rating (GCWR). Never tow more than the vehicle is rated to tow because handling characteristics (steering and braking) are affected. A poorly matched RV and tow vehicle can be very uncomfortable to drive in addition to being unsafe.

7. What about hitch requirements?
This is a very critical part of matching tow vehicle and RV. The working relationship between the tow vehicle and RV can usually be improved by proper weight distribution and hitching procedures.

8. Is a special license required to drive or tow an RV?
In most cases you need only your regular driver's license. However, you might need a special permit for length or weight, depending on the state you live in.

9. How should I equip my RV?
There are numerous options to choose from, so researching before you contact a dealer will save you time and confusion. Depending on where and when you plan to use your RV, you will want to compare the different heating and cooling systems, construction, and interior/exterior features.

10. What other considerations should I be aware of?

Access to plumbing, storage (interior and exterior), interior lighting (location and amount), options available (dealer or factory installed), interior decor choices . . . to mention a few.

— OTHER QUESTIONS TO CONSIDER —

11. Are all RVs constructed the same?

12. Have I attended a local RV show to compare brands or makes?

13. Are there legal restrictions on the length and maximum weight that can be towed?

14. Is it legal to have riders in towable units while they are in motion?

15. What kind of tow vehicle is needed for a fifth-wheel trailer?

16. Can I park or store an RV on my property?

17. When traveling, is it hard to find a place to park overnight?

18. Where should I purchase an RV?

19. What other costs should I be aware of in purchasing an RV?

20. Have I sought out lots of information and reading material and tried to absorb it all?

Dwight E. Bowers is the district marketing manager for International Vehicle Corporation, Bristol, Indiana. He has twenty-one years of experience in the recreational vehicle industry. He has held positions in sales and production management with major RV manufacturers, and he has worked closely as a manufacturer's representative in consulting with dealers and RV users nationwide.

53

Buy Your First Home

The purchase of a home will be the single most expensive decision most people will make in a lifetime. This investment could mean the difference in being able to save money during your lifetime for retirement and having a nest egg for retirement in the form of equity in a home. Discover the answers to these questions by talking to homeowners and other people knowledgeable about real estate. Some helpful books are available, too.

1. Why should I buy in the first place?
   The most common reasons for buying are establishing a fixed cost per month for housing, gaining tax benefits both federal and state against income, and developing a growing equity position in an appreciating asset.

2. Should I use a real estate agent or broker when I buy?
   Using a real estate salesperson doesn't cost; it pays. Attempting to buy without a professional's help is not cost-effective because you have no buffer between yourself and the seller when negotiating.

3. How should I get in contact with a good real estate broker or agent?
   Check with other satisfied sellers or buyers referring you to a qualified agent. Also, know a little about the reputation and knowledge of the salesperson. Don't play phone roulette by calling because you saw an ad in the newspaper.

4. How can I explain to the real estate agent what we are really looking for in a home?
   Many real estate professionals are taught to ask open-ended questions. These questions get information from you about what you are looking for in a home. If the only questions you answer are yes or no questions, you will be left with the

feeling that the salesperson doesn't know what you really want. Open-ended questions probe deeper, and you will feel better about working with a salesperson who understands your needs.

5. How large a home should I buy?
Buy with an eye toward reselling and developing a family. That would mean buying a three- or four-bedroom home instead of a two bedroom. The three- or four-bedroom homes have more resale potential because many families need more bedrooms.

6. Should I buy a fixer-upper?
You can save lots of money by investing "sweat equity." Sweat equity refers to your labor that reduces your initial investment when you buy. Many buyers avoid homes that need work but will purchase an already fixed property for more money, then change things anyway.

7. When is the best time to buy?
Most people buy during "hot" real estate markets. That is when herd mentality kicks in. During these times, writers refer to the market as a seller's market. Also during these times, prices and interest rates are usually higher because many people are competing for available money. Buy during holidays and when the market is slow—that's a buyer's market.

8. If I can, should I add the cost of repairs or cosmetic changes to the mortgage?
Avoid it if you can because you could be paying for those changes from fifteen to thirty years. That makes those changes more costly.

9. Should my family be involved in the decision because they are helping me buy the home?
Don't depend on family or friends for opinions on your purchase. In most cases, they have owned their homes for several years and have a higher opinion of what you should buy, and have forgotten how they started. Also remember, you probably can't afford what they have quite yet.

10. What are home warranty plans?
Home warranty plans cover plumbing, heating, and electri-

cal items for one year after purchase. They can be a great help to you while you adjust to a higher monthly payment from what you rented for.

— OTHER QUESTIONS TO CONSIDER —

11. **How long should I plan to own?**
12. **What locations should be considered when buying?**
13. **I see ads on TV—isn't that the company to call?**
14. **Should I stretch myself and buy more than I can afford?**
15. **Is buying a home an emotional decision?**
16. **Should I buy a home that is all fixed up?**
17. **Where can I get advice about potential defects in a home?**
18. **Is there an optimal time to look at a property?**
19. **When the real estate market is slow, what will I find?**
20. **Should we buy an old home and restore it?**

Augustine A. Sodaro is a California real estate broker, property manager, and investor. He holds a B.A. from Azusa Pacific University and teaches at Mount San Antonio College. Additionally, he is a member of the Inland Empire West Board of Directors, the California Association, and the National Association of Realtors.

— 54 —

Move Up to Another Home

Moving up to another home involves selling as well as buying property. In addition to questions you ask when you _buy a first home, you have another set of questions to answer. Keep these points in mind: shop for a qualified salesperson, know what you want, don't allow yourself to be pressured, get qualified by a lender so you'll know what you can (or cannot) afford, and be patient!_

1. When should I move up to my next home?

Once you own a property, you have some leverage. Buying during slow real estate markets might get you a better interest rate, but prices won't matter too much. If you sell during a "hot" market, you will get top dollar and then have to pay top dollar for the next home. Conclusion: buy when you are ready emotionally and financially.

2. Should I keep the home I have as a rental instead of selling?

Most homeowners don't have that option because they need the equity (money) in the present home to buy the new one. If you can keep it, decide that it isn't anything but an income generator for business purposes, and deemotionalize yourself from it.

3. Is it true that adjustable rate mortgages (ARMs) can buy me more home?

Because the starting or "teaser" rates are lower than fixed rates, that is correct. You should do two things before deciding to use an adjustable rate mortgage: (1) determine the highest the adjustable rate will go and figure out if you can pay that amount per month; and (2) determine that if you are only going to keep the property from four to six years, the fixed rate will cross over the ARM loan in about that amount of time, making the fixed rate cheaper.

4. Is buying a custom-built home a wise decision?

Keep in mind that most homes are custom built. They are constructed on a site and not made in a factory and assembled on the land. Most people confuse the quality of materials used in the construction as a determiner of what makes a custom home. Homes are built pretty much the same way from the slab to the roof. Also, you can't see into the walls to determine how they were put together.

5. **Can used homes be upgraded more cheaply than new ones?**
   Most of the time the answer is yes because you are not under any pressure to change or add things immediately upon purchase. You will, however, see builders now giving front lawns, sprinklers, and sometimes even allowances for window coverings to get their homes sold. Use a sharp pencil and keep your emotions in check with new homes.

6. **When should I buy our dream home?**
   When you can afford it. Or, put another way, working your way up through a couple of homes might get you your dream home. Keep in mind that most dream homes don't exist. Just about the time you think you have it, you want something it doesn't have.

7. **Should I waive the disclosure form?**
   Many states require disclosures because of sellers trying to cover over defects, but many disclosures will ask questions about permits, neighborhood problems, and other situations that would affect your buying that particular property.

8. **Should I fix up my home before I sell it?**
   It depends on what you mean by "fix up." Paint and soap and water will do wonders for a property, but certain things that are replaced will not get more money when you sell. The roof is a good example. Buyers expect a good roof but are unwilling to pay you for installing a new one. Your real estate salesperson can help you with this question because some answers are regional as well.

9. **What should I do about major repairs that need to be done?**
   Depending on the nature of the repair, you might want to offer a discount for the item instead of replacing it.

10. **How do we find out the worth of homes in the areas where we are wanting to buy?**
    Ask the real estate salesperson to get comparables of properties that have sold recently in the neighborhood you are interested in. The appraiser will need them for the institution making your loan anyway.

— OTHER QUESTIONS TO CONSIDER —

11. Should I try to make a good deal on a new house and possibly make a quick profit?

12. Is location important?

13. Should we pay extra for quality features in a home?

14. Should we buy a new home over a used one?

15. How should we handle pushy real estate salespeople?

16. If we find deferred maintenance, what should we do?

17. What happens if we discover toxic problems?

18. Should we shop for a home during the holidays?

19. Will buyers negotiate more during slow real estate markets?

20. How can I find out what my present home is worth?

Augustine A. Sodaro is a California real estate broker, property manager, and investor. He holds a B.A. from Azusa Pacific University and teaches at Mount San Antonio College. Additionally, he is a member of the Inland Empire West Board of Directors, the California Association, and the National Association of Realtors.

Marriage and Family

Become a Dad

Ours is a culture that acknowledges and rewards in special ways almost every male achievement but fathering. So, while asking yourself some questions beforehand may be an unusual exercise, it's an incredibly important one. You can avoid pain later in life by acting on the truths your answers to these questions will reveal.

1. **Have you and your wife discussed your views of what a good father does?**
   Fathering is one of the most powerful areas in which patterns from your families of origin will play out their differences in your home and marriage. Working out differences in marital expectations between you is one thing. Parenting style convictions are sometimes held even more tightly. Be sure you find common ground on issues such as discipline, caregiving responsibilities, and time patterns, especially during the child's first eight to ten years.

2. **Who or what has most shaped your understanding of fathering?**
   Frequently, our fathering patterns develop in response to good fathering models in our lives and in reaction to poor ones we've observed or experienced. Making a list on paper of the specific practices you wish to emulate or discard is a very helpful exercise.

3. **Do you feel you will be willing to set aside personal goals or activities that might interfere with your solid performance as a dad?**
   These days, experienced men recognize that it's virtually impossible to have it all. Priorities are needed, and tough-minded choices are the order of the day especially during a dad's and child's early years when the pressures typical to

becoming well-established in your career path collide with your child's need for time and attention. When your child is young, what you both miss if there's not enough time in the relationship is hard to notice. The toll of regularly missed moments tends to show up most much later when there's no way to change what happened.

4. What three men will top your list of candidates to be your fathering mentor?

Contrary to the prevailing mores in our society, the best fathers don't go it alone. They know that much of their strength, savvy, and security in turning in a great fathering performance flows from the wise counsel and feedback received from other dads who have already completed portions of the task. It's a serious mistake not to have at least one man during your various fathering passages with whom you can comfortably discuss what you are doing and experiencing.

5. At what will you be most consistently excellent, and what will be your most persistent fathering fault?

The very act of identifying your probable strengths and weaknesses can heighten your fathering. Writing down your answers to these questions where you will come across them every six months or so can really keep you on track. You will probably discover some of your identified strengths and weaknesses changing. Fathering, like life, is not static.

6. What are five of your most rewarding childhood moments that you would like your child to experience?

One reason it takes time to be a good dad is that kids don't choose their great moments or ask their most important questions on a schedule. If you're not hanging around as a dad fairly consistently, you're bound to miss some of their best stuff. So, keep in mind what you will want to help them experience.

7. Have you ever read about or sought out any specific training for being a father?

You wouldn't expect to be good at your chosen profession without getting some initial training. Fathering isn't really any different. Read a book; take a class; attend a lecture.

With a little searching you'll uncover a surprising number of available resources on fathering.

8. **What can't you wait to one day teach or share with your child?**
   Your answers on this list are another great window on the joys and priorities of fathering. Note next to each item the appropriate age bracket for learning or sharing this experience. It's a good start on your fathering plan.

9. **What legacies from your families of origin will likely affect your child?**
   We're a lot more aware these days of the impact of family systems, which reveal how behavioral patterns and predispositions to various physical diseases and psychological "dependencies" are passed from one generation to the next. Taking time to identify these factors can vastly enhance your joys and successes as a father.

10. **How much do you understand about the stages of child development?**
    Typically, moms know a lot more than dads about how children grow and develop. They talk and read a great deal more about it. Frankly, becoming familiar with the stages of growth and personality development can greatly enhance your confidence as a dad. Drop by your local library and read a chapter or two in a child psychology textbook. It's interesting reading, and you'll likely find a developmental chart to photocopy for future reference there.

— OTHER QUESTIONS TO CONSIDER —

11. **Do you believe the job of a father is more like that of a farmer or an architect (i.e., is nature or nurture more influential in raising children?)?**

12. **How would you rate your father's performance compared to the dad you would like to have had?**

13. **Are you really ready to grow up?**

14. **What will it cost to provide for your child?**

15. What six adjectives do you hope your child will one day use in describing his or her relationship with you?

16. Would you say it is more rewarding to be a parent or a child?

17. Are you ready for the relationship between you and your wife to be profoundly changed forever?

18. Have you read the instructions the Bible gives fathers?

19. Will you be a dad who hugs a lot and readily displays emotion and affection?

20. Besides being born, making you a "father," what other roles do you imagine your child will play over the years in enabling and strengthening your fathering performance?

Paul Lewis is president of Family University and the founder of its College of Fathering—Dad "U." For more than fourteen years he has edited and published the *Dads Only* newsletter. Among the books he has authored are *40 Ways to Teach Your Child Values* and *Famous Fathers*. Paul regularly speaks to live and media audiences across America on fathering and family strengths issues. He and his wife have five children.

— 56 —

Communicate with Your Teenagers

Talking to kids who don't like to talk isn't always easy. At best, it's like nailing jelly to a tree; at worst, it's not much better than getting a root canal. Quite frankly, many parents feel like giving up. Here are twenty questions on what to ask when you don't know what to say.

1. **On a scale of one to ten, how are you feeling?**
   If they say a five, ask them what would make them a six. At the root of most teenagers' frustrations is a confusion of feelings. Students often cannot express what they feel so they just clam up. Getting them to start with their feelings (regardless of their validity) helps get the communication process jump started again.

2. **What really makes you mad or frustrated? Why?**
   Frustration subtly robs us of our joy. This frustration is magnified when there seems to be no ability to change circumstances. Kids often feel they have no control over their problems, and so the resulting frustration just builds like a pressure cooker.

3. **What's your greatest fear in facing the future?**
   Most students don't consciously admit to being afraid. Behind the "I've got it all together" image is oftentimes a very "scared but I don't want to admit it" kid. Helping students process their fears brings these "nightmares" back into proportion.

4. **What is your most memorable family experience?**
   Remembering the good times helps people put life into perspective. We tend to focus on the negative instead of the positive. Positive memories bring us back into emotional equilibrium. Helping kids remember these family experiences will bring a smile to their faces.

5. **What gives you the most happiness in life right now?**
   Happiness is a by-product of what we have or don't have. To the degree that students perceive they have what they *want* or need, they will experience the feeling of happiness. Probing in this area may give you valuable insight into your teenagers.

6. **What do you look for in a genuine friend?**
   As students move from parental to peer influence during adolescence, the people they spend time with are extremely important. The acceptance of a genuine friend helps them through the tough times. Being honest, being a good listener, being available, and being loyal are some characteristics that kids look for in a true friend.

7. **If you could go anywhere in the world, where would you go and why?**

   Have your kids grown up in one place all of their lives, or are they seasoned travelers? Do they seek adventure, or are they content just to be around home? Traveling may be a key to unlocking the dreams that your kids have for themselves.

8. **What would you like to be doing twenty-five years from now?**

   What do your kids picture themselves doing in the prime of their careers? Are there ways you can help them move in that direction? Are they big dreamers, or do they tend to play it safe? Help them develop a positive focus on the future.

9. **Which three people do you most admire and why?**

   Our modern culture has deemphasized the significance of positive role models. This question may provoke your kids into thinking about why they admire or respect people. Is their answer purely based on media hype, or is there any substance to their choices?

10. **Who has had the greatest impact on your life personally?**

    This is a corollary to the previous question. Parents will be surprised how often their own names will come up if this question isn't asked by them directly. Kids are still looking for heroes. Teachers, youth workers, and coaches are likely candidates.

— OTHER QUESTIONS TO CONSIDER —

11. **How would you complete this sentence: I feel most alone when . . . ?**

12. **How would you describe yourself to someone who had never met you?**

13. **What causes the most tension in the family?**

14. **What is your earliest childhood memory?**

15. **What do you like the most and the least about school?**

16. **What are your three greatest strengths and weaknesses?**

17. **If you could do anything for twenty-four hours, what would it be?**

18. **If you were given $1,000,000 and had to spend it in thirty days, how would you spend it?**

19. **If you could ask God a question, what would it be?**

20. **If you died tonight, what would you consider the highlight of your life?**

John Erwin is the pastor to students and families at Grace Church in Edina, Minnesota. He has been involved with youth ministry for almost fifteen years, serving at Evangelical Free Church of Huntington Beach, California, as well as being the Christian education coordinator for the Evangelical Free Church, Southwest District. He ministers to more than 250 students on a weekly basis. His latest tape series is *Parenting... Is Not a Disease.*

— 57 —

Consider the Effects of Divorce

Since divorce has lifelong implications, you should consider the reasons, costs, and consequences. Because marital conflict becomes so emotionally charged, it is tempting to end the marriage without actually examining the situation systematically. Wisdom suggests a careful, thorough approach to such a serious step as divorce.

1. **What do I hope to gain by divorcing?**
   What do I really want? How will divorce improve my life? Is it my spouse's attitude I want to escape or the responsibility of children and family? Am I chasing a dream of an exciting single life? Sometimes people become caught up in the

immediate, surface reasons and lose sight of the bigger picture and the deeper reasons behind their decisions. They are involved in their own complicated life pattern that would be tripping them regardless of who the spouse was. They may be in a middle-age crisis, and their complaints reflect their discomfort with themselves. The spouse happens to be a part of this picture without being the cause and the primary villain. Searching out the *real* reason for wanting a divorce will be enlightening and helpful.

2. How accurate is my picture of life after divorce?

Some people picture divorce as the grand entrance into a fun, free life. But those who have been living the divorced single life say, "It is not a lot of fun out there! There are a lot of hurting, lonely people." They spend nights alone, have no money and no companionship, share the kids for holidays, rarely see old friends who do not want to take sides and are uncomfortable with the divorce, have conflict with the ex over issues not settled by divorcing, and so on. Many people realize—often too late—that divorce does not end and solve the problems; it merely changes them. Problems continue to exist; they are just different problems.

3. What will divorce cost me emotionally?

The emotional costs come in several areas. No matter how bad the marriage has been, there will be a sense of loss and grief because an important part of life has come to an end. Although it is possible to work out the grief, the "aloneness" is a frequent complaint from many divorced people. Going to the mall, church, or other places where there are couples can be excruciatingly painful. Some people choose to avoid this pain by jumping headlong into another relationship or a series of intense emotionally charged encounters, but this avoidance only postpones the inevitable pain and often causes additional problems in the healing process.

This aloneness can also relate to the absent children, especially for the parents who do not have custody. The reality of not being able to tuck their children into bed, not being there when normal childhood events happen, and knowing that "some other person" in the form of a stepparent will be seeing their children more than they do becomes quite evident once the dust has settled. Also, do they want the "divorce" label following them the rest of life? What will that feel like?

4. How will a divorce affect the children?

This question is a difficult one to answer. It depends on the children's ages and their personalities. One thing is certain, it is going to affect them, but the damage of a divorce must be weighed against the damage of staying in an unhealthy marriage. When conditions are definitely severe, leaving is often the best solution for the children. People say of a parent who stayed for the children, "I wish Mom (Dad) had left a long time ago. Staying for us kids hurt us more than if she (he) had left." Working with a professional counselor can shed specific light on this subject for your particular situation. Here is a second truth related to the children: when the couple can be supportive and congenial with each other after the divorce, there is less emotional damage to the children.

5. Do I realize the effect of a father-absent home on children?

Many father-absent families carry on successfully, but most professionals agree that families with both parents are stronger. Research reveals the following about mother-only families: they move more frequently, causing additional stress for the children; adolescents are more likely to be sexually active; adolescents receive less help with homework; adolescents are more likely to commit delinquent acts; children perform at a lower level on standardized tests of cognitive development; adolescents are more susceptible to peer pressure; and so on.

You may be the exception, but there is no crystal ball telling you how long your children will be with a single parent or the quality of a stepparent. Also, research shows that many dads stop visiting their children two to three years after the divorce—the pain is so great that it hurts less to avoid the kids than to see them for their weekend visit.

6. Did I grow up in a dysfunctional home with poor role models for marriage?

For persons who have grown up in dysfunctional homes with poor marriage models, understanding one's own distorted perceptions is especially critical because faulty learning has taken place. An individual should be especially cautious about a quick decision and determine to seriously examine the personal contributions to the conflict. Discovering and working out a negative emotional pattern usually require therapy and intense introspection.

7. **Do I clearly understand my role in the problems and how I have contributed to the decline in the relationship?**
   It is human nature to place the blame for difficulties on the partner in a bad marriage. Too often, a person sees quite clearly how the partner causes the grief and sincerely believes that "everything would be just fine" if the partner would only "stop being that way." Individuals typically are attracted to marriage partners who tie into their own set of problems, so in a subtle way they "need" their partners to have negative traits so they can continue to play out their own negative patterns.

   It is easy to focus on the partner and overlook one's own contribution. A spouse may spend years trying to fix the partner, which is an unending, impossible goal.

8. **Do I know enough about my emotional style and patterns to avoid repeating the identical pattern in my next relationship?**
   Most divorced people hope to remarry and "do it right" the second time. Some do, while others find themselves repeating the identical messy pattern they had tried to escape by divorcing. The fights are the same, and the painful feelings are similar.

   Correcting an emotional dysfunction requires more work than dumping a spouse and finding a new one. The person who "needs" to pursue closeness without achieving it may be attracted to a similar person the second time, and so he or she repeats the emotional pattern that is comfortable. Even someone who is aware of negative patterns may be attracted to a person who reinforces the negative side and has the very traits considered abhorrent.

9. Am I willing to commit myself to one year of serious effort at this relationship before making a definite decision?

It takes time to sort things out, and people do not make changes quickly. When trust has been violated, it takes time to rebuild it. Making a commitment of at least one year can bring some stability and reduce the seesaw wondering that drives everyone nuts: "I think I'll stay. No, I'll leave. I can't stay." If a couple seriously work at the marriage and have counseling for at least a year, they will have a pretty good idea whether or not it will work out. Not that everything will be solved at the end of a year, but if progress is possible, it will be evident.

10. Have I tried counseling?

Counseling is no magic cure, but it does provide a forum for discussion with a third party. Often the marital problem includes trouble communicating—the ability to explain and understand each other's point of view. Counseling professionals can introduce techniques and new ideas that do make a difference. Some say, "We can't afford it." Well, are you able to afford an expensive divorce? Some say, "I don't want to tell a stranger about my family problems." You'll have to explain your troubles to your lawyer if you divorce anyway. What do you have to lose? Counseling is an avenue that will clarify the problems, and if a person does divorce, counseling will help self-understanding and one's own role in the marriage failure.

— OTHER QUESTIONS TO CONSIDER —

11. How do I feel about being a divorced person?

12. Is physical, emotional, and/or sexual abuse being committed by either my spouse or me?

13. Is my partner or am I abusing any chemicals or involved in any other addiction?

14. Are my feelings about divorce being influenced by another person with whom I am involved?

15. What will divorce cost me financially?

16. How does this action fit in with my spiritual convictions?

17. **What does God want me to do?**
18. **How will I handle the pain?**
19. **Can I say, "I have done everything I know to do, and it still has not worked. I will never have to look back at this time and wish I had tried something else"?**
20. **Which set of problems do I want to live with?**

Donald E. Sloat, Ph.D., is a licensed psychologist in Grand Rapids, Michigan, who has been working with individuals and couples for over twenty years. He has presented papers and conducted national workshops on the dysfunctional Christian family in addition to authoring two books, *The Dangers of Growing Up in a Christian Home* and *Growing Up Holy and Wholly: Understanding and Hope for Adult Children of Evangelicals.*

— 58 —

Get Married

People live in happiness or hopelessness based on the single decision of a life partner. A person's sense of meaning and success are forever influenced by this decision. Children and grandchildren are also affected by this solitary decision. A life partner should not be chosen on the basis of feelings or looks. These are important, but attributes such as maturity in character, emotional stability, and spiritual values should be foremost in your consideration of a spouse. These questions will help you make that wise choice.

1. **What qualities do you see in your potential life partner?**
   Is there respect for parents? Do you see honesty, integrity,

responsibility, and a willingness to ask for forgiveness when wrong? Do you see an attitude toward people, work, and God that is maturing and growing, or do you see an attitude of self-centeredness?

2. **What do you need from a life partner?**
You should be able to write a list of your needs that you hope could be met and should be met by your marriage partner. Marriage is an exclusive relationship, and some needs should not be met in any other relationship. Does your potential life partner have the kind of attitude where character and maturity exist enough now to start the process of meeting the needs you have listed? Becoming mature is a continual process, but if the attitude does not exist now, the chances are not good that this attitude will exist after marriage.

3. **What does your potential life partner expect from a spouse?**
If the person can't articulate now what is needed in a marriage partner, that is a signal of little maturity. The person has probably followed feelings more than well-thought-out values. If the person can communicate what is needed, the question then goes to you: Are you willing to meet those needs?

4. **How does your potential life partner treat you now?**
You need to be careful and wise when you answer this question. Dating causes people to look, act, and be on their best behavior. People are often fooled by feelings of how well a person may listen and care and share heartfelt secrets. But after marriage, that person may not talk or act as before marriage. The major reason is a lack of character and maturity.

5. **What do you want to be and do after you marry?**
Think through your hopes for vocation after marriage because it will affect life-style, living location, budget, distance from family, and potential sacrifice on the part of your life partner for a short or a long period of time.

6. **What does your potential life partner want to be after marriage?**

Are you willing to make the necessary sacrifices and give the support needed for your partner to be fulfilled? Are you compatible, or do you think you will feel cheated?

7. Does your potential life partner keep a budget?
Finances can be a major cause of stress and pressure. To have the best chance for harmony and happiness, both people need to develop and live by a budget. A simple but practical budget provides control, a communication tool, and a clear guide for helping you accomplish what you both desire.

8. What does your potential life partner do to grow?
We have tremendous capacity waiting to be tapped and developed. If we don't set motivating goals to grow, we will shrivel up and complain. Growth goals are worthy of our effort. They help us look beyond our little perspective and challenge us to aim high.

9. What kind of social or recreational activities would be acceptable for you to do without your partner and vice versa?
Hunting, fishing, skiing, shopping, camping, hiking, golfing, playing tennis, and so on may be enjoyable together before marriage, but after marriage, one partner may have no intention of continuing the same activity. One reason may be that the person desires to be with you but will have plenty of "with you" time after marriage and won't desire to keep up the same pace. Do you both have an understanding? How long will your partner need to be gone, and will that be acceptable to you?

10. What habits does your friend practice to keep the spiritual life fresh, alive, and growing?
Does your friend pray? Read the Bible? Attend religious services? Is the person involved with a group that encourages spiritual growth? If not, sloppy habits as a single will not guarantee quality habits after marriage. Don't be fooled; a person who is capable of building a quality relationship with you must be a person who is developing in character, emotional stability, and spiritual values. By the way, to have a great capacity to build a quality marriage, you must be committed to these same goals.

— *OTHER QUESTIONS TO CONSIDER* —

11. What qualities do you see in your potential spouse's parents?

12. What qualities do you see in the siblings?

13. How much emphasis do you put on your physical relationship?

14. Is your potential life partner willing to set standards and boundaries on your physical relationship?

15. How do you feel about your differences in age, race, and culture?

16. What does your potential life partner believe about credit?

17. What is each person's debt level before marriage?

18. What motivates your potential life partner?

19. What social activities does your friend like to do and not like to do?

20. What does your potential life partner believe about God, spiritual authority, and doctrine that is worthy to live by?

Greg McPherson is the president of Life-Trac Family Ministries, Leavenworth, Washington, and coauthor of a communication tool *Preventing Divorce*. Greg has counseled more than twenty-five hundred couples and has given marriage seminars for over fifteen years. His objective is to "help you build quality family relationships...that will last a lifetime."

Place Your Child for Adoption

Making a decision about whether to place a child for adoption is probably the most difficult decision a person will face. Unfortunately, that decision is generally made at a very traumatic and emotional time, a time when rationally considering all of the ramifications of that decision is very difficult.

1. **What do you consider to be your responsibilities toward your child?**
   A parent has certain responsibilities in giving birth to a child, such as teaching and training a child, providing a stable, loving home, building self-esteem, and so on. You must consider what those are before deciding what is best for the child.

2. **What support do you have from your family?**
   The extended family can be a major factor in a child's life. We are often very influenced by those people and their attitudes.

3. **What involvement does the father of the child wish to have with the child?**
   Legally, the father has the right to be involved in decisions regarding the child. A father's input in the child's life is significant.

4. **What are your financial resources?**
   According to the November 12, 1991, issue of the *Los Angeles Times*, the cost of raising a child from birth to eighteen years of age will range from $131,170 to $233,400.

5. **If you decide to place your child for adoption, which type of adoption would you choose?**

In an independent adoption, you choose the adoptive parents with the assistance of an attorney. The state social service agency monitors the adoptive parents with the baby for approximately six months to ensure that the placement is in the best interests of the baby before the adoption is final. In an agency adoption, the agency handles the adoption, although you can be involved in selecting the adoptive parents.

6. What is the ideal family for the child?
You may wish to make a list of all the qualities and characteristics that you desire in the adoptive family, including siblings, extended family, age of parents, occupations, and so on.

7. What financial assistance do you need during your pregnancy?
In California in an independent adoption, the adoptive parents can pay for all maternity-related expenses, including health care costs, counseling expenses, maternity clothes, legal costs, living expenses during the pregnancy, and so on.

8. What do you wish the child to be told about you?
You may wish to give the adoptive parents input regarding when and how the child will be told about his or her birth parents. You may wish to write the child a letter, give the child a photograph, or send something special for the child that is precious to you.

9. Do you wish to see the baby in the hospital?
If you are planning to place your child for adoption, most hospitals have alternatives to being in the obstetrics unit at the hospital. You should tell your doctor whether you would like to see your baby.

10. Do you have a counselor who can assist you emotionally in making your decision?
You need professional help before and after you make your decision. Many counselors who specialize in this field have lots of experience to assist you.

— OTHER QUESTIONS TO CONSIDER —

11. What are your dreams and aspirations for your child?

12. What is the attitude of the family of the father?

13. If you decide to keep your baby, what provisions have you made for child care?

14. What are your goals and objectives for your life?

15. If you keep your child, what are your plans for school and for work?

16. What socioeconomic environment do you wish for the child?

17. Do you wish the adoptive parents to have certain religious beliefs?

18. Do you wish to meet your child in the future?

19. Is your decision based on guilt, fear, or your inadequacies, or is it based on love?

20. What would God have you do?

Susan P. McGann, Esq., is an attorney at law practicing in South Orange County, California. During her twelve years of practice, she has handled many adoptions including both California and interstate adoptions.

— 60 —

Talk to Your Kids About Sex

Many parents struggle with having to talk to their children about sex. When is the right time? What do I say? How do I say it? As I have spoken with parents and young people across the country, I have found the following to be the crucial questions for families to discuss.

1. Where did I come from?

This question can be put a thousand different ways, but it generally comes between the ages of six and ten and requires a relaxed, thorough explanation of sexual intercourse. Don't be caught unaware! Be ready with some basic answers regarding men's and women's bodies, intercourse, pregnancy, and moral standards.

2. Why is sex supposed to be so great?

Because God intended it as the ultimate expression of love between two people. It is the means of procreation and identification in a marriage.

3. What is happening to me?

When kids hit puberty, they can suddenly go bonkers! Explain to them that they are maturing physically and emotionally. They can expect to experience the passion and the peer pressure that come with that age. And the things they'll need most from you are encouragement and willingness to talk about the difficult stuff.

4. Why should I wait for marriage to be sexually active?

There are several good reasons: premarital sex hurts your self-esteem, leaves deep emotional scars, and can lead to sexually transmitted diseases and unwanted pregnancies. Premarital sex often hurts a relationship by destroying trust and respect and by making communication more difficult. More than that, it takes away the specialness of marriage. Many people are sorry they slept together, but I've yet to meet a couple who are sorry they waited.

5. Do you think I'm ready to go on a date?

You are if you know three things: (1) What kind of person do you want to be around, and what kind of person do you want to avoid? (2) What are your behavioral patterns? (3) Can you control yourself? It is imperative that you talk about these issues!

6. How can I handle peer pressure?

It's tough to go against the flow, but people of character are willing to stand up for what is right. Marines go through basic training so that under fire their training will take over and they'll know what to do. You need a similar experience—decide and discuss your behavioral standards *now* so that in a tough situation your training will take over and you'll do the right thing.

7. What about "safe sex"?
Lately "safe sex" has become a euphemism for "sex with a condom." Unfortunately, we're not even sure if a condom completely protects you from all sexually transmitted diseases, and we *know* it fails to protect you from the guilt, emotional pain, and decreased self-esteem that so many experience with premarital sex. The safest sexual activity is abstinence; nobody gets hurt or pregnant from that.

8. How do I cope with all these temptations?
People have been looking for an answer to that one for centuries. Here are some thoughts: know what turns you on; spend time with friends who share your values; decide what you will and will not do; keep your mind pure; and be willing to talk when you're struggling.

9. Is premarital sex really destructive?
Premarital sex often ruins relationships by destroying communication and trust. Solid marriages are built on these things, not on sex. Some people never discover how to have a deep, honest relationship because they always rely on sex. Sure, sex feels good. But isn't there more to life than that?

10. How can a couple talk about their physical relationship?
Sit down in a quiet but public place and say, "We've been going out awhile, and I really like you . . . so I want to ease some of the tension by talking about our standards. This is what I'm comfortable with. . . . Anything beyond that is out of bounds. How does that sit with you?"

— OTHER QUESTIONS TO CONSIDER —

11. Is it wrong to desire intimacy?

12. Is everybody doing it?

13. How far is too far?

14. Don't most people act like sex is no big deal?

15. Why is it so tough to talk with my parents about this stuff?

16. Is it ever okay to masturbate?

17. Do you think oral sex is all right?

18. How can I start over if I've had sex with someone?

19. What do I do about someone I really like who has a sexual history?

20. Isn't waiting until marriage to have sex terribly old-fashioned?

Jerry "Chip" MacGregor, Ph.D., is associate vice president of Trinity Western University, Langley, British Columbia, Canada. He is a popular campus speaker on the topic of human sexuality.

Money Matters

Buy Life Insurance

No longer can the consumer have blind confidence in America's financial institutions. You must take the initiative in researching the company's safety, performance, and reputation as well as the agent's qualifications and reputation. Consider these questions as you conduct your research.

1. **How much life insurance do I need?**
   A rule of thumb is five times annual salary plus enough to pay off a mortgage. A more personal computer analysis takes into account the surviving spouse's earnings, specific educational goals for the children, and income goals at retirement. Other factors are assumptions about retirement age, inflation, and earnings on investments.

2. **What kind of insurance should I buy?**
   A young family or a new business should generally buy convertible term. Whole life is lower in total cost for policies held more than ten years.

3. **What are the advantages and disadvantages of term insurance?**
   Term insurance initially has a cost of only 10 percent of whole life. A young family can buy $1,000,000 of term for $100 per month. Premiums increase with age and become prohibitive in later years.

4. **What are the advantages of whole life?**
   Premiums are level. Cash values build without taxes at attractive interest rates. Cash can be withdrawn tax-free for opportunities and emergencies.

5. **Can I do better by buying term and investing the difference between term and whole life premiums elsewhere?**
   Life insurance is a conservative investment with some companies paying 9 percent on their cash values. You would

need to earn more than 13 percent taxable elsewhere to match the 9 percent tax-sheltered earnings on whole life.

6. What optional benefits are available?
The waiver-of-premium benefit provides that premiums are waived (paid by the company) in the event of disability.

The accidental death benefit pays an additional amount if death is due to an accident rather than disease.

The additional purchase benefit protects insurability of children and younger adults by permitting the purchase of additional insurance regardless of health, dangerous hobbies, or military service.

7. What impartial sources of information are available?
Check A. M. Best, Standard & Poor's, Moody's, or Duff and Phelps. Ratings and analysis are available at a public library or from your agent.

8. What are the top rankings of safety?
A. M. Best A+, Standard & Poor's AAA, Moody's AAA, Duff & Phelps AAA.

9. What comparisons of companies should I request?
Request current and past company investment earnings, current and past mortality expenses, current and past operating expenses, and current and past lapses (dropped policies).

10. How do I select an agent?
The established agent should have the Chartered Life Underwriter (CLU) and Chartered Financial Consultant (ChFC) designations. A newer agent should be taking exams toward these designations. Choose an agent who provides satisfactory answers to the questions listed here.

— OTHER QUESTIONS TO CONSIDER —

11. What if I prefer whole life but can't afford the higher premiums?

12. If I want to be more aggressive by investing in mutual funds, should I buy term?

13. Do life insurance premiums have special tax incentives?

14. Why do older, wealthier people buy substantial insurance?

15. How do policy loans work?
16. Why should I pay interest on the use of my own money?
17. Does whole life have decreasing insurance due to increasing cash values?
18. In selecting a company, have I considered safety, performance history, and reputation?
19. Should I compare company illustrations?
20. Have I checked past performance?

Thomas L. Delahooke, CLU, ChFC, is past president of the Pasadena Estate Planning Council as well as past president of two professional associations. He is a life and qualifying member of the prestigious Million Dollar Round Table. In addition to being a leader in life and disability insurance, he is also an investment officer with Robert W. Baird, member of the New York Stock Exchange. He resides in Pasadena, California.

— 62 —

Invest in a Residential Fixer-Upper

Have you ever thought about buying a run-down house and fixing it up with the goal of making money by reselling it at a higher price? Many real estate gurus, such as William Nickerson, promote this concept as the road to wealth and financial security. If you have what it takes, I concur. On the other hand, you may have thought about buying a run-down house and fixing it up to use as your personal residence. In either case, based on my success, I believe that the following questions should help you work through your decision-making process.

1. **Will all your hard work and the cost of repairs and improvements really make you money?**

   Get an appraisal before you purchase the fixer-upper, determine its pre-fix-up value, and then tell the appraiser what you will do to fix up the property. The appraiser can also tell you the value of the property after it is fixed up.

   My rule of thumb is that I will not buy a fixer-upper unless the value of the fixed-up home is worth 15 to 20 percent more than my original costs plus repairs and carrying costs (i.e., all loan payments, taxes, insurance, and interest payments on repairs charged to credit cards). If I will be living in the house, I will accept as low as 10 percent more in value.

2. **Do you want a fixer-upper or a cleaner-upper?**

   Most fixer-upper buyers really want a cleaner-upper—a home that needs paint, carpets, decorating, and gardening with very minor repairs. Fixer-uppers often require more extensive repairs. Unless you are a skilled home repair person, avoid all homes needing major repairs.

3. **Have you hired an expert to help you evaluate the necessary repairs?**

   This is a must! In California, for $150 you can have a licensed home inspector inspect the house and give you a detailed report on the condition of the house and required repairs. In fixing up, surprises are bad and always costly. Experts help you limit the surprises.

4. **Have you contacted your local building and safety department about this property?**

   Each city or county requires permits for making structural changes or repairing electrical systems, plumbing, heating, cooling, and the roof. Check with your local government before you make an offer.

   Get copies of all the permits ever issued for the property. You may find that permits were not obtained for the additions. When applying for a government insured loan, such as FHA or VA, the appraisers cannot take into consideration any additions that were not constructed with permits and were not reported to the county tax assessor's office as additional square feet.

5. Do you want to use licensed contractors or unlicensed ones?

Although there are no guarantees that a licensed contractor is better qualified than an unlicensed handyman, most state governments require licensed contractors to be bonded. So, in the event your job is not completed, you can make a claim against the bond ($5,000 in California) to get the money to finish the job. Also, the licensing agency will work with you to settle disputes. Certain repairs that can have serious side effects if not done properly (i.e., electrical and gas connections, and major plumbing) should be done only by licensed contractors.

Be sure to check that all the workers on your home are covered by workers' comprehensive insurance or have some other form of insurance to cover accidents on the job. Also, be sure that your insurance will protect you.

6. What do you know about this particular property?

Often neighbors or local Realtors can tell you why this property is run down or vacant. This information will be a help to you when you make your decision to buy or not. Vandalism can be a serious problem in certain areas during the fix-up stage through occupancy.

7. Is your fixer-upper insurable?

Check with several insurance companies to see if you can get full coverage during the fix-up stage. Many insurance companies will not insure vacant houses. Don't buy any property without adequate insurance protection for fire, vandalism, and personal liability.

8. Have you had a termite inspection on the property?

Termite and dry rot repairs can be very costly and are required to be completed before a loan can be obtained. Most termite companies will do an inspection for $65 or less. Often the seller will pay for this inspection and the repairs if you negotiate for these items in your offer.

9. Will your lender loan on a fixer-upper?

Many lenders have guidelines that allow them to lend only on properties in good shape. The more repairs the fixer-upper needs, the more the seller will have to help with the financing by carrying back the mortgage.

FHA has a special loan program for major fixer-uppers. There is also the FHA Title I loan program for fix up after you own the property.

10. **If you plan to live in the fixer-upper, how much chaos and disorder can you stand and for how long?**
Talk to several people who lived through a major remodeling or fixing up of a personal residence. Their insight will be most revealing. Remodeling and living in a home that is in disarray will cause stress.

— OTHER QUESTIONS TO CONSIDER —

11. **Why do you want a fixer-upper?**

12. **What are your skills in home repair?**

13. **How much time are you willing to spend on repairs?**

14. **Do you know someone who can help you think through the entire fix-up process so you can develop a plan?**

15. **What are your financial resources?**

16. **Do you know reliable contractors?**

17. **Can you really count on those people who are going to help you?**

18. **Have you checked on the cost of repair supplies lately?**

19. **Does your fixer-upper require major remodeling?**

20. **If you're married, are both spouses committed to a fixer-upper?**

Bruce S. Herwig, Esq., is an active real estate attorney and real estate broker in San Bernardino, California. His personal real estate portfolio consists of thirty properties. In the last ten years Bruce has fixed up over fifty homes and several apartment buildings.

Invest Internationally

The last fifteen years have seen significant developments in the financial world, and in the last five years we've experienced nothing less than extraordinary developments in the political world. When coupled with advances in technology and communications, national barriers to investing continue to dissolve. The following twenty questions will help as you seek the knowledge you'll need to put your money to work wisely and safely in the international arena.

1. What must my investing accomplish for me?
In the pension business, we refer to defined benefit plans, where a specific end result is targeted, or to defined contribution plans, where a specific sum is periodically set aside and the end result is not explicit. An individual should have elements of both approaches.

2. What effect will inflation have on my investing?
Here the investor's worst enemy is unmasked! Inflation, which in the postwar period has come to be accepted as a fact of life right along with death and taxes, is actually a more insidious foe than Uncle Sam's annual cut of your profits because its effects are not explicit. Instead, they sneak up on you.

A 6 percent investment—which takes twelve years to double the number of dollars—would require thirty-six years to double your buying power! And that's with a relatively modest 4 percent inflation rate and no taxes. Assuming you believe, as I do, that no growth in your buying power over time is hardly different from a loss, even so-called safe investments, such as U.S. Treasury bills, turn out to be not very safe at all in light of taxes and inflation.

International investments are even more complicated. You have U.S. inflation *and* inflation in the foreign country tampering with your buying power. That, in turn, will affect the value of the country's currency, the interest rates, and the economic growth rate, all three of which can have a measurable impact on the value of your international investment.

3. **Will my investment fund be required to make periodic or even emergency disbursements?**

Of course, an emergency is by definition unpredictable, but some probability can be assigned (a healthy thirty-year-old is less likely to require funds for a medical emergency than is the not-so-healthy seventy-five-year-old). An example of periodic disbursements would be the twelve quarterly tuition payments from your college expenses fund. In the investment business we call this liquidity.

The level of liquidity required will vary as the years pass, but along the way the answer to this question will help in making investment choices. The liquidity requirement need not be met individually by every investment within a portfolio, but as a general rule, foreign investments are less liquid than their domestic equivalents. When international investments are included, the domestic investments must carry a proportionately larger part of the liquidity burden.

4. **What are the historical returns from different countries and different classes of investments over various time periods?**

In investing, awareness of how different types of investments have performed in the past is critical to formulating a strategy today that has a good chance of meeting your goals for the future. Similarly, awareness of historical performance for different countries is also critical. As a general rule, returns from financial assets in developed countries are similar in character to like returns in the United States.

5. **What are the historical risks incurred in different countries and by different classes of investments over various time periods?**

As a general rule, risks from financial assets in developed countries are equal to or greater than like risks in the United States. The benefit of using international investments comes from the fact that, most of the time, when the U.S. investment "zigs," the international investment "zags." The result of having both in the portfolio is lower volatility (risk) and yet, over time, the higher returns accrue to your benefit.

6. **How should I allocate investable funds among the available countries and investment classes?**
   This is *the* key strategy question. Numerous academic and real-world studies have concluded that asset allocation—the distribution of your funds among investment types and countries—is the primary determinant of your long-term return. Using your policy as the guide, determine the types and amounts of the various investment classes and countries that should make up your portfolio. Recognize that no single investment, and probably not even any single investment class, will meet all of your policy criteria. But several investment classes taken together should balance one another so that your portfolio *does* fit your policy. Don't forget inflation and taxes as you work through this one!

7. **What impact can currency values have on the investment?**
   In five years or less, the fluctuation in the value of the foreign currency, relative to the U.S. dollar, can be the dominant factor in the performance of an international investment. For example, in February of 1985, the U.S. dollar could be exchanged for about three and a half deutsche marks, the German currency. Three years later, the dollar could only buy one and a half deutsche marks. In such a period of dramatic weakening of the dollar, a German investment by an American investor would perform fabulously. If you had known that the dollar would weaken so much, you might have taken $1,000 in February 1985 and exchanged it for 3,500 DM (deutsche marks). Three years later, at the beginning of 1988, you could have converted your 3,500 DM back into $2,333! That's over 30 percent annual appreciation! But don't forget, it goes the other way, too.

8. **What is the risk of foreign government interference?**
   With most developed countries, this is a nonissue, although the word *interference* is broad and could be something as simple as adverse tax policy changes or central bank intervention in the interest rate arena. With less-stable countries,

possibilities include restrictions on withdrawal of capital, expropriation of the interests of foreign investors (you!), or even nationalization of local companies. In the nineties, some of these possibilities may seem farfetched, but once again the point is to get you to weigh the chances. A good example here is investing in Eastern Europe. Even though the world is hopeful, these young, inexperienced democracies have some rough days ahead of them, and just about anything is possible.

9. **Is the available information compiled in accordance with known standards?**
Financial statistics from foreign countries are rarely compiled with an intent to deceive, but accounting standards aren't really standard from country to country. For example, an American company and a German company with essentially identical operating results (sales, cost of goods sold, etc.) can have greatly different financial statements. If the statements are taken at face value in your evaluation, the conclusions may or may not be valid.

10. **Is the cost of converting income or capital gains from the foreign currency into U.S. dollars reasonable?**
Not only is there a varying exchange rate to deal with, but there is also the *cost* of exchanging your foreign currency profits for dollars. This cost is really nothing more than the currency trader's payment for taking the risk of converting one country's money to another's. With many currencies (e.g., English pound, deutsche mark, Japanese yen), this cost is negligible. But with other, less-common currencies, the cost can be substantial. It's worth knowing the answer to this one before you have to pay for it.

— OTHER QUESTIONS TO CONSIDER —

11. **Have I formulated an investment policy to guide my individual investment choices?**

12. **How much time do I have to reach my goals?**

13. **What effect will taxes have on my investing?**

14. **Are there any other special considerations or circumstances that need to be factored into my planning?**

15. **What role in my strategy would this specific international investment play?**

16. **What effect might settlement delays have on the investment or on my sense of well-being?**

17. **Is there sufficient information available on which to base a decision?**

18. **Is the information available on a timely basis and at a suitable frequency?**

19. **How will foreign taxes affect my returns?**

20. **For a specific investment, what is the economic position of the home country?**

Kurt R. Winrich is a Chartered Financial Analyst (CFA) and president of Winrich Capital Management, Inc. (WCM), a nationally known southern California–based investment management firm. Since its founding in 1976, WCM has specialized in investing for employee retirement plans and has grown in size by more than twenty times.

— 64 —

Invest in Vacation Property

One of the most emotional decisions we make is the selection of a home. The decision to purchase a second or vacation home may be even more so. For most people today, home ownership is their largest form of equity development and their major lifetime investment. Fortunes have been won and lost in real estate investment. And although 97 of the top richest 100 people in America made it in real estate, care in this investment decision making is critical.

1. **Can I really afford a vacation home?**
   Take your total gross income before deductions and multiply it by 36 percent. Subtract from that figure your existing long-term debt payments (car, home, credit cards, etc.), and the remainder would be available for this mortgage. Call your local mortgage broker to confirm and get a prequalifying letter.

2. **Am I at the point in my equity development that this investment makes sense?**
   Most people in their thirties should acquire property for appreciation to build equity. Then when they hit their mid-forties to mid-fifties, they should switch over to income properties that will cover college tuitions and retirement needs. Second homes usually should come after these needs are being met.

3. **Is tax policy an important element of this decision?**
   Depending on your annual income, you may get a better tax break on an investment property instead of a second home deduction. Consult your tax accountant.

4. **How secure will the property be in my absence?**
   For rental properties, how reputable and stable is the property management company? Read the contract carefully and especially note the fees and add-ons. Make sure it is bonded. Check references. For a vacant home, you need to check on ways to protect it from vandalism and break-ins.

5. **What is the maintenance fee going to be like?**
   Whether a single-family home or condo, there will be maintenance costs. For a condo, read the last three meetings' minutes of the association and then ask the property management company about projected increases in monthly or one-time fees. For a single-family home, be sure to check with local authorities on future assessments (i.e., roadwork, sewers, etc.).

6. **Is there any pending litigation on this project?**
   Many times associations sue the developers for problems on

the project. The attorney's fees will be passed on to all residents in the project.

7. What percentage of the units are in foreclosure?
In down markets, you can make a good deal in a vacation project. But if many units are in foreclosure or have been foreclosed on, the values of the units will not appreciate soon, and maintenance fees will go up when fewer units are having their obligations serviced.

8. Are there support services for what I need?
At different ages in your life, you need different support systems. How far away are hospitals, entertainment, police, schools, recreation, and so on?

9. Who is going to use the house?
If your kids or your parents are going to use it, you must make sure they express their thoughts. Many times your needs are different from theirs, and you don't want them to dread the annual vacations you'll probably be locked into.

10. Who will be the owners?
Many vacation homes are held by partnerships and multi-family units. The best way to lose friends is to get into something that ends up a burden on one of the units. Have written buyout plans and set a date (i.e., five years of holding, and then selling or buying each other out with a fair market price established by two competent appraisers).

— OTHER QUESTIONS TO CONSIDER —

11. Do I really plan to hold this long term, or is it a specu-lation?

12. Would it be better to come back each year to this location and rent?

13. Is appreciation an important factor in this decision?

14. Is income a significant factor in this decision?

15. What is the tax picture going to be on this property?

16. How does the general community view this project?

17. Who really are my neighbors?

18. Have my spouse and I really slept on this decision?
19. Have we consulted a friendly third party?
20. Before I sign, have I read everything?

Hal Jones, chairman of ERA Jones Properties Int'l., one of the largest real estate firms in Hawaii, built the firm in five years to be number one in the franchise in the U.S. He has been named 1992 president of his brokers' council and designated president of an international brokers' council. Mr. Jones does business extensively in Asia as well as Hawaii. He is a former state legislator for Hawaii and was chosen out of twelve hundred legislators to be Outstanding Legislator for 1986 by the American Legislative Exchange Council.

— 65 —

Invest Your Hard-Earned Money

Planning is a key element to success in any endeavor. And although it will never be as precise as, say, the physical sciences, investing can nevertheless be approached in a systematic and logical fashion. In that way, you can come as close as possible to "guaranteeing" success. Consider these questions before you invest.

1. **Should I periodically and systematically invest a portion of my hard-earned money for my and my family's future?**
   Yes. (That was easy, wasn't it?)

2. **What must my investing accomplish for me?**
   In the pension business, we refer to defined benefit plans, where a specific end result is targeted, or to defined contri-

bution plans, where a specific investment is periodically set aside and the end result is not explicit. An individual should have elements of both approaches.

3. **How much time do I have to reach my goals?**
   This is known as the time horizon, and the answer to this question goes hand in hand with the answer to the second question. Together they determine the vehicles used, the route taken, the speed traveled—and by implication the *risk* incurred—on your journey to your goals. Time is the investor's greatest ally, and the more of it you have, the better off you are. So start early!

4. **What effect will taxes have on my investing?**
   Uncle Sam likes to share in your success. Both federal and state taxes should be factored into your investment decisions. And it's astonishing what a difference taxes can make! For example, a 6 percent investment will take just about twelve years to double. But in a 35 percent tax bracket, that same 6 percent investment requires eighteen years to double, fully half again as long! Fortunately, the government has given us a few options (tax-free bonds) and opportunities (IRAs, 401(k)s, etc.). Depending on your tax situation, you can choose from taxable, tax-deferred, and even tax-free investments.

5. **Will my investment fund be required to make periodic or even emergency disbursements?**
   Of course, an emergency is by definition unpredictable, but some probability can be assigned (a healthy thirty-year-old is less likely to require funds for a medical emergency than is the not-so-healthy seventy-five-year-old). An example of periodic disbursements would be the twelve quarterly tuition payments from your college expenses fund. In the investment business we call this liquidity. The level of liquidity required will vary as the years pass, but along the way, the answer to this question will help in making investment choices.

6. **Are there any other specific considerations or circumstances that need to be factored into my planning?**
   Take an inventory of any constraints or requirements that

haven't yet been covered. Examples might be social concerns (such as avoiding nuclear utility investments), ethical
concerns (such as avoiding investments that support ethically controversial activities), or even legal constraints (your
investable funds might be in the form of a trust that has
specific, legally enforceable directives or prohibitions). No
need for action here—just an acknowledgment and record
of these types of items.

7. **What are the historical returns from different classes of
   investments over time periods roughly equivalent to my
   time horizon?**
   In investing, awareness of how different types of investments
   have performed in the past is critical to formulating a strategy today that has a good chance of meeting your goals for
   the future. For example, if your investment goals lead you to
   a need for 15 percent average annual return, it's a good bet
   you *won't* accomplish that with U.S. Treasury bills. T-bills
   have returned close to 15 percent in one or maybe two years
   this century, but most of the time they have generated something between 3 and 8 percent.

8. **What are the historical risks incurred by different classes of
   investments over time periods roughly equivalent to my
   time horizon?**
   The flip side of question seven, this one informs you about
   the "cost" of the historical returns. Neglecting this aspect
   can be dangerous.

9. **How should I allocate investable funds among the available
   investment classes?**
   This is *the* key strategy question. Numerous academic and
   real-world studies have concluded that asset allocation—the
   distribution of your funds among investment types—is the
   primary determinant of your long-term return. Use your
   policy as the guide, and determine the types and amounts of
   various investment classes that should make up your portfolio. Recognize that no single investment, and probably not
   even any single investment class, will meet all of your policy
   criteria. But several investment classes taken together
   should balance one another so that your portfolio *does* fit

your policy. Don't forget inflation and taxes as you work through this one!

10. Should I adjust my policy and/or strategy to conform to my (or some expert's) current view of the economy and/or markets?

We're starting to venture into areas of diverse opinion here, but I think mine are reasonably sound. First, in regard to investment policy, the answer is a resounding no. Your policy is intended to be a statement of what you need to achieve, how much time you have to do it, and what limitations you have to deal with along the way to reaching your goal. Policy should change only when one or more of those changes significantly. In regard to investment strategy, the answer isn't so plain. Many will argue—and rather persuasively—that you should set your allocation once and leave it alone until such time as your policy changes. I'm in the camp believing that *moderate* adjustments to strategy in light of economic and market cycles can be beneficial.

— OTHER QUESTIONS TO CONSIDER —

11. Have I formulated an investment policy to guide me?

12. What effect will inflation have on my investing?

13. Have I formulated an investment strategy to implement my investment policy?

14. Should I consider employing professional advisers either in the formulation of policy and strategy and/or in the ongoing management of my investment program?

15. Does this specific investment comply with my investment policy?

16. What role in my strategy would this specific investment play?

17. Do I know what I'm getting into?

18. What are the reputation, background, and history of the firm that's behind the salesperson?

19. What is motivating the salesperson to get my money into this investment?

20. What does a trusted adviser think about this investment?

Kurt R. Winrich is a Chartered Financial Analyst (CFA) and president of Winrich Capital Management, Inc. (WCM), a nationally known southern California–based investment management firm. Since its founding in 1976, WCM has specialized in investing for employee retirement plans and has grown in size by more than twenty times.

Planning

Book a Hotel or Conference Center for a Meeting

Choosing the right hotel for your next conference can create a feeling of helplessness. You are unsure how to effectively communicate with the hotel to get the right atmosphere and have your needs met at the best price. The following list of twenty questions will help you work through the process of selecting a conference site and negotiating the contract.

1. **Is the location of the property one that has a reputation for providing good service?**
   The number of hotels with a facility that looks good but does not provide service is increasing because of the economy. The expansion of the hotel industry in the eighties produced many quality properties that, in the nineties, won't be able to sustain the level of service planned for because of the pressure for profit. A trusted reference for rating hotels in the United States is the *Mobile Guide*, found in bookstores and at Mobile service stations.

2. **Is the property location in an area where the needs of the conferee can be met?**
   Are there affordable restaurants and recreational features? Is transportation convenient? Is there accessible parking? Is it in a safe location? Is it central to the conference location and other properties if overflow properties are needed? Many factors influence a conference's success. The location is one of the main ingredients that will communicate to the potential conferee a special time away from home. With the baby

boomer generation aging, the level of expectation for a fun and relaxing time away from home is rising. They are willing and able to pay more for comfort and service.

3. **Is the meeting space adequate to meet your needs?**
Meeting space in a hotel is critical for a conference. A hotel with the level of service you are expecting will have a working knowledge of the meeting space. The sales representative can explain the space and its use to you in an understandable way. If the size of the meeting room is adequate for your conference, choose the room shaped like a square to allow the greatest flexibility in seating design. Rectangular-shaped rooms create a box-car-style meeting; conferees in the back have a hard time seeing the speaker and audiovisual presentations. With the industry realizing a reduction in cash flow, the condition of the carpet, walls, and so on will help you determine how the property is maintained and the commitment of the management to service.

The hotel's sales staff can explain the best way to set up the chairs to maximize your conference's impact. Ask if the hotel has enough chairs to set the meeting room theater style for your anticipated attendance. If not, require them to supply chairs of the same type. Rented chairs (most likely to be plastic) are uncomfortable for sitting a long time. As you look at the meeting space, consider the way your conferees will move between meetings. Can it be done in a timely way?

4. **If the meeting room will meet your needs, is it equipped with proper sound support, lighting, and temperature control?**
The meeting room needs to have solid sound-resistant walls for the privacy of your meeting and protection from noise bleed from other meetings. Inquiring about the group meeting in the room next to you will help in minimizing unexpected interruptions. Request to see the hallway from which the hotel supplies the room with equipment and food to determine if the room is close to an area from which noise can be generated and interrupt your meeting. There should

be a sound system installed in the room that will allow a lecture. In most facilities it is provided free. A lighting control panel permits you to use different types of lighting. Climate control, or the awareness of how to have the room temperature adjusted, is a valid area of concern for you. The temperature needs to be cool when the room is empty; it can become very uncomfortable quickly if it starts out warm.

If after viewing the meeting space, you know that a specific meeting room is necessary for your conference to be successful, and the sales representative agrees with you, place the specific meeting room by name on a diagram in the contract you sign. The purpose of the diagram is to protect you from a change in meeting room names by the property.

5. **How does the time of week of the conference give you the greatest rate advantage?**
   If your conference falls on a weekend—when most business travelers are home—the rate for the room should be less than on weekdays. Even on weekdays the occupancy has highs and lows. Monday, Thursday, and Friday nights tend to be slow. This principle is true in most properties catering to the business traveler.

   In resort properties or properties located in cities with a high weekend attraction, the weekend rate may be higher. Generally, at these properties the slow time will be Sunday or Monday.

   The time before and after major holidays (i.e., Easter, Thanksgiving, Christmas, New Year's, July 4, etc.) is an excellent time to secure lower rates. Because of less travel, hotels are very slow and are seeking *any business*.

   A common understanding in the hospitality industry is that you can control two of the three: rates, space, or dates. The hotel will control what is left. If you choose rates and dates, the property can choose the space for you. In holiday periods the demand for space is so low, space is almost always available. The industry standard is one complimentary room for every fifty occupied.

6. Does the rate quoted include food?

Some properties quote rates to include food, which is generally favored in resort areas. There are three food plans: (1) Full American Plan (three meals daily); (2) Modified American Plan (two meals daily, breakfast and dinner); and (3) European Plan (no meals). Most conferees don't need three meals daily because they aren't that active. One way to help the conferees is to plan a brunch about 9:15 to 9:30 after your first meeting.

7. Is the contract prepared by the hotel for the conference a good representation of the partnership formed between you and the property?

With the amount of disputes happening in the courts today, most contracts prepared by the property lean in favor of the property. As you negotiate with the sales representative, keep in mind that when the contract is prepared, it should contain what you have agreed to in a language you can understand.

If you see this hasn't been done, you can prepare an amendment to the contract modifying it to better explain the agreed-upon areas. Make note of the amendment on the original contract, and indicate that the contract isn't official until the amendment is properly executed. Some properties will request that the amendment be placed in the body of the contract for easier flow and assurance that these areas will be seen by the departments at the property that have to service your conference.

If you make a change to the original contract, call your sales representative and explain what you are doing. If you change a contract in *any way*, the original agreement expressed in the contract is null and void. You possibly will have to renegotiate the entire contract. *Keep the sales representative informed.*

8. Is the conference services department assigning you a qualified person who understands your business and will be with you through the entire conference?

A property that has conferences on a consistent basis will have a Conference Services Department. The Sales Department will track your conference until the contract is signed, then turn your file over to the Conference Services Department.

The Conference Services person first reviews your file after you finish signing the contract. This is for your benefit to determine if there are any questions regarding your contract. You can also expect a letter of introduction or a phone call. The actual processing of your file begins ninety days before your conference begins.

The Conference Services person must attend the preconference meeting. By then, the person should know your conference needs thoroughly.

9. **When the conferee registers for the conference, do you need to send a rooming list to the property, or do you need to have the conferee register with the property using reservation cards or 800 numbers?**

The advantage of having the conferee register with the property directly by using a reservation card or calling the 800 number is that your administrative needs are reduced. The disadvantage is that you don't know if the conferee has registered with the property and when the number of rooms needed for free meeting space is realized. The conferee may instead locate a lower rate at another property and commute to the conference.

The advantage of the rooming list is that you know where the conferee is staying. The disadvantage comes if the hotel requires a first night's deposit that you must process. If you have rooms held until 6:00 P.M. the day the conference begins, you won't have to collect the first night's deposit because the conferee will either call and guarantee the room personally or be at the property before 6:00 P.M.

If more than one property is involved in your conference, you may have to ask the registrants to state their preference to be placed in the headquarters property.

10. **When can the conference be cancelled without penalty to the conference organizer?**

The cancellation clause needs to be specific regarding the damages the hotel will pay to the conference if the hotel cancels the conference (because of high-revenue business). Consider including the difference in rate at another property of like type and the costs of notifying the conferees and reprinting the brochure and everything else caused by the cancellation. If no property is available, consider financial damages equal to the amount of thirty days' cancellation with the property by the conference organization and a future conference at the property at half the conference rate.

If the conference organizer cancels, establish a one-year penalty, a six-month penalty, a ninety-day penalty, and a thirty-day penalty in the contract. A cancellation clause is important for both parties because it defines the damage before it happens and is easy to understand.

— OTHER QUESTIONS TO CONSIDER —

11. What are the objectives of this conference?

12. Do the lodging rooms reflect the expected comfort level of the conferees?

13. What types of beds and how many of each does the property have?

14. Are the recreational activities offered included in the rate?

15. What percentage of rooms need to be occupied to receive free meeting space?

16. How is the property staffed on weekdays versus weekends?

17. When does the property want to have the preconference meeting to review your conference?

18. When is the control of the rooms held by the conference returned to the property to be sold to the general public?

19. Is the conferee required to give a first night's deposit for the room held?

20. What type of deposit is required, if any?

Enoch Williams is the founder and president of Arrowhead Conferences and Events, Redlands, California. He has had over fifteen years of experience setting up, negotiating, and networking in the meeting market. In the past year, Enoch has booked approximately eighty thousand hotel room nights.

— 67 —

Brainstorm (Plus, Sort Your Ideas)

Before deciding on the practicality of any idea in a brainstorming session, get all of your ideas on the table. By answering the twenty brainstorming questions, you will be able to do this. You may want to have the group respond after each suggestion—no matter how farfetched—with a rousing "Why not!" After you have many fresh new ideas on your list, sort out your best ideas using the idea-sorting questions. Unlike other chapters in this book, this one offers no answers because you adapt it to your situation.

1. **What is the one word, sentence, or paragraph essence of our idea (many words could be substituted for idea, such as *program, project, department,* etc.)?**
2. **Why are we doing what we are doing?**
3. **What are our five most fundamental assumptions?**
4. **What changes would we make if we had unlimited time to accomplish the task?**
5. **Where will this idea be ten, fifteen, twenty-five, fifty, or one hundred years from now?**
6. **What if we had unlimited staff?**
7. **What changes would we make if we had double our current budget?**

8. How can we double the income and cut our costs in half?

9. Which part of the total idea warrants extra funding?

10. Which part could we drop and not really miss?

11. What is the ultimate blue sky potential of the idea?

12. What five things could keep us from realizing the full potential?

13. What are our greatest strengths?

14. If we had to start over, what would we do differently?

15. What if this idea is one hundred times as successful as we plan?

16. What course of action would we need to take to be number one in our entire field?

17. Where will our market be in the year 2000?

18. What ten things do we want to accomplish in this area by the year 2000?

19. How do we, as a team, feel the environment will have changed for this idea by the year 2000?

20. In our most idealistic dreams, where will our team be in the year 2000?

Use these questions to help you sort out your best ideas.

1. Which idea best meets our needs?

2. Which has the highest future potential?

3. Which would be most cost-effective in the long run?

4. Which best fits our overall masterplan?

5. Which is most realistic for our staff today?

6. Which could help us win rather than just get by?

7. Which has the lowest front-end risk?

8. Which would work best day to day?

9. Which facts are still missing before we can properly decide?

10. Which is really worth the overall risk involved?

11. What are the predictable roadblocks?

12. How do our senior executive and board feel about the project?

13. Where would we get the funding to do it right?

14. Why have people who have tried similar ideas in the past failed?

15. What are the side effects—good and bad—of the idea we are considering?

16. Would I put my personal money into this project or idea?

17. Is the timing right?

18. Are we able to protect, patent, or copyright this project or idea?

19. Would we have to stop something we are now doing to take on this project?

20. How can we test the idea before committing major resources to it?

Bobb Biehl has logged one-to-one time with over fifteen hundred executives in the past few years. As the founder of Masterplanning Group International in Laguna Niguel, California, he is asked frequently to help make decisions involving millions of dollars, thousands of people, and years of programming. Bobb currently serves on the board of directors of three organizations.

— 68 —

Conduct a Major Event

Deciding to conduct a major event is no small decision. Major events involve major investments of time, energy, and dollars and affect your organizational reputation. Do your research carefully. The following twenty questions will help your research process and your decision making.

A "major event" is any event that is major to you. It could be a weekend retreat for one hundred people or an international conference involving thousands. Note that the pronoun we *is used in the questions. Major events are not planned and conducted by one person. It takes a team.*

1. What organizational need is this event going to meet?
Will this event help you achieve your organizational purpose, vision, or goals? Do you have a need to bring your people together? To sell an idea, service, or product? To teach something? To give visibility to the organization? Focusing on meeting a need will keep the event significant and fuel your motivation in running the event.

2. Is this event the best way to meet this need?
We tend to repeat past activity without asking, Is there a better way? When any event becomes highly predictable, it loses its attraction. Instead of a national conference, should you do regional events? Instead of a week-long event, should you do a three-day event or two-week event? Consider alternatives.

3. Is the right location available?
Your choice of location plays a significant part in the success of the event. Your choice affects not only the budget but also access to the facility, attendees' expectations, limits on programming, and your success in meeting the event purpose.

4. Is an appropriate time available on our calendar?
Timing is crucial. The weather and cultural activity at the event location are both issues to consider, along with your organizational calendar. What dates would be best for your organization and your people?

5. What can we learn from the events of other organizations?
If others have been down the trail you are about to take, learn from their experiences. What things do you want to avoid or copy? How were they organized? How did they promote their event? What can you do to make your event better?

6. **What action steps will be necessary to conduct our event?**
   As you consider the various elements of your event, brainstorm and identify the action steps necessary to conduct a successful event. Make a checklist of these action steps and review them regularly. This will help you track progress and keep you focused on the essentials.

7. **What major areas of logistics will we have?**
   Think through what it will take organizationally to conduct a successful event. Some typical major areas to consider are program, facilities, promotion, registration, finance, transportation, food, and insurance.

8. **What will the timetable for this event look like?**
   Develop a projected timetable from beginning to end. When will you begin to plan, book facilities and resource people, promote the event, receive registrations, coordinate logistics, conduct the event, evaluate the event, and close the financial books? You need a projected timetable to plan around your organizational calendar. You also need to know when to establish cut-off days or go-no-go days for the event.

9. **What will the event cost?**
   Project the possible expenses for each major area of the event. Consider the dollar cost as well as the manpower and hours required. Consider the impact on the overall organization and its focus. Total your projected expenses and add 10 percent. You will need the buffer.

10. **Why *shouldn't* we conduct this event?**
    "If you don't have a case against it, you don't have a case for it"—this principle from Peter Drucker can save you many headaches. Knowing the potential problems will help you prepare and avoid them. You may even decide not to conduct the event before you suffer great loss.

— OTHER QUESTIONS TO CONSIDER —

11. **Why are we considering this event?**
12. **Have we identified the people we want to attract to this event?**
13. **What are their needs?**

14. Can we attract these people?

15. Are resource people available?

16. What can we learn from our past events?

17. When we imagine the event taking place, what does it look like?

18. Who will direct the event, and who will coordinate major logistical areas?

19. Can we afford this event?

20. Does our answer to why we are considering this event still make sense?

Ed Trenner is senior consulting associate of Masterplanning Group International and lives in Orange, California. Nearly thirty years in non-profit organizations have provided Ed the opportunity to plan or coordinate hundreds of special events from local one-day events to week-long national conferences. He is the author of the *Successful Event Planning Checklist.*

— 69 —

Consider What to Do Before Retirement

Retirement can and should be a time for growth through new opportunities, new friendships, a deeper understanding of your own needs, and a greater emphasis on strengthening relationships. However, these benefits come only through planning in advance for the desired life-style and activities of retirement years.

1. What are my expectations for the retirement years?
Expectations for the retirement years vary. Even husbands'
and wives' thoughts for that period of life differ. By each
spouse writing a statement of expectations, a basis for discussion emerges. Common goals may then be established.

**2. If married, what will be the impact of the large segments of
time we will spend together?**
Planning on activities you enjoy doing together as well as
those each of you enjoys doing independently will smooth
daily interaction after retirement. A couch potato married to
one engaged in multiple activities may lead to problems. Or
two couch potatoes may become bored and irritated with
too much togetherness.

3. Do I have a budget for later retirement years?
With inevitable inflation, planning a proposed budget for
later retirement years is essential. Depending upon income
from pensions and other sources, saving money during the
early retirement years may be necessary to provide sufficient
capital for the later years. Projections enable prudent
planning.

**4. Will it be necessary for me to work full-time or part-time,
or will I want to be employed?**
Because of the work ethic many people follow, paid work is
attractive even during retirement. However, a retired person
who seeks employment is often shocked to find that services
are no longer worth top dollar. Employment offers at minimum pay can be disillusioning. Explore possible employment opportunities in advance if you plan to remain in the
labor force.

**5. How much medical coverage will I need, and how will I
pay for it?**
Consider the insurance needed to supplement Medicare. If
your employer's medical plan will not cover you during
retirement, get information on various plans for a comparison. Depending on your health, you may wish to consider
nursing home insurance, which is less costly when taken at
a younger age.

6. **Where would I like to live during retirement?**
   If you will continue living in the same location, will you want to go to another area for the winters? For the summers? Or you may wish to move to another community. Before moving to a new town, spend time there throughout the year so that you can assess the desirability of living there.

7. **What considerations should I face before moving to a new city or town?**
   Analyze costs of living. Consider the impact of leaving old friends or family as well as the opportunities for forming new relationships. Find out about state taxes. Study all options, including renting or buying property.

8. **In addition to cost, what are the problems in maintaining two homes?**
   Even if two homes are feasible economically, moving back and forth presents problems. Oftentimes people who spend a part of each year in different places feel that they don't really belong in either place. Also, consider how long you will be able to handle the responsibilities and the travel.

9. **What preparations should I make for my estate before going to an attorney?**
   A married couple need to talk freely and make decisions together before seeing a lawyer. Write down your wishes on the distribution of your estate, and decide on an executor or trustee. Reviewing the existing will or trust and listing desired changes will save valuable time with the lawyer.

10. **What other legal advice do I need?**
    The advice of a trusted attorney may help you avoid estate taxes and provide updated information on the state's most recent living will stipulations. Request advice on a power of attorney and its appropriateness.

— OTHER QUESTIONS TO CONSIDER —

11. **What inner resources (faith and belief in self) will enable me to adjust?**

12. **What social support will I have during retirement?**

13. **How will I spend my time if I am not gainfully employed?**

14. What talents do I have to offer as a volunteer, and what agencies might use my services?

15. What is the status of my health and that of my spouse?

16. Do I have my personal business matters organized?

17. Do I have a trusted religious adviser or other professional for counseling?

18. What plans should I make for my death?

19. If married, what are the consequences if one of us dies?

20. How much income will I need to maintain my current standard of living?

Adele Schrag, Ph.D., is a retired professor of business who lives and volunteers in the retirement community of Sun City West, Arizona.

— 70 —

Create a Master Plan for an Organization

A master plan is a written statement of a group's assumptions about its direction, its organization, and its resources. Having such a plan allows the board of directors, the senior executive, and the executive team to "play off the same sheet of music."

1. **What have been our milestones so far?**
   Your future goals are based on the level of your past achievements. Milestones are also helpful to review whenever it seems that you are not making as much progress as you

wanted to make. And they are great orientation/briefing points for new team members.

2. **What are our three greatest organizational roadblocks currently?**
As a leader, you want to know at any point in time your three greatest roadblocks and then focus your resources on removing them.

3. **What are our three greatest organizational resources currently?**
Use your greatest resources to eliminate your roadblocks!

4. **What are our goals (realistic, measurable targets of accomplishment for the future) or our primary problems to be solved?**
You can list either your top three *goals* or your top three *problems* for the next ninety days...one year...two years...three years.

5. **Do we have the right person in the right place?**
Consider the persons in the organization and the areas of responsibility. Then for each position, decide to hire someone, leave the person in place, transfer the person, or fire or release the person. But the bottom line is, get the right person in the right place.

6. **What are our five to ten vital signs indicating the health of our organization?**
If you were on an island and could get only five to ten bits of information per month and be able to tell if the organization were healthy, what would you ask to see? Ideally, you will chart these leading indicators of your organization's health for board reports and timely management decisions.

7. **What reports do we need?**
You really need to ask only five questions to track the progress of any person or team reporting to you. In relationship to your goals,
   1. What *problems* are you having?
   2. What *decisions* do you need?
   3. What new *plans* are you making?

4. What *progress* have you made?
5. How are you doing *personally*?

8. What meetings do we need?

Discuss and agree on the types of meetings (board meetings, staff meetings, planning retreats) you need to have on a team. And agree on their frequency.

9. What refinement does our organization need?

Once your evaluation is complete, you begin the process of refining each vital element of your organization. Start with the elements that make the largest difference first.

Use process charts or flow diagrams to get a clear look at the process you are using. Then refine each piece to improve your bottom line results.

10. What should we document as progress before we go back and start over?

Mark your trail! Consider all the issues raised in all twenty questions. The first year you do a master plan takes the most time (like the first time you create a budget). The next year you are just refining based on last year's actual experience.

— OTHER QUESTIONS TO CONSIDER —

11. About what needs do we feel deeply emotional and committed to meeting?

12. Why do we exist?

13. What will we do to meet the needs we see?

14. *Who* is responsible for *what*?

15. *Who* is responsible for *whom*?

16. What is our budget?

17. What are our cash flow projections?

18. What is our income statement?

19. What is our balance sheet?

20. Are we achieving the quality we expect and demand of ourselves?

Bobb Biehl has consulted with over one hundred clients (churches, nonprofit organizations, and for-profit corporations) since he founded Masterplanning Group International in 1976. He has created thirty-five resources (books, notebooks, tapes) in the area of personal and organizational development. He frequently lectures at seminars, conferences, and universities, both domestically and internationally.

— 71 —
Direct or Delegate a Major Project

The likely success or failure of a major project is influenced more by the decisions and actions taken before the work starts than at any other time. The key issues apply whether you are directing (managing, controlling, and/or supervising) or delegating (assigning, authorizing, or entrusting another to act in your place) the project. In either event, be sure to ask yourself these questions.

1. **Has the need or desired result been defined in a clear, concise sentence or statement?**
   A short word picture of the desired result can often clarify most of the issues of the who, what, when, where, and why of a project. Questions can then be asked. The discipline of writing the desired result to obtain agreement on the issues will save much time as the work goes forward.

2. **What resources will I need/have (to provide to another person as my representative) to accomplish the project?**
   Is there a list of the items that you will need and/or have to

accomplish the work? Has the list been reviewed and agreed upon by all concerned? The list should include people, money, facilities, tools, equipment, and intangibles (advisers, etc.).

3. **Is this project best done by me, or can I delegate it to another person?**
You should have a reasonable expectation that you can successfully complete the project. Equally important, if it is to be delegated, your representative should have the same expectation for its successful completion.

4. **Do I know enough about the project to successfully delegate it to someone else?**
There must be enough information for you to be able to undertake the project successfully before you can delegate it to another person. Be sure that you have exhausted the available information before you turn it over to another person.

5. **Will the person selected be able to successfully complete the project?**
No person has all of the knowledge, resources, and experience to complete every possible project. Each person will need help or support at some point. Each person must also have the opportunity to succeed *and* the freedom to fail if the person is to benefit from the project. Your support and help must be available in the event of success *or* failure.

6. **Have I furnished my representative adequate information and guidance on the project?**
The information and guidance should include all of the relevant things that you know or would need to know if you were to carry out the project yourself. The list of items may grow over time, and it may need continuous updating.

7. **Have I considered and explained the risks and pitfalls of the project?**
Every project has one or more risks and the possibility of failure. These risks should be considered before the work begins, or they should be uncovered and explained as the project goes forward.

8. **If I am delegating the work, have I given my representative every resource at my disposal to further the chances for success?**

   Often you can help more than you realize by providing resources to your representative. The resources may include physical items (money, etc.), or they may be the names of persons who can provide information and assistance.

9. **Am I willing to take time to help with overcoming unforeseen obstacles as the project goes forward?**

   Every project will be confronted with unforeseen obstacles, and they will arise at the least convenient times. If there is not time to deal with and overcome obstacles, time and talent may be wasted needlessly, and frustrations may arise that you could have avoided. Allocate time for these problems so that frustration or loss of momentum can be avoided.

10. **Am I willing to give full credit to my representative if the project is a success?**

    The best test of your maturity in assigning projects to others is your willingness to give full credit for the success of the project after it is completed. Don't stumble on this point because you may not have many project opportunities in the future!

— OTHER QUESTIONS TO CONSIDER —

11. **Is this a project that I would be willing to do?**

12. **Have a specific time of performance and date of completion been determined?**

13. **Am I willing to accept the full responsibility if the project does not succeed?**

14. **What special training, gifts, abilities, or motivations will this project require?**

15. **Have I considered all of the possible candidates for the project?**

16. **Have I considered the problems that may be encountered as the project goes forward?**

17. **If I have decided to delegate, am I monitoring the progress and helping my representative at regular intervals?**

18. **Am I willing to provide time to answer routine questions as the project goes forward?**

19. **Am I willing to admit error if I have delegated the project to the wrong person or if the project is not a success?**

20. **Am I willing to keep good records so that the project can be reviewed and improved upon the next time the need arises?**

John B. Mumford is the managing director of the Washington Group—Consultants, a Virginia-based firm that has served more than fifty for-profit and not-for-profit national and international organizations in market research, corporate strategy, finance, turnarounds, ADP planning, human resource development, real estate, and business planning. The firm was founded in 1982.

— 72 —

Go on a Personal Planning Retreat

To gain or regain a clear focus, it helps to get away from your schedule (the pace, the rat race, the grind) and ask yourself a few questions that can lead to a profoundly simple personal focus. Next time you decide to get away to clear your head, try asking yourself these crystallizing questions.

1. **What have been the major milestones in my life so far?**
   Start focusing your future by remembering the accomplish-

ments of your past. Not only will you find it encouraging, it also provides a basis for your future goals.

You may want to categorize your milestones according to the seven basic areas of life: (1) family/marriage milestones; (2) financial milestones; (3) personal growth milestones; (4) physical milestones; (5) professional milestones; (6) social milestones; and (7) spiritual milestones.

2. What is the single-word focus of my life?
It is amazing how different the focus of your life is when you shift this single-word focus. Imagine for sixty seconds how different your life would be if you focused on family, money, God, parents, or service. What is your single-word focus?

3. What is my greatest strength?
Most likely if you are reading this chapter, your response will be, "Candidly, I do a lot of things above average, but I really can't say what I do the very best." This may take a while . . . thinking it through . . . talking it over with friends . . . reevaluating based on additional experience.

Once you define your greatest strength, you take a great step toward focusing your future. Look for ways to maximize the strengths, talents, and gifts you have been given.

4. If I could do anything, if I had all the time, energy, money, staff, and education I wanted and I knew I couldn't fail, what would I do?
This question stretches your mind in new directions because it changes the assumptions you are making as you consider your future. It is one of my personal favorite brainstorming questions.

5. What are the three greatest roadblocks in my life keeping me from turning my dreams into reality?
People should have a crystal clear understanding about the three areas holding them back to be able to work at removing these roadblocks effectively.

6. What are my three greatest resources in life?
Once your resources are clearly understood, you know how to deal with your roadblocks more effectively.

7. **What are the three greatest decisions facing me before I move into the future?**
   A very high percentage of stress in life is caused by indecision. By identifying your major decisions clearly and making them wisely, you are able to move on.

8. **What great ideas do I have that I would like to see accomplished in the future?**
   Never lose a good idea. But don't pursue all of your great ideas at once or you will end up feeling overwhelmed and exhausted.

   Separate your ideas into the categories listed in question one, and then pursue the best of your ideas. Later pursue the rest of your ideas.

9. **If I could reach only three realistic, measurable goals or solve three major problems, what three would I reach or solve in the next twelve months?**
   Concentrate on the big three, and deal with smaller goals or problems later.

10. **What three things could I do in the next ninety days to get me 50 percent of the way to my one-year goals?**
    You can use this question in this type of retreat reflection, and you can modify it and use it in one hundred different ways in daily life.

— OTHER QUESTIONS TO CONSIDER —

11. **Why am I on the face of the earth?**

12. **What needs do I feel deeply about?**

13. **Before I die, what are the three to ten things I would most like to be?**

14. **Before I die, what are the three to ten realistically measurable things I would most like to do?**

15. **Before I die, what are the three to ten things I would most want to have?**

16. **Before I die, what three to ten individuals, organizations, or causes would I most like to help?**

17. If I could do only three of the things listed in the previous questions, which three would I do?

18. If I could do only one of the things listed in the previous questions, which one would I do?

19. How do my goals fit with my spouse's goals or my team's goals?

20. If I could complete only three to ten things next week, what should I do?

Bobb Biehl has helped over one hundred senior executives from start-up enterprises to multimillion-dollar multinational corporations focus their future. He has a tape series called *Focusing Your Life*, which has sold thousands of sets. And he has lectured frequently on the topic, both domestically and internationally.

— 73 —

Make a Major Decision

The following questions are designed to help you make any major decision you are asked to make anywhere, at any time, for the rest of your life. By the way, not every one of these questions will help every time, but any one may be just what you need to make a wise decision in a specific area.

1. In one sentence or less, what is the basic decision I am trying to make?
Write it out. This single exercise can put together all of the pieces of the puzzle flying in your head. You may discover there are two to five decisions you are trying to make all at once. List your decisions in priority order, and make them one at a time!

2. Is my head clear; am I thinking straight?

Try never to make a major decision when you are feeling physically or emotionally exhausted. Remember the all-time great coach Vince Lombardi's wisdom: "Fatigue makes cowards of us all."

When you are fatigued, your decision making becomes fearful, introspective, and negative. Avoid it!

Try never to make a major decision when you cross several time zones on a transcontinental or transoceanic trip. Conventional wisdom says to give yourself a minimum of forty-eight hours to adjust. In jet lag things often seem extremely important or emotional; the next day your mountain may seem like a mole hill. Be extremely careful.

Avoid making any decision after a great loss (death, fire, accidents, etc.). Your thinking may not be clear for days.

3. What facts should I get before I make this decision?

The reporter's questions "Who? What? When? Where? Why? How? How much?" are worth their weight in ink! And remember Dr. Peter F. Drucker's quote: "Once the *facts* are clear, the decisions jump out at you."

4. Should I seek outside counsel on this decision?

As you consider a major decision, you may find it helpful to make a list of your top three most respected advisers in this particular area. Then imagine what each would most likely advise you in regard to this decision. You may want to actually contact them to discuss their perspective on this decision.

5. How do I feel about this decision?

Typically, how we feel plays a vital role in the decision-making process. We live with our feelings long after the decision has been made. Get in touch with your *true* feelings about any major decision *before* you make it!

6. What are one to three options/alternatives for this decision?

Dr. Ted W. Engstrom, president emeritus of World Vision International, says, "An option of one is really no option at all." By definition, a *decision* is "a choice between two alternatives."

What are your real options? No options . . . no decisions! No options . . . find some!

7. What are my lingering questions?

Many times you will find that the one or two lingering questions turn out to be the keys to making a wise decision. What are your simple questions and silly questions about this decision? List them. *Pay attention to them!*

8. Are there any hidden agendas in this decision?

What are your hidden agendas? Who has the most to gain from this decision? *Don't* assume that the person with the most to gain by this decision is giving you objective counsel. The safest assumption is that the person is selling you, not just helping you!

9. Can I subdivide the major decision into subdecisions to limit risk?

When you turn one 50,000 piece (people, dollars, days, etc.) into ten decisions of 5,000 pieces each, you are limiting your overall risk substantially.

What are five to ten natural subdecisions in the major decision you are planning to make? How can you try one to three steps before you make the final major commitment?

10. Have I done my homework?

Have you verified what the results have been for others as they have made this decision? Have you checked references? Have you actually interviewed previous users of the product or service?

— OTHER QUESTIONS TO CONSIDER —

11. Have I given myself twenty-four hours to let this decision settle in my mind?

12. Is the timing right for this decision?

13. Will this decision deal with a symptom or the cause of the problem?

14. What would be the ideal in this situation?

15. How will this decision affect my overall masterplan?

16. Does this decision maximize my strengths?
17. How is the assumed budget affecting the wisdom of the decision?
18. How does this decision affect my family?
19. What assumptions am I making that may or may not turn out to be true?
20. What are the spiritual implications of this decision?

Bobb Biehl has logged one-to-one time with over fifteen hundred executives in the past few years. As the founder of Masterplanning Group International in Laguna Niguel, California, he is asked frequently to help make decisions involving millions of dollars, thousands of people, and years of programming. Bobb currently serves on the board of directors of three organizations (Duane Pederson Ministries, Focus on the Family, and Mentoring Today).

— 74 —

Plan an International Conference

The world is becoming a smaller place. Multinational companies and organizations are increasing. More and more people are seeing the need to plan and organize large international conferences to bring people from various countries together. For some, it is a mission purpose. For others, it is the challenge of expanding markets and new business opportunities. In any case, before you print your brochure for your proposed conference, you may want to ask yourself the following questions.

1. **What is the purpose of the conference?**

   This decision is the most important one to be made. All of the planning will flow from it. At the time when most conference planning should begin, few people are interested in giving input. As enthusiasm grows and the time nears, many people come to the front with suggestions of new things to be included in the program and ideas about delegates and speakers who should be invited. When the purpose is clear, all future decisions can be made based upon whether or not the idea contributes to the purpose of the conference—and whether you can afford it.

2. **Have you identified the people you want to attend?**

   There are basically two kinds of conferences in terms of promotion and recruiting: (1) by invitation only, and (2) open registration (anyone can register until the facilities are filled). In the second kind of conference, people will be attracted by the program being offered, location, ease of entry, and cost. If your organization or company is paying the cost of the transportation and conference for each delegate, the location is always secondary. People will come no matter where you hold the event. However, if you are trying to recruit people to come at their own expense, you must determine very quickly your target audience. How much can they afford? What kinds of accommodations do they expect? How far will they travel to attend? What is the general level of interest in the type of conference you are offering? A conference providing investment counsel to medical doctors has a much different profile from a week-long conference teaching political science to high-school students. The expectations vary widely, and the promotion will vary widely.

3. **Will the delegates be paying their own way or coming at company expense?**

   Someone must pay for transportation, room, food, transfers to and from the airport, registration fees, special banquets and events, materials, and miscellaneous personal expenses. If the delegates are coming at their own expense and the target is to recruit large numbers from some of the poorer countries of the world, much of the planning must be done to minimize costs. It is possible to plan such a high-quality conference in a high-priced venue that the very people you want to come are excluded by the cost.

4. **What meeting venues are available near the housing locations?**
Obviously, you will want your meeting space together with your housing if at all possible. Once you outgrow the hotel ballrooms, you will be investigating convention auditoriums, exposition halls, and sports arenas. You should select a venue that will provide the best environment for your plenary sessions. The most important thing is to be able to hear the speaker well. If you are going to be using a lot of media, you will need to check to see if the room can be darkened. This is sometimes difficult if conferences are being held in the summer months and the meeting hall has many windows. It may not be dark until nine or ten o'clock at night.

5. **What are the program objectives?**
What do you want the delegates to be able to do, remember, or be convinced of by the end of the conference? Are you going to try to inform, inspire, or sharpen a skill? Is feedback important? Do you want time for questions and answers and group discussion? Giving information and inspirational content can be done in large plenary sessions. If you want to allow for questions and do more individual work, you will have to think about breaking the conference into smaller groups. If breakdown rooms are a problem near your plenary hall, you may want to hold them in the individual hotels to minimize transportation problems.

6. **How many delegates will need translation of sessions and materials?**
This is one of the most basic aspects of an international conference. In your registration form, ask what languages they understand and whether or not they would like to have translation if it is available. Some delegates are reluctant to indicate that they need translation in case they might be rejected for not speaking English well. Don't try to save money in the area of translation. It is better not to invite

delegates if you are not prepared to make sure they can understand the sessions and the materials.

7. **What speakers, musicians, or endorsements are needed to attract the delegates to the conference?**

   Delegates are not always attracted to the "meat" that you want to give them in your sessions. People are interested in the frills of what will be happening at the conference. Certainly, the announcement of outstanding speakers is always an advantage—even if the speaker is there only one session.

8. **How will the conference be funded?**

   If you are going to try to fund the conference from the registration fees, you will have to figure your overall level of fixed costs at an estimated attendance number. Above this number, the added cost of each delegate up to the plenary session room capacity will be only the cost of programs, name tags, materials, in-city transportation, and so on. Divide your total budget costs by the number of delegates expected for the conference. If the amount is more than is affordable by your target audience, you may have to seek scholarship help or eliminate some more costly aspects of your planned program.

9. **Will other companies or organizations be invited to exhibit or participate?**

   If an exhibition area is planned, appoint someone immediately who will handle all setup arrangements between those coming to exhibit and the congress or meeting hall. You will also need to involve an exhibition company to build the exhibition area itself and provide the tables, signs, and so on. This area can produce income for the conference if handled properly.

10. **Will there be media presentations that must be prepared beforehand?**

    Consider which subject matter should be illustrated with media. You should consider the use of multimedia slide shows on several big screens. That makes the biggest impression on the audience since you can construct three to five fifteen- to twenty-foot screens that can cover an entire side of a hall. If you are going to do a video presentation, be sure that you have a good quality video projection unit. Some video projectors are not effective if there is any ambient light in the hall. Also, if your conference is going to have more than three thousand participants, you may want to consider video projection of the speaker's face. You should have two screens for this angled toward the corners of the room.

— OTHER QUESTIONS TO CONSIDER —

11. What city is most central to the most delegates?

12. Where will the delegates stay during the conference?

13. How will the delegates be transported between the housing and meeting locations?

14. Where will the delegates eat their meals?

15. How much time is needed to accomplish each program objective?

16. How will the conference be promoted?

17. How much time is required to recruit the number of delegates desired?

18. Is publicity desired before, during, and after the conference?

19. Will there be a postconference follow-up plan?

20. What are the organizational functions that must be staffed?

Paul Eshleman is the director of the Jesus Film Project, Campus Crusade for Christ International, Laguna Niguel, California. He has directed or consulted on some of the largest international Christian conferences held during the last twenty-five years.

75

Plan a Seminar

In our busy information-driven world, there are numerous opportunities to share what we know and understand with a vast market that needs and wants our information. Prior to any seminar planning, explore what people want, what they will be willing to invest to get it, and what it will cost to produce. Use the following questions to help you sort out your ideas and count the cost before investing the resources.

1. **Why would I want to attend this seminar if I had the opportunity?**
   Be entirely honest with yourself at this point. Given the value of what may be received, what is it going to cost people in terms of time, energy, and money? Work to make the value of the seminar so irresistible that people will gladly pay any price to receive what you have. Until it's irresistible, people will continue to question the price. Magnify this "hook" in all your marketing literature to get people to commit.

2. **What are the costs of producing this event?**
   Once you have decided the idea feasibility, consider the financial feasibility of carrying out the idea. Get a realistic handle on your input costs—meals, room rental, decorations, materials, supplies, speaker honorarium, travel, insurance, sound system, marketing/promotion costs, and the cost of your invested time. Include another 10 percent for hidden costs. You should get a good idea of the costs involved.

3. **How will we market this event?**
   Strongly consider the means you intend to use to inform others of the pending event. Common avenues are bro-

chures, fliers, press releases, public service announcements, newspaper ads, and television and press interviews. Talk about what life will be like after investing their resources in your materials. People expect results, and it is motivating to perceive those results in your marketing literature.

4. What is our timetable?

Most events fail for lack of two things. Either they are undercapitalized, or they have tried to do too much in the time allotment at their disposal. To be effective with a large event, you will need four to six months. In a shorter period, you will need more people and more money to do it right.

5. Are there any legal or liability questions we should investigate?

Check for any copyright restrictions, zoning ordinances, special insurance requirements, fire codes, assembly and/or health permits, and other regulations you may be responsible for. A little homework before the event may save costly solutions later.

6. What if it is twice as successful as we think it will be?

Before committing the time, energy, and money to your intended activity, count the potential cost. Think through some what-if scenarios. Can the facility handle twice the number of registrations you think you'll get? How difficult will it be to get additional materials? Are you prepared for the visibility this event could potentially generate for you and your business?

7. Can we deliver what people will expect?

Do a reality check on the anticipated audience's expectations. Test your seminar idea with several people. Specifically ask them what they would expect from their investment. Once you have good feedback, honestly evaluate whether your material will deliver the desired result.

8. If this works, what will we do next?

Is your seminar idea a one-shot deal, or could it be developed into a series of events? If your seminar really hits, people may want more. You will want to be ready with an answer on the next series that will soon be available. Take the time to think through what you would like to do next, and weave it into your original seminar format.

9. **How can we test the idea before we commit major resources to it?**
In any start-up situation it is good to test the effectiveness of the idea prior to its actual rollout. Find a small group of people who would be willing to attend an abbreviated session. Let the group know you are testing an idea and you want feedback from them on what could make this seminar even more effective. In doing so you will be more confident in the actual implementation of the seminar idea and enthused because you've seen it work.

10. **What difference will this seminar make twenty years from now?**
To the extent possible, focus on how this seminar idea will make a difference in people's lives for the next twenty years. You will have great motivation and determination at the onset of your seminar planning, and the thought of that impact will keep you motivated in the midst of all the planning turmoil.

— OTHER QUESTIONS TO CONSIDER —

11. **What do we want to accomplish with this seminar?**

12. **Who will make up the intended audience?**

13. **How will we underwrite these costs?**

14. **Is this the best timing?**

15. **What if the idea doesn't sell?**

16. **Should we have a planning committee?**

17. **Where is the ideal location for this type of event?**

18. **Has something like this been done before?**

19. **Have we considered getting outside help with this event?**

20. **Will outside help be expensive?**

Terry Fleck is a consulting associate with Masterplanning Group International in Indianapolis, Indiana. He also serves as executive vice president of the Indiana Pork Producers Association. In both experiences he has been involved in seminar creation and implementation.

Politics

76

Run for Public Office

People who seek public office are asking to be given a sacred trust. Anyone who is thinking about becoming a candidate ought to start by frankly examining personal motives and capabilities.

1. Why do I want to run for office?
Am I out to change the world? Or just participate in the process? Many candidates are primarily attracted to the notoriety and status of public life. What's my motive?

2. What am I trying to accomplish if I am elected?
Are there issues or policies I deeply care about? Am I a reformer? Do I want to cut taxes or raise them? Do I want to throw the rascals out? What's my ultimate objective? How will I know if I'm successful?

3. Am I financially able to run?
Many candidates end up paying for part, sometimes a large part, of their campaign costs. Can I afford to do so? Also, can I afford the time off from my work to campaign and, if elected, to serve in public office? How will my employers (partners, creditors) react to this idea?

4. Can I stand the pace?
Running and serving mean long hours. Being on city council or in the legislature or other public office means constant demands on my time for meetings, speeches, and so on. Is it realistic for me to add twenty or thirty hours a week or more to my present schedule? What can I cut out if I have to do so?

5. Can my family and I survive defeat?
Losing an election hurts. But in every contested election, somebody loses. How will I feel if that happens to me? Will I

end up an emotional basket case? How will my spouse and kids handle the loss?

6. Can my family and I survive victory?
Divorce is fairly common among political couples. Apparently, a lot of marriages just can't survive high-voltage political life. Is our marriage solid? What can we do to be sure that the price of public office won't be our family?

7. Can I be bought?
The media constantly report on political leaders who have been bribed with money or sex or political advancement. Will this happen to me? What precautions can I take to keep my bearings?

8. Can I stand the other temptations of power?
Will I become arrogant like so many others in public office? After I've been in office awhile, will I become a member of "the club" and identify more with my fellow officeholders than with the people I represent? Bottom line . . . what kind of person am I anyway?

9. What will I have to do to win the election?
What promises will I have to make? Who will I be allied with? Will I have to criticize my opponent? Will I feel comfortable about doing so?

10. How will my campaign affect the willingness of others to run?
Will people in my community feel good about my campaign? Win or lose, can I run the kind of race that will encourage other good people to take an active part in the political process? Or will the campaign leave a residue of bitterness and disappointment?

— OTHER QUESTIONS TO CONSIDER —

11. How much do I know about the job I want to run for?

12. How does my spouse feel about my running?

13. How thick is my skin?

14. Are there skeletons in my closet?

15. Is my ego the right size?

16. **How will I react to frustration?**
17. **Who can I turn to for advice?**
18. **What will my friends think if I run for office?**
19. **What will I have to give up?**
20. **When will I quit?**

Bill Armstrong, a Colorado businessman, was elected to the Colorado House of Representatives when he was twenty-five years old. He went on to win two terms in the Colorado Senate, three terms in the U.S. House of Representatives, and two terms in the U.S. Senate. He retired from the Senate to return to private life and is now in TV broadcasting and mortgage banking. Bill believes that running for public office is a noble calling.

— 77 —

Support or Oppose a Political Issue

Young people and older people alike are becoming increasingly aware of their duties as citizens in a democracy. They are learning that they must be involved and cannot abdicate their citizen responsibilities. Over the past two decades, many moral, ethical, and family issues have become politicized. These issues have moved into the public policy arena.

1. **What is *politics*?**
   Webster's Ninth New Collegiate Dictionary's definition is "the art or science concerned with winning and holding

control over a government...competition between competing interest groups or individuals for power and leadership (as in a government)...the total complex of relations between people in society."

2. Why should I care about political issues?

Fundamental ideas or philosophies lead to political issues, which eventually become public or governmental policy. These policies can lead to the betterment or the detriment of our lives and communities. You might say, ideas have consequences.

3. Do I know how to extrapolate an idea?

Extrapolation is taking a concept or theory to its full, complete, and logical end. Often an idea sounds good at first blush, but when taken to its logical conclusion, it is revealed to be fallacious, absurd, or dangerous.

4. What is strategy?

Strategy is *how* we do something versus *why*. Strategy has everything to do with planning, executing, and winning. A strategic plan would include the following: (1) timing; (2) resource and liability evaluation; (3) anticipation of adversarial actions yet unseen; (4) a game plan; and (5) performance evaluation and feedback.

5. How important is strategy when considering a political issue or candidate?

Strategy is critically important. Whereas we might morally or ethically support a political issue, on the basis of strategic thinking, we may choose not to support that issue because it would not be doable. Therefore, it would be a waste of precious resources, time, and energy.

6. Does it matter what kind of people are involved in a particular issue?

Of course it does! That is like asking if you want an unprincipled, slovenly, behind-the-times doctor or an intelligent and diligent one. It might be a good cause but with the wrong people leading it.

7. Who is seeking what in this political issue?

What benefits are to be derived, or who will be deprived by

this issue? In the political realm, discerning motivations can be as difficult as it is revealing.

8. **Do I know the relationship between economic and political freedom?**
Property rights, ownership, and the profit motive all relate to the free choices of free individuals. It is virtually impossible to have political freedom without economic freedom or vice versa.

9. **Where does this statement come from, and what is the undergirding philosophy?**
We hold these truths to be self-evident, that all men are created equal, that they are endowed by their Creator with certain unalienable rights, that among these are life, liberty, and the pursuit of happiness.

This statement is from the Declaration of Independence adopted in Congress, July 4, 1776. The undergirding philosophy is that human beings are endowed by a Creator and therefore have certain rights that no government has the moral right to take away. The Creator, not any earthly government, gives these rights.

10. **What is relativism, and how does it relate to politics?**
The philosophy of relativism states that there is no universal truth. All potential solutions are relative. There are no absolutes. It is the basis of what is sometimes called situation ethics. It breeds a politics of utilitarianism or "the end justifies the means."

— OTHER QUESTIONS TO CONSIDER —

11. **Does the issue at hand concern administrative problems, or is it more fundamentally ethical and moral?**

12. **Does the political ideology or philosophy lead to a public policy that fosters life or death?**

13. **What is the undergirding philosophy of this political ideology?**

14. **Where is the power in this political situation?**

15. **Does this political issue affect the poor?**

16. Does this political issue affect widows and orphans (or divorced women and their children)?

17. If these political issues touch the poor, are these policies compassionate and understanding?

18. Does this issue foster individual freedom or dependence on government?

19. What is the relationship between freedom and responsibility?

20. What is my political philosophy?

Douglas G. Kay is president of National Institute for Healthcare Research. NIHR is a research and public policy think tank in the Washington, D.C., area. He was previously the director of public policy for Focus on the Family and a candidate for the Oregon state legislature. He is active in California politics.

— 78 —

Vote

With the prevalent belief today being that government serves only those who serve the government, it is easy to see why Americans have become so disenchanted with the political system. However, it seems to me that the very people who complain about the injustices of government are the same people who don't take the time to vote. If people will come to realize that their vote can change the way that government operates, the opportunity for our children to retain the same freedoms and equalities of our parents will continue to be possible.

1. **Do I understand my rights as a voter as set forth by the Constitution?**

   The Constitution clearly states in the Fifteenth and Nineteenth Amendments that no person can be denied the right to vote because of race, color, or previous conditions of servitude, or on the basis of sex. However, discrimination against Afro-Americans continued through the 1960s, and so the Voting Rights Act of 1965 was introduced to set the record straight in eliminating voting restrictions.

2. **Can I lose my right to vote?**

   Yes, you can lose your right to vote! People have lost their voting privilege as a result of being convicted of certain crimes, losing their citizenship, or not reregistering to vote after moving.

3. **What is the difference between the primary and general elections?**

   A closed primary allows registered voters to cast a ballot to nominate candidates from their party to run against opponents nominated from the other party. On the other hand, an open primary allows voters to cast a ballot without disclosing their party affiliation. A general election offers all registered voters the opportunity to choose their public officials from all persons represented on the ballot.

4. **Can one vote really make a difference?**

   Throughout my life, I have been told by many people that one vote cannot make a difference. According to the 1988 census, only about 70 percent of the population of voting age in America was registered to vote, while only about 60 percent of those individuals voted. That means less than 45 percent of all Americans of voting age voted at that time. With such a low voter turnout, your vote carries more weight now than ever before.

5. **Who can I contact to receive the most accurate information on the candidates or the issues?**

   Often, community centers and women's groups will hold forums to give the public the opportunity to ask the candidates questions regarding the issues, their candidacy, and their qualifications for office. Or you can contact local legislators, church leaders, and any special interest groups that you may align yourself with.

6. Should I be a one-issue voter?

Many vital issues face our society today. Voting for a candidate who agrees with your position on only one main issue could prove to be disastrous. Candidates can change opinion on an issue once the polls of public concerns have been released. So keep an eye out for inconsistencies.

7. What is an incumbent, and is that person the most qualified?

An incumbent is the individual elected to the same office that is now open for new election. We must hold all incumbents accountable for their past voting records. Ask yourself, Did this individual stay within the agenda/platform announced in the campaign, or did the person succumb to the political pressures of special interest groups or organizations?

8. Should I vote for the person whose name appears most frequently around town or in the news?

Money talks. Publicity for candidates can be bought. Just because a candidate is well financed does not necessarily mean that person stands for issues in your best interest. To have the best person in office, voters must send the message that they will not be fooled by lavish campaigns.

9. Why should I bother voting when all politicians are corrupt anyway?

It seems that every day you pick up the newspaper, a politician has been caught taking bribes or helping campaign contributors secure contracts with the government. It cannot honestly be stated, though, that all politicians are corrupt. That is why it is so important that Americans get involved in the election process.

10. Is it necessary to vote on every issue or for every position?

Although you should stay informed about the issues and the candidates, there are times when voters have not been completely informed about all issues and/or positions presented on the ballot. For instance, information on certain propositions or candidates for the judiciary or party central committees is often not made available. In such instances, it may be a wise decision to concede on the issues/candidates you are doubtful about and vote only on the ones you feel certain about.

— OTHER QUESTIONS TO CONSIDER —

11. **Am I registered to vote?**

12. **Do I know what I am voting for?**

13. **Will society benefit from my vote?**

14. **Should I vote for a Republican, a Democrat, or someone with another party affiliation?**

15. **Should I vote for a conservative, moderate, or liberal?**

16. **What groups or organizations are supporting the candidate or issue?**

17. **Does the candidate or organization answer questions directly?**

18. **Is the candidate or organization willing to take advice from the people being represented?**

19. **What is the candidate trying to accomplish?**

20. **Did I vote?**

Daniel Batty works as a project coordinator for Hunsaker & Associates, Inc., of Irvine, California, where he is responsible for the coordination of the civil engineering phase of development projects. Dan is active in politics and believes that as Americans, we are called to play an active role in government with the least of these roles being voting.

Potpourri

Devise an Organizational Security System

Having a sense of security when it comes to you, your family, and your assets is difficult at best. These twenty questions will stimulate your thinking and enhance your awareness, enabling you to develop a proactive and practical approach to the security issues of your everyday life.

1. **What has been the level of security experience in my family?**
   Each family or business has a history that closely relates to its socioeconomic makeup. What crimes have family members personally experienced? Have family properties or individuals been the targets of criminal or civil activities? If so, ask what corrective actions were taken to prevent an occurrence of a similar incident. For example, if your home was burglarized, what did you do to prevent it from happening again?

2. **Do I reside or work in an environment that exposes me or my family to additional security risks, such as robbery, theft, or assault?**
   Contact the community relations bureau of the local law enforcement agency and ask about crime statistics in your area and surrounding areas. Ask what type of safety and security education is available from the agency.

3. **What can I do to minimize exposure to theft, fire, or accidental injury?**
   Inspect the fencing, locking mechanisms, lighting, wiring outlets, burglar and fire alarms, smoke detectors, windows, and pathways. Contact your casualty insurance carrier, and determine whether you are protected from all aspects of loss due to any of the listed areas if negligence is present.

4. **To what extent do I secure my home or business from intrusion?**

   The most reasonable approach to securing any building is using your window and door locks. All locks should be easily activated in case of emergency and you need to exit quickly. A professional locksmith can advise you on the type of equipment best suited for your location. You may find your property can be better protected with proper lighting, an alarm system, involvement in a neighborhood watch program, and so on.

5. **Should I leave a key outside my home or business in the event of a lost or forgotten key?**

   "Secret" locations for hiding a key are so limited and used so frequently that intruders seldom have difficulty finding an outside key. Lock boxes similar to those used by Realtors are available at lock or hardware stores.

6. **Have the adults and children in my home been properly trained in responding to first aid emergencies?**

   Contact the local fire department or Red Cross to find out when community classes are provided. All family members should be trained in CPR, basic first aid, and procedures when calling 911 or other emergency numbers.

7. **What type of a preparedness plan do I need in case of a natural disaster that will significantly disrupt my home for a period of time?**

   Private businesses and public agencies have information packets and supplies available that will assist you in preparing to respond to such incidents. You should have supplies readily available to support your family for a three-day period. Also, telephone numbers for friends and relatives out of the area should be placed with the supplies so you may call to inform them of the condition of the family. Telephone calls into the area may not be possible; outgoing calls are more easily completed. Contact your children's school to learn about the disaster preparedness plan and what to do if your children are at school when a disaster occurs.

8. **What is my need for competent legal counsel?**

   A need may arise for legal counsel for any family member due to civil and criminal action. Last-minute arrangements may prove to be costly and a waste of time. Network with friends and business associates to obtain referrals. Make appointments to interview several professionals, choose someone whose position you respect, and establish a fee.

9. **What is my liability when I sign for my minor child's driver's license?**

   Obtain a copy of your state's vehicle code, and review the section relating to the responsibilities and liabilities of parents or guardians. Depending on the state, the parent may be responsible for insurance coverage and/or the costs of medical expenses and car repair. In some cases, a parent may be liable for the child's driving negligence.

10. **What is my liability when I or my family members allow others to drive my registered vehicles, and what is my liability for passengers?**

    Legal counsel and your automobile casualty insurance carrier will assist you in understanding these areas and how best to protect yourself in these circumstances regarding the limits of liability coverage with your automobile and homeowner's insurance.

— OTHER QUESTIONS TO CONSIDER —

11. **What does security mean to me, and what do I need to feel comfortable in today's environment of increasing crime?**

12. **Do I have a plan if there is an intrusion into my home while it is occupied?**

13. **What are local and state laws in regard to keeping firearms in my home or business?**

14. **Do my family members know how to minimize the potential of an assault in a public place?**

15. **Does my family know how to properly answer the phone in response to solicitors or nuisance calls or how to respond to strangers at the door?**

16. Do my children understand about "stranger contact" and how to respond if they are approached by strangers?

17. Have I trained my children about inappropriate touching and what action they should take if it occurs?

18. Do I have a fire exit plan for my family?

19. Have I made legal arrangements for custodial care of my minor children, and are funds and resources adequately available?

20. Have I considered holding family meetings to discuss security issues?

Dale Walters is the owner of Walters and Associates, Laguna Hills, California, an organization specializing in security risk analysis, consulting, and private investigations for individuals, groups, and corporations. He has twenty-one years of experience in law enforcement, five of which were spent as head of the Security and Fire Division for West Coast Attractions with the Walt Disney Company, Disneyland, the Disneyland Hotel, and the *Queen Mary*.

— 80 —

Host an International Student or Guest

Hundreds of thousands of international students, visiting scholars, and other international visitors arrive in our country each year. They are among the brightest and best of their nations. Will they leave thinking of Americans as self-centered individuals unconcerned about people from other countries? Or will they be positively affected by Americans who reach out to them in friendship? Will they carry a positive image of the United States to their home countries? I hope that after reading these twenty questions, you will consider reaching out to internationals in your area.

1. **Am I the type of person suited to host an international student or guest?**
   Most international men and women are looking for warm, caring American friends willing to make their stay in the United States more enjoyable. They are not looking for ethnocentric individuals who feel superior to and lack an interest in people from other cultures.

2. **How many international students are studying in America?**
   Conservative estimates place the number of international students in the United States at about 450,000. The students represent nearly every country of the world.

3. **How would I go about hosting an international student?**
   Contact a foreign student adviser at a college or university in your area and express your desire to meet an international student.

4. **Would an international student be interested in my friendship?**
   Many international students are lonely, having left family and friends behind in their country, often for the first time. Most would love to have an American friend, yet only three of ten international students see the inside of an American home.

5. **What are some of the different ways people reach out to internationals?**
   Some invite international men and women—and their families—into their homes to share a meal, perhaps during a holiday. Others meet international students at the airport as soon as they arrive, offering transportation and help in finding housing and other immediate needs. Some even open their homes for international students to live with them for a period of time. Many choose to commit to a one-to-one relationship with an international student in which the two agree to meet on a regular basis.

6. **If I invite an international to my home for a meal, what should I serve?**

   First, be informed and sensitive about any religious or cultural dietary restrictions. As a general rule, for instance, Muslims will not eat pork, Hindus will not eat beef, and few Asians or Africans care for cheese or canned tuna. It's best to serve a safe meal to begin with. Spaghetti is always a favorite, and fish, poultry, and lamb are usually acceptable. Vegetables and fruits are also generally appreciated.

7. **Could you suggest some activities an international might especially enjoy?**

   Cultural experiences—such as attending a friend's wedding, celebrating special holiday traditions, or going to a state or county fair—are all good ideas because they help the international receive a broader perspective of life in America.

8. **How can I communicate effectively with an international?**

   Be a good listener and demonstrate a genuine interest in the individual. If your international friend has a limited understanding of English, speak clearly and carefully. Also, try to avoid idioms or slang terms—"hit the road," "get on the ball," "play it by ear"—and use jokes and humor, which may be misunderstood, sparingly.

9. **What are some practical ways I could assist an international?**

   Students, especially newly arrived ones, appreciate help in getting acclimated to a new culture. You could assist by helping the student understand the area's transportation system, open a checking account, learn the language, locate housing and used furniture, understand local customs, meet other people, or maintain cultural or religious customs.

10. **What are some typical needs of international students?**

    Brand-new students need a wealth of information about how to get things done personally and academically in this new and confusing system. Examples might include such things as which institutions deliver the best services, where the best buys can be found on various items, and what the culture considers acceptable ways of asking for things. After students settle into America, their greatest need is for a support system—people to love, praise, counsel, rejoice and cry with, and regularly encourage them. Americans can introduce the students to those among their friends and networks who can also befriend them.

— OTHER QUESTIONS TO CONSIDER —

11. If a foreign student adviser gives me the name of an international student, can that person provide helpful hints before my first meeting with the student?

12. Is there a typical international student?

13. Would an international be interested in participating in our family's normal daily routine?

14. Do most internationals enjoy talking about similarities and differences between the two countries?

15. Are there common cultural differences Americans and internationals experience?

16. Are there common problems international students face in this country?

17. Is being judgmental of the international's culture or beliefs the primary mistake to avoid?

18. In addition to learning about another culture, can I expect to benefit in other personal ways by hosting an international student or guest?

19. Are internationals interested in talking about religion?

20. Should I share my religious beliefs with my international friend?

Gordon D. Loux, L.H.D., is president of International Students, Inc. (ISI), Colorado Springs, Colorado, a Christian service organization established in 1953 that works closely with foreign student advisers and other college and university officials to assist international students in practical ways.

81

Print Something

You may need to have something printed: social invitations, an organizational newsletter, publicity, or your own book. Whether it's at a quick print shop or a full-line printer, you need to be able to answer certain questions about what you want printed. Most printers will be glad to show you examples of what they can do, and they will typically prepare a cost estimate for your approval before doing any work.

1. How many copies do you want printed?
The more copies, the lower the cost per copy. If you're in doubt, order a few more than you think you'll need because it is expensive to go back to press for just a few copies.

2. How many pages will be in the final printed piece?
One side of a sheet of paper is called a page. There will always be an even number of pages, even if they are not all numbered. Printing something with many pages can be done more economically if the number of pages fits with the printer's equipment. In other words, a piece with four, eight, twelve, or sixteen pages might be more economical to print than something with six, ten, or twenty-two pages. Ask the printer for guidance.

3. What type of paper will be needed?
Paper has several characteristics including weight, thickness, and coating. A heavier paper is generally thicker. Paper weight affects price, ease of folding or binding, durability of the paper, mailing weight and cost, whether the printing ink on one side will be visible through the paper, and other factors. Coating generally refers to whether the paper has a slick or rough surface. Discuss paper carefully with the printer.

4. **Will the printing be done in black ink only, or will other colors be needed?**

   The more colors used, the greater the expense but also the greater potential for an eye-catching piece. Avoid using black ink on dark-colored paper or light-colored ink on a light background—these combinations will be hard to read.

5. **How will the printed item be held together?**

   The item could be held together by stapling (one, two, or three), perfect binding (like a thick magazine), case binding (like a book), or hole-punching (to be inserted into a notebook).

6. **Will photographs, artwork, or other illustrations be included?**

   These items require additional work and are charged for separately. The more there are, or if color is used, the greater the expense. If the printer must adjust the size of the photo or illustration to fit the space, there is usually an extra charge. In many cases, try to provide duplicates, not originals, to avoid loss or damage. Ask the printer about options.

7. **If the piece is to have a cover (such as a book or magazine), what kind should it be?**

   Soft covers come in various weights; hard covers also have variety and are more expensive but more durable. Some printers have to send off to other companies for hardcover bindings, so production time could be increased.

8. **Will the typeface be legible on the chosen paper or background color?**

   Evaluate the size of the type and its style. Too small a type size or an unusual typeface may be hard to read, especially when used for a mass of text. Anything to be read by persons with poor vision should be larger and spaced more openly. Many styles of type are available, but most situations can be handled with a few conventional typefaces. Unusual styles probably need the guidance of a graphic designer.

9. **Who owns the materials used in the printed work?**

   Generally, you own and should get back whatever you provided. The printer retains whatever he provided. If you have special concerns or needs, discuss them in advance.

10. **Should the printed piece be copyrighted?**

Copyright exists in the work as soon as it is created. Seeking formal copyright from the U.S. Patent and Trademark Office is not needed on many printed items, although it may be appropriate to include a copyright statement ("Copyright," year, owner's name). Applying for a copyright will depend on how the printed item will be used, whether the organization requires it, and other factors.

— OTHER QUESTIONS TO CONSIDER —

11. **What size will the finished piece be?**

12. **What color paper will be used?**

13. **Will the printing be done on one side of a sheet or on both sides?**

14. **Will the piece be folded?**

15. **Will cutting or hole-punching be required?**

16. **How quickly must the work be done?**

17. **Do you need to lay out or design any of the pages in a special way?**

18. **Who will proofread and give final approval to the item before it is printed?**

19. **Where and how will the printed material be delivered?**

20. **How will the work be paid for?**

William L. Needham is the vice president of administration with a printing firm in Tallahassee, Florida, which does $35 million in printing per year with a staff of approximately four hundred. He is also a writer and editor.

82

Seek Free Publicity for Your Organization

Free publicity can be a great way to acquaint people with your organization. Media people are usually on the lookout for interesting, well-written, and informative items. This is especially true with print media, including newspapers, magazines, and other periodicals. At press time, with a half-column to fill, your press release might be just what an editor needs.

1. **What do I have to say that would interest or help others?**
   That is the key! If it's newsworthy, it will get printed. Editors don't like what are called puff pieces, filled with glowing adjectives about your organization. On the other hand, keep Dizzy Dean's words in mind: "If you done it, it ain't braggin'."

2. **What sort of things might be newsworthy?**
   Probably more than you think: personnel promotions or retirements; appointment of new officers or directors; relocation or expansion of facilities; development of new services or products; significant dates (e.g., twenty-fifth anniversary); upcoming events; noteworthy achievements (e.g., new sales or earnings records); a need for volunteers or donated materials; community activities; awards; human interest items; and so on.

3. **What's the most effective way of getting free publicity?**
   In most cases, a press release will suffice. If you have something really important to announce, you may want to host a press conference. But be certain it's *really* newsworthy before you take that step.

4. **What specific audience do I want to reach?**
   Don't waste an editor's time by sending material unsuited to

that publication's audience. An article on aging, for example, should be aimed at *Modern Maturity,* not *Seventeen.*

5. What's the best time to do it?
That, of course, depends on your message. If you're promoting an upcoming event, you'll want to give the editor of a monthly publication a lot more advance notice than for weekly or daily publications. The same is true if your material is seasonal. Don't wait until November to send in that Christmas article.

6. How do I locate the most receptive publications?
Local newspapers and magazines are usually your best bet. Two annual publications, *Writer's Market* and *Christian Writers' Market Guide,* list the specific requirements of thousands of publications. Most libraries should have both volumes.

7. What are the best media to use?
They include newspapers, magazines, radio and TV stations, community bulletin boards, newsletters, and so on. And be sure to gear your presentation accordingly. Press releases are fine for print media, but for radio or TV prepare ten-, thirty-, and sixty-second messages suitable for public service announcements.

8. What other means of publicity should I consider?
Service clubs, civic, church, and other groups often need speakers. Offer them the services of people in your organization, along with a list of suggested speech topics. Not only are you getting free exposure, but in some cases you may receive small honoraria.

9. What "hidden" costs am I likely to incur?
Your campaign may bring you lots of "free" publicity but make sure it's worth it. Writing articles, preparing and giving speeches, and sending out releases take time; do a cost-benefit study. That free publicity may cost more than you think.

10. How do I keep from wearing out my welcome with editors?
Send only pertinent, well-prepared data; don't inundate them with irrelevant matter. Refrain from calling them often.

Be considerate of their needs. Establish yourself in their eyes as an "expert" in your field; you'll become a resource for them rather than a pest.

— OTHER QUESTIONS TO CONSIDER —

11. **How much information should I provide?**
12. **Should I include photographs?**
13. **Should I try a one-shot approach or a campaign?**
14. **Who is best qualified to prepare our message?**
15. **Who is best qualified to deliver our message?**
16. **What results would I like this publicity to generate?**
17. **How do I generate response?**
18. **How will I handle media inquiries?**
19. **Whose counsel or advice should I seek before proceeding?**
20. **What are the possible pitfalls?**

Bob Kelly is a free-lance writer and founder/president of Kelly Communications, Inc., a newsletter publishing firm in Colorado Springs, Colorado. He has written many books and articles, and he is a former bank president and newspaper editor/publisher.

Religion

83

Attend Church

Looking for and choosing a church home can be an exasperating experience, especially if you don't know where and how to begin that selection process. Today, there are numerous kinds of churches with varying theologies, ministry philosophies, programs, and styles to choose from. The following is a list of twenty questions to help you sort out the issues and choose the right church home for you and your family.

1. Am I comfortable with the style of worship?
The style of worship reflects, to some degree, a church's values and who it is trying to reach out and minister to. The fact is, there is no right style or wrong style of worship. There are fine churches of liturgical style, traditional style, and various contemporary styles. A key question on this issue is, Do I feel comfortable with the worship style *this* church employs?

2. Are my kind of people here?
Often, choosing a church is more a cultural question than a theological one. We tend to settle in places, and with people, we can relate to.

3. What is the vision of this church?
Vision has to do with the future and the direction of the church. The questions of vision are, Does this church know where it's going? and Can I get excited about helping it move in that direction?

4. What is the style of leadership at this church?
Churches have various styles and structures of leadership. Some are congregational rule, some are governed by elected or appointed boards, while others are led by one person. Knowing the style and structure of leadership, un-

derstanding how decisions are made, and personally respecting and valuing that style are important issues to work through before finalizing your choice of a church home.

5. **Is there a place in this church where I can know and be known by a group of people?**
   Sometimes individuals can get lost in a local church, especially if it's a large congregation (over three hundred). Anyone can find a "home church" to attend and be anonymous in. A "church home" is different. It involves relationships and support and care with and for others as a community of believers.

6. **What has been the history of this church?**
   Sometimes where a church has been can tell you a lot about where it's headed, especially in the last five years, and if the leadership has remained the same. Has it grown or declined? Why or why not? Are there existing problems or different "camps" within the congregation? Look before you leap!

7. **What is going on in and through the church other than on Sunday morning?**
   Look through the church bulletin. It will tell you a lot about what a church believes in but more about how it acts. Also, examine the church budget. Where it allocates its funds will also tell you a lot about what it does and values.

8. **What is the "feel" of this church?**
   Is it reverential and still or alive with activity? Is it joyful and exciting or peaceful and quiet? Is it empty or crowded? Depending on the kind of church you are looking for, these are some things people "feel" quite early in their looking period.

9. **What are the expectations for membership?**
   Once you know what's involved in choosing a church home, is this the kind of place where you can and will get involved?

10. **Can I live with the things I don't like about this church?**
    No church is perfect. In fact, if you find the perfect church, don't join it—you'll ruin it! The key is that you have investi-

gated and been honest with yourself about what's important and you can commit yourself to a body of believers moving in a particular direction.

— OTHER QUESTIONS TO CONSIDER —

11. **What does this church believe doctrinally?**

12. **What is the stated purpose or mission of this church?**

13. **What programs does this church have to offer to my children? My teenagers? My family?**

14. **What opportunities for service does this church afford me?**

15. **What is the reputation of the church in the community?**

16. **Can I identify with the leadership of this church?**

17. **What was my first impression of this church?**

18. **What are the priorities of this church?**

19. **Does this church have a strong youth ministry?**

20. **What are the style and personality of ministry at the church?**

Denny Bellesi is the founding and senior pastor of Coast Hills Community Church, Aliso Viesto, California, an interdenominational church that has grown in size from thirteen to two thousand in its seven-year history.

84

Call a Minister to Your Church

One of the more important decisions affecting the work of the kingdom of God in the world is the one that attempts to correctly match a pastor and a local church. From a church's perspective, here are twenty questions that should be answered in that process.

1. **When and how were you called by God to be a pastor?**
   Calling becomes the backbone of stability in time of crisis. One should clearly understand and be able to articulate that calling.

2. **What do you consider the greatest difficulty (or disappointment) of your present pastorate? Why?**
   Are the difficulties or disappointments spiritual in nature, or temperamental, relational, or financial? Do they reflect management inadequacies?

3. **Why do you wish to leave your present pastorate?**
   Pinpoint desires, frustrations, and personality or temperament traits.

4. **Why do you wish to pastor this church?**
   Is it superficial (a step up, more pay), or is it deeper (calling to community)?

5. **Are you comfortable with the demographics of our city and our congregation?**
   Age, race, income level, personality, and style—all play their part in good relationships.

6. **What is your philosophy of ministry? Of worship? Of leadership training?**
   How does this philosophy blend with the church's past/present/future direction?

7. **What changes have occurred or do you expect to occur in your ministry style?**
   One may be in the midst of a philosophical change that is not apparent in an evaluation of one's previous ministry. Try to avoid surprises.

8. **How would you handle a major disagreement with an influential board member?**
   Observe the level of comfort or discomfort with the question while you analyze the answer. The question could be changed to the wife of a leader or another staff member. Since confrontation is a real part of church life, one's approach to it is significant.

9. **How do you stimulate and monitor growth in your life?**
   Along with prayer and devotional habits, consider reading habits, exposure to others through training seminars, accountability to a superior or a mentor, and so on.

10. **Is the salary package we offer adequate for your present needs?**
    Financial pressure is a major distraction from good work. Deal with it up front. Inform the candidate about your policies regarding an annual review of compensation.

— OTHER QUESTIONS TO CONSIDER —

11. **What was your prepastoral background or rearing (church or nonchurch; traditional or nontraditional)?**

12. **What training have you had to be a pastor?**

13. **What has been your average tenure in your pastorates?**

14. **What do you consider the greatest joy (or success) of your present pastorate? Why?**

15. **Have you ever lived or pastored in a city of this size?**

16. **What do you see as the church's role and your personal role in the community as a whole?**

17. **How would you approach and establish vision and goals for this congregation?**

18. **What do you see as the role of your family in the ministry of this church?**

19. How do you feel about loyalty and cooperation with denominational emphases (if applicable)?

20. What do you expect from this congregation and its leadership?

Ray Smith has been president of the Open Bible Churches denomination (over three hundred fifty churches) for twenty-one years. He has also pastored three churches, one of which he founded. Earlier he served as superintendent of South Dakota, and then of the Mountain Plains Regions. Throughout his years in denominational leadership, he has helped place many pastors.

— 85 —

Plant a Church

One of the most strategic means of fulfilling the Great Commission of Jesus Christ is through the ministry of church planting. That strategy began with the apostle Paul and other early church leaders and has continued to this day. Although there are some well-trained and gifted church planters, many churches are begun by Christians who respond to the needs of the particular neighborhood or community as they are guided by the Holy Spirit. God can use you to plant a church!

1. **Why would anyone want to plant a church?**
   A significant number of churches are closing every week in the United States. In fact, we are told that one hundred thousand churches will close in the United States within the next ten years.

2. How many people are needed to plant a church?

Believe it or not, only a few people who feel prompted by the Holy Spirit to form a small nucleus may begin to pray, plan, and prepare for the planting of a new church. I am aware of churches that have been planted by as few as two families or five to six people.

3. Is there a best way to plant a church?

There are several effective approaches to church planting. One of the most effective has been beginning with a small group Bible study.

4. How do we begin?

I would encourage you to begin by getting together with other people who are interested in planting a church in your area or community to pray and seek God's guidance regarding how you should proceed. In short, you can begin with a small Bible study in a home on a weekly basis. Many churches have begun with just a handful of people studying the Word of God, seeking guidance from the Lord, and praying about the vision that God has given for Church planting.

5. Who should teach the beginning Bible study?

Although you or one of the other persons in your small group may be gifted as a Bible study leader, it is usually best to have a pastor or someone who has had special biblical training or special gifting from the Holy Spirit to give leadership to such a nucleus of people seeking to plant a church. If you belong to a denomination, contact your bishop, district superintendent, or area representative for guidance. Often a pastor of an established church within driving distance is a good resource to lead your study.

6. When should we make the transition from a home Bible study to an actual worship service?

When your group reaches a size of twenty-five to forty people, you may want to prayerfully consider beginning a Sunday morning gathering. At that time, the format should go through the transition of focusing on a significant worship time as well as the proclamation of the Word of God. When public services begin, make a public announcement to the community, and invite others to be involved with you. Of course, you can begin the worship experience in your Bible study on a week night and make the transition when you feel the group is ready for a Sunday morning.

7. How could we afford to pay a pastor?

It is wonderful to see how God leads and provides in this basic area. For example, if you have had a pastor leading your Bible study who is available on Sunday morning to lead your worship service, your initial problem is solved. Frequently, you find a pastor working at a full-time job who can begin to pastor your flock on a part-time basis. In addition, many denominations will provide a pastor for a church that is being planted. That is why you should be involved with your denominational representative just as early as possible in your church planting process.

8. What is another approach to planting a new church?

Another exciting approach is called the mother church approach to church planting. In this situation, an existing church serves as the mother to plant a daughter church. Usually, a nucleus of fifty to one hundred people volunteer to go from the mother church to plant the new church. Often an associate pastor of the established church becomes the pastor of the new church plant. In addition, the mother church is often able to supply financial assistance and other kinds of assistance over a period of time. Once again, your denominational representative and/or your pastor can help you.

9. What is your favorite approach to church planting?

Since both churches I was involved in began church planting with Bible studies, I have a special place in my heart for that approach. However, I am excited about any and every legitimate approach that will plant churches and win new people to faith in Jesus Christ.

10. What special counsel do you have for us about church planting?

I would pray that you would do it! Begin prayerfully seeking the guidance of the Lord. If you become involved in a church planting ministry, you will be involved in one of the most exciting ministries available today in the United States—or in the world. I wish you God's best as you DO IT!

— OTHER QUESTIONS TO CONSIDER —

11. What topic should we choose for Bible study?

12. What should be the duration of the study?

13. Where would/could we meet when we begin worship services?

14. How do we begin the mother church approach?

15. Are fifty adults enough for an effective "daughter/son" church plant?

16. What kind of long-term commitment should be made by those who volunteer to be part of the church plant?

17. What are other important factors to be considered with the mother church approach to church planting?

18. Are telephone campaigns and visitation campaigns other effective approaches to church planting?

19. How should the telephone be used to plant a church?

20. How should visitation be used to plant a church?

Paul A. Cedar, D.Min., is an author, pastor, evangelist, and church leader who has been involved in local churches all of his life, including two church plants. Dr. Cedar serves currently as the president of the Evangelical Free Church of America, Minneapolis, Minnesota, which has a vigorous ministry planting new churches in the United States and abroad.

Recreation and Travel

Choose a Summer Camp
for Your Children

Each summer approximately ten million kids will attend camps in the United States. Summer camping has been noted by reliable surveying statistics to be the most effective institution in America for affecting lifelong value development. Dr. Willis Tate, president of Southern Methodist University, once said, "The moods of a lifetime are often set in the all but forgotten events of childhood." The events of childhood that camping affords young people develop friendships, memories, and spiritual values that give life its greatest fulfillment. Ask these questions of the director before choosing a summer camp for your children.

1. **How is your staff selected?**
   At a camp the counselors are everything. They can influence a camper positively or negatively for life. A counselor needs to have a rigorous interview and reference process to ensure that only the highest quality people fill the staff positions.

2. **What is the staff-camper ratio of your camp?**
   The national average is one counselor for seven campers. Our camps operate comfortably with a one-to-four ratio.

3. **Does your camp have a written risk management plan?**
   The fun things in camp often involve risk. Risk is a good thing and produces memorable moments and the development of courage and self-esteem if it is managed properly.

4. **What standards and precautions do you have in place to ensure safety in high-risk activities?**
   Every good camp should have a strict set of safety standards for each high-risk activity. It should also have a detailed plan and people trained to maintain those activities.

5. What are your typical menus like?

Milk at camp should always be abundant. Meats, vegetables, and whole grain foods should be served at each meal. Camp is a place to get healthier and to learn how to get and stay that way.

6. What is your camp's statement of purpose?

Learn a camp's statement of purpose or mission statement. Be sure you are comfortable with it because it is the base upon which all camp policy is built.

7. What is your cost per day of camp?

A good private camp costs about $60 per day; $80 per day is very expensive. Camps sponsored by churches and other institutions are sometimes operated for $30 to $40 per day.

8. What national organizations does your camp belong to?

The American Camping Association and Christian Camping International are valuable associations for camps to belong to. Such reputable organizations demand a certain degree of standards and quality control for participating camps.

9. How do you handle homesick campers?

Homesickness in the first days of the term is normal. Don't stress out over a homesick letter. If a camper is swarmed with love and kept busy, the loneliness should subside by the fourth to seventh day of the term.

10. How do you handle camper discipline problems?

Healthy, happy kids have rules and a guideline system to ensure their observance. If a camp offers a responsible system of punishment (i.e., running, push-ups, talks, etc.), it is proven to work well, but the director should monitor it carefully.

— OTHER QUESTIONS TO CONSIDER —

11. What is your standard for religious commitment of your counselors?

12. Are your staff members allowed to drink on nights off?

13. What questions do you ask your staff applicants about personal sexual and moral issues?

14. **What is your accident/safety history?**

15. **How much emphasis do you place on food service?**

16. **Are campers allowed to eat all they want?**

17. **How much do you spend per meal per camper?**

18. **What religious viewpoint do you stress at your camp?**

19. **What specific daily and weekly activities do you have to support that viewpoint?**

20. **What was your camper return rate last summer?**

Joe White, Ed.D., has been the president of Kanakuk-Kanakomo Kamps, Inc., in Branson, Missouri, for fifteen years. The Kamps serve some 10,000 kids annually and employ 1,100 summer staffers. Joe received his Doctor of Education from Southwest Baptist University and is the author of *What Kids Wish Parents Knew About Parenting, The Gift of Self-Esteem, How to Be a Hero to Your Teenager, Looking for Love,* and *Surviving Friendship Pressure.*

— 87 —

Go on Vacation

A vacation can be the greatest or the worst thing that happens during any given year. The most important question to keep the experience positive is, Why are we really going?

1. Why this vacation?

If your objective is rest, don't go to Europe. Go somewhere (preferably close to your own time zone) where you can escape the pressure of business without adding the pressure of wanting to see everything in town.

Westbound travel is easier on the body clock than eastbound. (Don't ask why; it just is—probably circadian rhythm or something.)

If you're going on vacation to see foliage (fall trees or cherry blossoms), the exact week can be critical. Ask someone who knows. Don't guess.

Local tourist bureaus can furnish a wealth of information. (Each state, country, or city has one—usually with an 800 number.)

2. What is my budget?

If budget is limited, should you shorten the tour and go first class or lengthen it while staying in cheaper hotels? Nothing is more pertinent than budget. As with anything else, plan and then add another 30 percent. Price guides are always a year old, and generally speaking, we have had limited success with less-expensive hotels and restaurants in guide books. However, they are useful in getting a general idea of prices, and they are very helpful in sightseeing where attractions don't change much from year to year.

Know the currency before you arrive. Find out if it's a one-way exchange. Don't change any more money than you think you will need.

Shortening the tour and going first class will depend on the country. In less-developed countries I would stay in the better hotels. In countries where travel is common (Germany, Italy, England, France, etc.), budget hotels can be a positive experience.

In pensiones and budget hotels, it is not considered rude to ask to see the room before you check in: do it!

3. How much lead time do I need?

For a lengthy safari to Africa, the planning needs to be more extensive than for a weekend in the Caribbean. A group tour, which can be difficult for a family, requires little planning and is probably a good choice for a last-minute trip. Airline tickets are a major factor in destination choice, with the lowest fares requiring purchase several weeks in advance. Visas for the more exotic places can take many weeks. If, however, you're camping, I would generally avoid places requiring reservations three to six months in advance because they will probably be crowded when you arrive.

4. What are our main interests?

There is nothing worse than going on a trip about which you are excited and finding that no one shares your interests. Get the family involved in planning from the beginning. No matter where you go, there are things that can interest everyone. (Make some obvious choices for each and take some chances on others. You may be pleasantly surprised.)

5. Should I purchase a complete tour or put it together myself?

If you are adventurous and don't mind some stress (will I find a hotel when I arrive in a city I have never been to before? . . . you usually will), do it yourself, or perhaps make a reservation for the first night. If you are traveling to Eastern bloc countries, the requirements for prepaying reservations are beginning to loosen. The price you can negotiate on arrival will be considerably less. However, in busy months you may have difficulty finding accommodations.

6. Should I use a travel agent?

Many people think that dealing directly can save money (airlines, hotels, etc.). For the most part, that's not true. A good travel agent can save you many dollars, to say nothing of time and energy. The mistake is in thinking that the person can do everything for you. To have a better chance at a successful vacation, do your homework. Know something about your destination, and the travel agent will be able to better determine your needs.

7. Should I rent a car or use local transportation?

It depends on your physical condition, age of your kids, the country you're driving in, and whether or not you are staying in a major city.

If renting in Europe, make your reservations before leaving. They are about half as expensive. Also, check with your insurance company to see if you are covered in a foreign country.

Don't forget to get an international driver's license through AAA before you leave. (It's not always required, but it's best to have it.)

8. Should I make hotel reservations and prepay?

If you have been to the city before, you have little risk in prepaying. If you haven't, my recommendation would be (unless it's a high season) to have a reservation the first night and then look around on arrival. You may find something better. One look is worth a thousand pages in a guide book.

Unless you will be staying in one place, avoid prepaying if possible. In the U.S. most hotels will hold until 6:00 P.M. without a guarantee.

9. Have I made three checklists?

The first one includes what needs to be done prior to departure: tickets (especially if time related), visas, shots, planned destination activities, and so on.

The second includes things to close, shut off, or notify before leaving home.

The third includes things to be taken (critical if you're camping). Leave half home (except if you're camping). The greatest hindrances to your vacation are too much luggage, poor planning, and too much luggage.

When traveling with small children, especially in countries where the cuisine is not familiar, carry a jar of peanut butter.

10. What special equipment should I take?

In most countries, U.S. video equipment cannot be played back on local TV sets. Be sure to purchase the correct power adapters to use your battery charger, electric razor, and electric hair dryer before leaving the U.S.

— OTHER QUESTIONS TO CONSIDER —

11. When am I going?

12. Does everyone in the family want to go?

13. How long do I have?

14. Do I want a structured vacation?

15. What have I planned for rainy days?

16. What passports and/or visas do I need?

17. Have I planned for "open" time?

18. **Have I talked to at least three people who have made the trip?**
19. **What are the best buys at our destination?**
20. **Have I left a detailed itinerary with someone back home?**

Lloyd Murray has been a commercial airline pilot for twenty-five years. With his wife, Roma, and three boys, he has had the opportunity to travel about the U.S. and the world. During these thousands of travel days, Lloyd and his family have experienced all types of vacations, from camping to castles, staying in the best, the worst, and everything in between. He and his family reside in St. Louis, Missouri.

— 88 —

Have a Party

The anticipation and planning that bring a group of people together to celebrate, enjoy one another's company, relax, forget their troubles, and just have fun can be an exhilarating experience. Like all good things, the party will take thought and preparation, but when you make it happen, the rewards can be great. The following questions have helped me focus and take action when planning a party. It is my hope that they will do the same for you.

1. **Do I have to have a planned prearranged party?**
   Many exciting, delightful parties have been thrown together at the last minute. Some people enjoy and respond to spontaneity. In our society today most people are extremely busy, and though they would like to be able to come on short notice, they are just unable to do so. You will be able to plan a successful "jiffy" party to the degree that you are instanta-

neously creative and the people you would invite are available at a moment's notice.

2. Which people would it be best to bring together?

The chemistry of personalities, common interests, acquaintances, and needs can explode into fireworks of fun and excitement or bomb into the ashes of boredom and disinterest. Mix and match your guest list thoughtfully and carefully.

3. In what way can I "break the ice" at my party?

Even the most carefully constructed guest list will include some people who are shy, insecure, and unacquainted. Planning a brief noncompetitive activity that will urge your guests to interact as they arrive can create a more relaxed atmosphere.

For example, a few days before the party, ask each guest to provide you with a childhood photo. Mount each photo on a large board to be displayed in a prominent place the day or night of the party. As the guests arrive, direct them to the board and encourage them to try to match the pictures with the persons.

4. Is it necessary to use name tags?

Name tags are generally suggested only for very large parties or when guests are either slightly acquainted or complete strangers. Tags can be used as ice breakers, however. For example, we often preprint name tags in couples (i.e., Mickey Mouse/Minnie Mouse). As the guests arrive, we let them choose a name tag randomly. As others come in, they are to try to find their mated tag and introduce themselves to the person they match. This activity stimulates conversation and helps people become familiar with one another.

In smaller party situations, name tags are unnecessary if the host or hostess can plan to introduce and/or help the guests get to know one another.

If you are having a dinner party, place cards will help people find their seating and will give you an opportunity to situate them according to interests and acquaintance.

5. Will an activity make the party more enjoyable?

This answer depends on the people invited. If all those present are reasonably well acquainted and will have an interest in common, it can be fun to plan an activity followed by food and informal socialization. For example, my husband and I are athletic. For Super Bowl Sunday we often invite our family and friends to participate in a bike ride, a game of volleyball, or a round of tennis or golf in the morning, followed by food and game viewing in the afternoon in our home.

6. **What about a theme for my party?**

Often parties create their own theme by virtue of their nature (i.e., birthdays, dedications/christenings, graduations, engagements, weddings, etc.). Or you can be imaginative and create your own unusual theme.

One year though our theme, Halloween, was predetermined by the holiday itself, our approach to the celebration for our children was completely outside the norm. Our neighborhood decided to have a block party instead of the usual trick or treat. At each house on our street, the parents planned an activity for the children (e.g., bean bag toss, haunted house, pinata, mask creating and painting, etc.). We gained permission from our city police department to block off our street. We began at one end of the block, and as the activity finished, that house closed down, and we all went to the next. We ended at the last house on the block with apple bobbing, music, dancing, food, and informal socialization. All the parents were costumed, too, and pitched in at each home to help with the activity. It was an event we and our children still talk about.

7. **What about music?**

In my opinion, no party is complete without music. It can stimulate action or act as a relaxant. As a stimulant, music can be central to the party with a performance by a talented friend, as a sing-along, or for dancing. Music can be played softly in the background coordinating the theme of your party or just as a panacea for the socialization taking place.

Many parties today, especially weddings, hire disc jockeys to provide and play the guests' favorite tunes. A disc jockey with a broad knowledge of music and sensitivity to people can make your party the most remembered event of the year.

8. How do I decide on the beverages?

Your choices will be determined by the tastes, preferences, and ages of your guests. Punches go a long way, and punch bowls often create interest and stimulate conversation.

The food section of your local community and city newspaper frequently prints new and exciting recipes for punches. They almost always offer seasonal and special occasion punch bowl ideas. Sparkling grape or cider drinks can be used for a festive party toast, and there's nothing quite like the aroma of flavored coffees, fresh ground and brewing, to add the perfect touch to a party's end.

9. How should I decide on the food and how to serve it?

The food can be determined by palate and/or theme. Select with your guests' preferences in mind, and plan to provide variety. You may serve informally, as a buffet, or formally, waiting on individuals at tables. Cooking at tables with hot pots can be an inventive way to allow your guests to serve themselves.

Consider placing a lazy Susan in the center of each table with a selection of foods to be mixed and matched at your guests' preference. Be creative! Surprise your guests with the most novel way you can think of to appease their appetites.

10. Who will be responsible for cleanup?

The most unpleasant part of a party is usually the cleanup. Unfortunately, the host or hostess must be responsible for this part of the party, too. You can enlist the help of party participants and your children, do it all yourself, or hire someone. We have been most fortunate to have people volunteer to help at the end of most parties. Some of our best times have been the day following a very large party when we have been so exhausted we opted to put off the cleanup until the next day. Many times our guests have volunteered and returned to help, and our cleanup has turned into an intimate, extemporaneous "day after" party.

— OTHER QUESTIONS TO CONSIDER —

11. Why do I want to have a party?

12. What kind of party will it be?

13. Where will my party be held?
14. How do I invite the guests?
15. How many guests will I want to invite?
16. Will the guests be expected to dress in a special way?
17. Will a game liven things up?
18. Have I sought information about unusual games?
19. What kind of decorations will make a difference?
20. Should I prepare hors d'oeuvres?

Anne Batty is a former schoolteacher. As coordinator of many children's and adult ministries, activities director of tennis clubs, manager of a fitness center, mother of three sons, and grandmother, she has had countless opportunities to plan parties. A free-lance writer and editorial assistant, she resides in San Clemente, California.

— 89 —

Travel Overseas

When traveling anywhere, especially outside your home country, you should keep several general objectives in mind. First, decide before boarding the airplane that you are going to enjoy the trip whatever happens because many unplanned things will. Second, decide that you will learn from the beauty of other cultures rather than lose the opportunity to grow because you are troubled by variance from what is familiar. Third, decide, in the words of Saint Paul, to "redeem the time" by making the most of every day. And finally, master the following twenty questions to assure a satisfying experience.

1. How should I interpret the official state department cautions?

Take them seriously. That doesn't mean you shouldn't travel when your government suggests not to. I haven't been able to do that. Yet, if your reason for travel is recreation or education, you would do well to pay close attention to advisories. And unless you have a compelling reason not to, abide by them.

2. Can I travel anywhere in the world I want to—no matter what my government thinks?

North Americans can. I have an old American passport that specifically forbids me to travel in Albania and Cuba. I have another with specially stamped permission to do so. Those were stricken by legal action. It is difficult to visit embargoed countries for the simple reason you are not allowed to spend money there. Most people can fulfill their travel urges without running into this problem. But make sure that the items you purchase can be legally brought back home. Not doing so can be terribly expensive.

3. What is the best way to pack?

Lightly. Roll clothing whenever possible to reduce bulk. Keep liquids in plastic bags. (My wife taught me that trick after an expensive shoe polish spill.) I like hand bags with lots of pockets. Yet, a hard case comes in handy with breakables you might purchase en route. So I travel with a convenient hand bag and a small hardside. Then I have a carryon with all my valuables, documents, computer, and camera, and I can travel as long as necessary.

4. What do I do if I encounter beggars in less-developed countries?

I seek local advice from a friend whenever possible. An outsider rarely knows validity of the need. Beggars in some cities are organized by racketeers using maimed or blind children and adults. Locals usually know the score. If in doubt, you rarely go wrong giving an alm to the poor, and you might feel better about it.

5. How can I keep jet lag from ruining my trip?

High-speed travel across multiple time zones slows or

speeds up your biological clock, depending on whether you are traveling east or west. Jet lag occurs when your body arrives before your vitality. Your body clock doesn't move forward or backward like the one on your arm. It takes an average of one day for every hour of time zone change you experience.

You can help yourself by following a few simple rules. First, don't overeat on the day before travel or en route. Second, drink water every time you think about it while on board a plane. Refuse coffee and alcoholic beverages. Third, as soon as you get on board, start eating and sleeping as much as possible on your destination time. If you can't sleep, rest anyway. Fourth, schedule arrival in early evening when possible. Schedule a few hours of sleep at your destination if you arrive in early morning. Then conform to destination sleep and eating times, and keep telling yourself all is normal.

6. Should I make an effort to "go native" in dress, food, and the like?

For the most part, follow your inclinations. Locals know you are not one of them, though they usually will appreciate your effort to identify. And they will understand if your taste in food is different, though they will appreciate your trying and, hopefully, liking one of their favorite dishes. Whatever you do, be yourself. African robes don't fit my personality. But I love African shirts, a middle ground for me. Remember, people want to relate to you, not what you wear or eat.

7. How can I keep from getting sick?

There are six simple rules. First, secure required vaccinations well in advance and a gamma globulin shot a couple of days before departure. Second, take an effective antimalarial drug if going into a malarial area. The Centers for Disease Control in Atlanta is your best source of information on shots and antimalarial drugs. Third, drink only boiled and filtered water unless you are absolutely sure tap water is safe, and you will have eliminated your number one threat to a happy trip. Secure a lightweight filter-purifier from your local travel store. I always carry one. Fourth, don't listen to resident Westerners or missionaries in the area; they are notorious for coming home loaded with parasites. Fifth, eat only peeled or cooked fruits and vegetables, refrain from salads, leave off milk unless you know it is reliably pasteurized, and make sure meat is fully cooked. Sixth, carry along medication for nausea and diarrhea—just in case.

8. What do I do if I become engulfed in a civil crisis or a natural disaster in the country I'm visiting?

When in crisis- or disaster-prone areas, register with your embassy. In times of serious crisis, this can be a major benefit. And if civil disturbance or natural disaster occurs, the paramount rule is to stay inside or get inside if you are away from your accommodations. Your hotel or friend's home is probably as safe a place as you can be. If you hear gunfire, stay away from windows and doors.

9. If I have a host or hostess in the country, should I take a gift or offer to pay for the costs incurred by my visit?

It's always in order to express gratitude. How one does it is the issue. Most non-Western cultures do not follow the "I have received, therefore I owe" concept. Non-Western friends usually are complimented by your acceptance of their invitation, or they wouldn't have invited you. Reflecting that you think they expect something in return can be insulting.

Yet, expressing appreciation is always appropriate. A hostess gift on arrival is a safe option, especially if it is a token gift of something special from your home area. An offer to share the cost of gasoline with your friend when you are touring the countryside can be as normally done as you would at home and appreciated because of the high cost of fuel in most places. And if hired staff at the hotel or elsewhere do a special favor, a monetary gift is in order. Be on guard, however, about tipping at meals. A service charge is usually already added to your bill.

10. What is the most important thing I can do to get the most out of my visit to another country?

Bone up on the culture. If you want to understand what is going on from the time you arrive to the time you leave, you have to know what people are doing and why they are doing it. People like people who seek to understand them and express appreciation for their ways. *Culture* by definition is "the behavior patterns of a society."

You can learn "their ways" by using two easily accessible resources—your local library and people in your community who come from the country to which you are going. Read all you can get your hands on as long as it is prepared by reputable sources. And invite natives of the country who now live in your community to coffee or tea and ask them about their homeland. They will count it a compliment to be asked. You will have a head start on understanding the country to which you are traveling, and you might learn of new contacts who will make your trip the rich experience you want it to be.

— OTHER QUESTIONS TO CONSIDER —

11. Why am I going on a trip out of the country anyway?
12. Is this the best time for the itinerary I've chosen?
13. What about passport, visas, and all those legal things?
14. What kind of clothing and other things will I need?
15. Is it safe to check my luggage rather than carry it on board?
16. What do I do if I get sick?
17. If I want to participate in Christian worship, where do I go?
18. Should I check about insurance—life, health, theft—before I leave?
19. In case of emergency where do I turn?
20. How much should I fear assault or robbery?

Jerry Ballard, Lit.D., has traveled worldwide half of his time during the past fifteen years. Thirteen of those years were as chief executive officer of World Relief Corporation (WRC), the international assistance arm of the National Association of Evangelicals. Since resigning from WRC leadership, Jerry continues to travel worldwide providing advocacy for the poor and training for effective executive leadership. He resides in Wheaton, Illinois.

Rites and Rituals

Make Funeral Arrangements

Few crises can seem more frightful than having to face a death in the family and thus make funeral arrangements. For many families, funeral customs may be prescribed by religious or cultural traditions, and for others, family traditional practices are the norm. Yet there is still a myriad of details to work out and decisions to make for each individual death. These twenty questions are presented to lighten the burden when it is time to make funeral arrangements.

1. **What is a funeral?**

   A funeral is a celebration. We celebrate the fact that a person lived, walked this earth, and touched many people. In most instances, families will arrange services in conjunction with clergy, respecting the religious preference of the deceased. Military or fraternal ceremonies are often held by themselves or combined with religious services at the mortuary chapel, church, or cemetery. In any case, the type of ceremony should be governed by what is most meaningful and satisfying for the surviving family members.

2. **What are the duties of a funeral director?**

   The funeral director (and mortuary staff) arranges for the removal of the deceased from the place of death to the mortuary, fulfills the legal requirements of filing the death certificate with the local health department, and provides for the care of the deceased by embalming or basic sanitation.

   The director consults with the family, clergy, cemetery, transportation firms, newspapers, and florists to carry out the final arrangements as requested. In addition, the director provides mortuary facilities for visitation and funeral services and necessary transportation.

3. How are funeral charges based?

Any mortuary will break down charges according to the following items. *Mortuary service charge*—for the use of the staff and equipment—includes a list of ten to twelve items that may be selected depending on the type of service desired. *Merchandise* may include a casket, burial vault or cremation urn. *Cash advance items* include sales tax on merchandise only, certified copies of death certificates, obituary notices, or any other charge that may be advanced for the family.

4. How do cemeteries charge?

Cemetery charges are based on location of the grave plus opening and closing charges and a one-time charge for perpetual care of the cemetery grounds. For eligible veterans and their families, burial at no charge is available at Veterans Administration cemeteries.

5. Is embalming necessary?

The law requires embalming if the body is transported on any common carrier (i.e., airline or train transportation). Also, embalming is necessary if the body is to be viewed prior to or at the time of the funeral. The purpose of embalming is to delay decomposition and to sanitize the body long enough to carry out the services. The goal is not to preserve the remains as done in ancient Egypt.

6. What about cremation?

Cremation is the process of reducing the body to ash. The body and casket (or cremation container) are placed in an industrial-type furnace and burned three to four hours at temperatures ranging from 1200 to 1600 degrees F. The ashes are then placed in some type of urn.

7. How can I avoid getting involved with the coroner?

Generally, it is the coroner's duty to investigate any unattended death. That means the deceased is not currently being treated by a doctor and includes accidental death, homicide, suicide, or death by infectious disease. The body is normally removed to the coroner's facility where an autopsy may be held before the body is released to a mortuary. The coroner may further conduct a hearing to gather testimony and evidence before issuing the cause of death. Since these procedures are required by most state laws, they cannot be avoided. However, for *natural* death, the attending physician is required to sign the death certificate within fifteen hours, thus the coroner involvement is eliminated.

8. How do I obtain certified copies of the death certificate?
The mortuary staff prepares the death certificate from the vital statistics information given by the family. It is then taken to the attending doctor's office for the cause of death to be entered and signed by the doctor or coroner, as the case may be. The mortuary staff files the document with the local health department to obtain the permit for disposition (burial permit). Certified copies are ordered at this time, and there is normally a seven- to ten-day wait before they are mailed to the next of kin.

9. What about preplanned or preneed funeral arrangements?
More people today are making prearrangements than ever before. It is no different from making a will. A visit to the mortuary office is necessary to record your instructions and sign the legal papers. Several copies of the document are provided to the family, trust officer, or attorney so all interested persons are informed.

10. Isn't giving funeral instructions in my will sufficient?
That definitely is not recommended. Too many times the will is locked in a bank safety deposit box or is not found for days or weeks after the death; and even if available, the burial instructions are very general and incomplete. As our society becomes more complex, greater emphasis is placed on getting legal forms signed and witnessed, which is all accomplished by a preneed funeral agreement at a mortuary. In regard to a will, it is sufficient to state that "instructions for my funeral are on file with _____ Mortuary."

— OTHER QUESTIONS TO CONSIDER —

11. What is the difference between a funeral and a memorial service?

12. What is direct cremation?

13. Under what circumstances is an autopsy necessary?
14. Can I donate my body to science?
15. At what age should children attend a funeral?
16. Is the obituary notice a legal requirement?
17. What burial benefits does the government pay?
18. Who is eligible for burial in veterans' cemeteries and where are they located?
19. Can I prepay funeral expenses?
20. If a funeral is prepaid, what happens if the death occurs out of state?

Joseph A. O'Connor, Jr., has been a California-licensed funeral director for over thirty years. He was a former managing partner of three Cunningham & O'Connor Mortuaries in Los Angeles County. In 1975 he opened O'Connor Laguna Hills Mortuary with his wife, Jane. Their son, Neil O'Connor, is a fourth-generation family member to continue in the family funeral service.

— 91 —

Plan Your Wedding

When starting to plan their weddings, most brides already have an idea of what they want them to be like, but their first questions usually are, "What do I do?" and "Where do I begin?" They want to know how to personally translate their dreams into reality. Checklists, worksheets, and other organizing tools lead brides through any questions until all the details are covered and the necessary decisions are made. That eliminates the frazzled nerves and confusion most often associated with being a bride and planning a wedding, and the result is an organized and relaxed bride!

1. **Where should I begin the wedding planning process?**
   Three decisions must be made immediately: (1) the budget, (2) the ceremony site, and (3) the reception site. All other details of the wedding depend on them. The locations of the wedding and the reception plus the number of guests all hinge on the amount of money budgeted for the wedding.

2. **How do we determine whose responsibility it is to pay for the various wedding expenses?**
   Traditionally, the bride's expenses are stationery, bridal attire, groom's wedding ring, music, flowers (except her bouquet), photographs, bridesmaids' gifts, and reception. The groom's traditional expenses are the marriage license, bride's bouquet, bride's rings, his wedding attire, clergy fees, rehearsal dinner, and honeymoon. Today, though, the budget can be handled in a number of ways: by the bride's parents, by the groom's parents, by both sets of parents, by the parents in conjunction with the bride and groom, or by just the bride and groom.

3. **What do I need to know about the ceremony site?**
   Regardless of where you choose to have your wedding—at a church, in a garden, hotel, or private club—the following information is essential to the planning process: (1) the number of guests it will accommodate; (2) restrictions concerning the music, the use of candles and flowers, and the throwing of rice or birdseed; (3) any guidelines for the photographer, including when and where pictures may be taken; (4) whether the ceremony site has any wedding accessories (arch, candelabra, kneeling bench); (5) any available sound equipment for amplification and for recording the wedding; (6) the dressing areas for the bridal party; and (7) the charges for the use of the facility.

4. **What should I look for in a reception site?**
   First of all, it should be a place that can be easily decorated and the right size for the number of expected guests. It may provide the food, beverages, and the wedding cake as part of a package. It should also have a floor plan that ensures good traffic flow around the serving tables, seating, and entertainment areas. Finally, the fees, estimated cost per

person, payment schedule, and cancellation policies must be clearly stated in the contract you sign.

5. Is it important for us to get premarital counseling?

Yes! Your growing relationship is of primary importance and vital to your future happiness. Getting to know each other better and nurturing your relationship can help you grow in love, trust, understanding, and commitment. Premarital counseling is usually offered by churches or reputable family counseling centers.

6. How large should our guest list be?

Determining the size of the guest list depends on several factors: (1) the amount of the budget, (2) the size of the ceremony and reception sites, and (3) the percentage of invited guests who usually attend (percentages are available in our book). More guests may be invited to the reception when the ceremony is small. Equally divide the number of guests to be invited between families before anyone starts drawing up a list, and give them a deadline for completion. It is always easier to add names later if space is available rather than try to delete names and risk hurt feelings.

7. Should I use a wedding coordinator?

Wedding coordinators are available for whatever part of the wedding you would like them to plan. Their costs vary but usually depend on the amount of time spent planning your wedding. You can usually handle the wedding preliminaries yourself, but a wedding coordinator is especially valuable on the wedding day. A relative, close friend, or church wedding hostess can orchestrate all the details and keep the day running smoothly.

8. What important information should I look for in the contract with the caterer?

Before signing the contract, make sure it specifies what is being served, the number of people serving, the per-person cost, the payment schedule, and a release clause if you need to cancel. If possible, taste samples of the food to be served. Also, find out if the caterer is familiar with the reception site and the facilities to prepare and serve food.

9. **What information do I need to give to the florist?**

You will need the following information when visiting the florist: your wedding gown color and style, fabric swatches of bridal attendants' dresses, colors of mothers' and grand-mothers' dresses, style of wedding, diagrams or pictures of ceremony and reception sites, length of aisle, and any restrictions concerning the use of flowers and candles. The florist can help you stay within your budget by choosing flowers that are in season, by using more greenery, and by controlling the size of arrangements and corsages.

10. **What should I do to avoid having things get too harried or out of control?**

First of all, get organized and stay organized—taking one day at a time. Second, take plenty of time to relax and enjoy each other. Third, stay focused on the essentials of your planning rather than on the total of the details. Remember, the relationships that are being formed (the bridal couple, parents, and future in-laws) are more important than all the planning.

— OTHER QUESTIONS TO CONSIDER —

11. **How soon should I decide on ceremony and reception sites?**

12. **Who should perform the wedding ceremony?**

13. **Is it a good idea to sign up at a gift registry?**

14. **How can I personalize my wedding?**

15. **How soon should I order the bridal gown?**

16. **What should be considered when selecting the brides-maids' dresses and accessories?**

17. **When should I order invitations?**

18. **What kind of music should I select?**

19. **Should I hire a professional photographer?**

20. **Should I have the wedding and reception videotaped?**

Kathleen Goble and **Cecily Shea**, a mother-and-daughter writing team, successfully planned Cecily's wedding and later coauthored *Goble & Shea's Complete Wedding Planner for the Organized and Relaxed Bride* (Questar Publishers, Inc., Sisters, Oregon).

Self-Improvement

92

Improve Your Personal Image

When you develop your image and style, professional or personal, you indicate your status, your level of sophistication, your trustworthiness, many of your hopes and fears, your state of mind, and your educational "club." Whether intended or not, you do reveal your personal image. Style is the totality of your look from hair style to shoes. Consider the points raised by these questions as you improve your image.

1. **What is the first step in determining my personal image and style?**
   Consider these five factors that determine your personal image and style: (1) the response of your skin, eyes, and hair to color; (2) body frame; (3) life-style; (4) budget; and (5) profession.

2. **How often should I evaluate my skin care and makeup application?**
   It should be redone once a year by a trained artist who will keep your life-style, face shape, and new makeup trends in mind when individualizing your image.

3. **Is there a perfect "figure" for a woman?**
   The fashion industry calls it a figure eight shape, and it can be created for every figure by how one dresses. Determine where you gain weight, and minimize contrasting color and pattern lines in that area of your body. Make your shoulders and hips look balanced. A structured belt will create a smaller waistline, and you'll have the illusion of a figure eight frame.

4. **When do I know that my clothes fit properly?**
   Can you sit, kneel, and bend without straining fabric and

seams? Anything worn too tight makes you look heavier. But if there is too much room to spare, you portray a picture of ill health. It also cheapens your look.

5. **How do I complete my personal image after buying an outfit?**
   The final touch is through accessorizing. Women, determine one focal point area. (Draw attention away from any figure flaw.) Accessory colors should be duplicated at least once but not more than four times. Jewelry application begins with earrings and moves to necklace and next to bracelet and watch. Men, coordinate the texture and color of your briefcase, wallet, watch, belt, and shoes.

6. **Are there guidelines when selecting new glasses?**
   Definitely! You must not overlook the eyewear issue. The color of your frames should complement your hair, skin, and eyes. The shape should not repeat your face shape. The size should be in proportion to your face, and your pupil should be in the middle of the lens. If eyewear is necessary, develop a collection of different frames.

7. **How can a businessman use his attire to make a more impressive statement?**
   Quality classic suits are always in style, but use your tie to individualize your look and express your personality. Your tie is your focal point; use its color to make your statement. A tie worn too long looks sloppy. If worn too short, it signifies a lack of success. Tie it so the tip touches the top of your belt buckle. A silk tie is always most impressive.

8. **When is the best time to shop?**
   That is determined by how much you have to invest in your look. Custom clothing doesn't go on sale, but department stores have regular sales where quality can be purchased reasonably. Plan to shop at preview sales. Always check the designer rack. Try on the most expensive looks. Wait four months and copies will be available at less expense.

9. **What do I look for in a quality garment?**
   Quality garments are natural fiber fabrics. All patterns should match at the seams. There must be room in the

seams for the garment to be altered. Look for bound button-holes. The seams should not be frayed at the edges, and the garment must be lined.

10. **How often should I dry-clean my quality garments?**
    Most people have a tendency to overly dry-clean. Hang your clothes outside your closet to get rid of any stale odors. Too much dry cleaning strips fabric of natural oils and shape.

— OTHER QUESTIONS TO CONSIDER —

11. Have I determined the colors suitable for me so that I can coordinate my wardrobe?

12. Do I use style and quality to enhance my professional image?

13. How long has it been since I changed my hair style?

14. Does my hosiery blend in with my clothing?

15. Do my shoes go with my quality wardrobe?

16. Is my look consistent?

17. To create a coordinated, sophisticated image, do I strive not to combine more than two patterns?

18. Is 5 to 10 percent of my yearly budget too much to spend on my wardrobe and image?

19. Do I consider the texture and fabric when buying clothes?

20. Do I have my clothes altered to get a custom fit instead of accepting them "off the rack"?

Sue Cappelen, owner of Designer's Touch, Bakersfield, California, has consulted and trained in the image and fashion field throughout the United States. Her services have been offered on Princess Cruise Lines, for major corporations, hospitals, television series, and individuals. She also works with a well-known southern California plastic surgeon. Her favorite saying is, "Your image is an outward expression of your inside feelings and attitude."

93

Select and Read a Book

More information has been produced in the last thirty years than in the previous five thousand. We live in the information age, and we are all information processors. The secret of processing information is narrowing your field to what is relevant to your life, that is, making careful choices about what information merits your time and attention. Below are twenty questions to ask before, during, and after you read a book.

1. How much time should I invest in this book?

Should I ravage, scan, read, or study this book?

- Ravage. Allow about ten minutes to examine the table of contents, read the promotional copy on the dust cover, and thumb through the chapters.
- Scan. Allow about one hour to rapidly turn the pages and dip into occasional points of interest.
- Read. Determine the type of material to be read, such as light novel or technical. Time yourself as you read the first ten pages. Estimate how long it will take you to read the entire book at this same speed, and pace yourself to meet this goal.
- Study. After reading the book, return to significant portions. Underline and interact with the author by making notes in a journal. Frequently reflect on your notes, and share your insights with interested friends.

2. How can I read so that I have maximum retention of information?

You can answer this question by asking others. Where can I read with as little distraction as possible?

What instrumental, not vocal, music can I play softly in the background? (Music opens the right hemisphere of the brain and increases your capacity to absorb information.)

What overview do I get from reading the table of contents?

How can I visualize the information presented? (For most people it is easier to remember a picture than to recall abstract thoughts.)

What response should I write in the margin (only if I own the book) or in a journal?

Why should I accept the fact that all information is interpretation? (This idea will free you to understand things in a way that works for you.)

3. **With whom will I try to share the lessons of this book?**
Select one person before starting. Note others as they come to mind as you read. This personal focus will greatly increase your retention of the information.

4. **Of what valuable information do the things I've underlined remind me?**
Learning means making connections. Knowledge consists of two parts: What you know that you know, and what you know that you do not know. Only as you relate what you know to what you do not know will learning take place.

5. **What terms do I need to understand better?**
One major hindrance to learning is pride that keeps us from admitting that we do not know something. Another hindrance is laziness that prevents us from taking the time to look up the meaning of new or obscure terms.

6. **What kind of questions should I ask to uplift my spirit?**
Don't ask, "What's wrong with this book?" Don't ask questions that can be answered with yes or no.

7. **Will this book help me achieve my long-term goals?**

8. **Will this book help me achieve my short-term goals?**

9. **Will *not* reading this book affect my life?**

10. **Can I use the information in this book to improve the quality of my life and the lives of others?**

— OTHER QUESTIONS TO CONSIDER —

11. **What is the most significant lesson in this book for me?**

12. **What is the author's purpose?**

13. What do I need to underline so that I will remember it?

14. Will this book help me improve my roles in life?

15. On a scale of ten (with one being low and ten being high), how important is it for me to read this book?

16. On a scale of ten (with one being low and ten being high), how urgent is it for me to read this book?

17. What is missing from this book?

18. How would I change this book to improve it?

19. What questions would I like to ask the author?

20. If I knew that I would be dead in six months, why would reading this book be a good use of my time?

Archie Parrish, D.Min., is founder and president of Serve International, Atlanta, Georgia. Archie is a firm believer in the maxim that all readers are not necessarily leaders, but all leaders are readers.

Skills

94

Give a Sermon, Speech, or Presentation

If you are one of those people who is comfortable in front of others, that's great! You'll find this list of questions will help you organize and prepare more effectively. However, if you are like most people—a bit nervous about speaking before a group—I've created this list especially with you in mind. Learn to work through the questions and you'll find yourself becoming much more confident and comfortable the next time someone says, "Could you say a few words?"

1. Do I care about what I'm saying?
You know what makes a good movie? EMOTION—a love story that touches your heart, a tragedy that causes you to cry, a comedy that creates genuine laughter. Bad acting is really just false emotions. Evaluate your idea: Can you *feel* anything about your topic? Does it get you excited? Does it make you weep? If not, start over.

2. How should I introduce my presentation?
Never begin with an apology or a lengthy explanation. Tell a story or a joke that introduces your idea. Getting your talk started properly will grab the audience's attention and build your confidence.

3. How do I make my speech come alive?
Walt Disney once said in every movie he tried to do two things: make people laugh, and make people cry. Follow Walt's example. Look for stories (from books, from your life, from today's paper) that illustrate your point.

4. How should I end my speech?
Like a boxer, try to end it all with a haymaker. Never just say, "Thank you." Save your best illustration for the end, and let

them walk away pondering it. Many people find it helpful to write out, word for word, their introduction and conclusion. That way they know *exactly* how to begin and end.

5. What things will most improve my presentation?
Preparation and practice. Spend adequate time preparing what you want to say, then practice it until you need only an outline with a few notes as reminders. (It always comes out different from the way it sounded in your head.) Practice in front of a mirror, with friends, with a tape recorder, or in an empty church, but don't get caught trying to give it for the first time in front of a big group of people.

6. How good is my verbal presentation?
Remember MacGregor's prescription: "Always check the five *P*'s."

- Pitch. How high or low you speak reveals your emotional tone. For example, I can change my pitch when I say yes to sound angry, loving, bored, or excited. (By the way, if you want to sound emotional, *drop* your pitch.)
- Pace. Try speeding up or slowing down at intervals so you don't lull them to sleep. Change commands attention!
- Pause. Stop and be silent once or twice. It allows time to reflect, and it brings attention back to you.
- Power. Yell once or twice. Whisper once or twice. Change commands attention.
- Pepper. Learn to use vibrant, descriptive words. Don't say, "I drove my car," say, "I zipped along in my red '57 Chevy."

7. Do I have to be funny?
Unless you're paid to be a stand-up comic, don't tell jokes. Instead, let the humor flow out of the stories you tell. That kind of gentle humor creates a rapport with the audience.

8. What if I have to answer questions afterward?
Ask yourself, What questions might they ask me? Have a ready response. Treat questions with respect: look at people while they're asking, listen to the entire question, and repeat it so that everyone can hear it. Take your time formulating

your response, but be brief in answering. Be willing to admit "I don't know" when you don't.

9. What if I'm asked to speak impromptu?

Try radio commentator Paul Harvey's idea. Begin by saying, "There are three things that come to mind..." As you're talking about the first point, try to think of a second point, and so on.

10. How can I build my credibility?

Credibility stems from the impression you leave with your audience. Know what you're going to say, practice it, and work on looking confident when you first go up to speak. If you come across as personal and meaningful, you'll be credible.

— OTHER QUESTIONS TO CONSIDER —

11. What do I want to say?

12. What do they need to hear?

13. Are my thoughts organized?

14. How do I move from one point to another?

15. How good is my nonverbal communication?

16. Should I use a visual aid?

17. Do I need to do anything special in preparing a Bible talk?

18. What will help people remember my talk?

19. How can I really get to these people with my message?

20. Will practicing and believing in my presentation help me overcome my nervousness?

Jerry "Chip" MacGregor, Ph.D., is associate vice president of Trinity Western University in Vancouver, British Columbia, Canada. Long associated with Masterplanning Group, Chip is a well-known speaker in churches and conferences, and he has taught the principles of effective speaking in seminaries across Canada, the U.S., and Asia.

95

Organize Your Office, Home, and Time

Disorganization in our offices, homes, and schedules can play havoc with our lives. Getting organized physically, emotionally, and spiritually will add quality, meaning, and purpose to our everyday living.

1. Why are so many people struggling with disorganization?
There are two reasons. First, very few people have been trained in how to manage their paperwork or kitchens or closets. Organization is a skill and can be learned. Most people feel they are disorganized because their parents were or their grandparents were. But actually they are disorganized simply because they have not been trained. Second, we simply have too much stuff, too much paperwork, too many clothes or dishes. We are saturated with abundance, and we have lost the ability to maintain our possessions.

2. After I organize a drawer, why does it look good only a day?
Most people don't realize that they have actually rearranged, straightened, neatened, or cleaned; they have not reorganized.

3. What's the difference?
Most people instinctively know to remove all the articles from a drawer and group them. They usually then eliminate what they don't need. They stand back, look at all the articles left that are neatly grouped, and say to themselves, "That's the way I want my drawer to look." Then they put it all back in the drawer. The step they forgot was to put the articles in containers and then place the containers in the drawer. Take a look at your knife, fork, and spoon drawer.

Your utensils are grouped and contained. Use that same concept to organize your tools, toiletries, paperwork and files.

4. **How can I stay focused and finish my organizational tasks?**
Many people see the whole job, and it becomes too overwhelming. Break each room into small bite-sized steps, and spend only thirty minutes to an hour on each step. Also be sure to disconnect the phone.

5. **How will I know when I'm organized?**
Organization is having a place for everything and using containers that hold only one type of article or one subject.

6. **Can you tell me the steps to getting organized?**
Let's say you are organizing a desk drawer:
   1. Remove all items.
   2. Group as you remove the items.
   3. Eliminate what you don't need.
   4. Contain the items by using a drawer tray divider.
   5. Assign the container a place in the drawer.

7. **What do I do with all those loose pieces of paper on my desk?**
Using the container principle, you use letter-tray stackables and organize your papers according to the action you are going to take on them (i.e., to do, to boss, to call, to secretary, to delegate, to copy, to spouse, etc.). The stackables are for papers you will address in the next five days. Papers that will take longer should go in a file in an action drawer.

8. **What is a preferred time management trick?**
I continually use the philosophy of worst first. Whenever I have several jobs to do, I always pick the worst first. Then I reward myself with something I enjoy. I am motivated all through the day, and I also get through the worst so I can enjoy the rest of my day.

9. **Is there ever a time that you don't do worst first?**
Yes, first thing in the morning, I do what I love the most. That gives me energy to start my day. I eat, have coffee, read, and pray. That way my morning is off to a great beginning.

10. **What is the most important tip you can offer that will give me time and greatly enhance my quality of life?**
Keep your family life balanced with your work life. Remember, if it's not working at home, it will eventually fall apart at work. Make it a rule to take off one whole day every seven days. This fantastic time management trick will literally save you energy, time, and money. One day off totally refreshes you for the following week, increasing energy and productivity as well as enhancing your family life.

— OTHER QUESTIONS TO CONSIDER —

11. **Am I sentimental about my possessions, or am I addicted to possessing *things*?**

12. **Have I pared down my possessions as an efficient step in getting organized?**

13. **Do I have a file cabinet to help me manage my paperwork?**

14. **Do I have a planner notebook I can use to organize my time?**

15. **How can I use a planner notebook to fit my life-style instead of making my life fit its style?**

16. **Have I determined my peak energy time so that I can do my most important projects then?**

17. **Do I plan my route when I run errands?**

18. **Have I compiled a list of professional and personal items I need to take with me when I travel?**

19. **Am I eating balanced meals and avoiding alcohol so that I can work efficiently?**

20. **Am I getting exercise so I'll have more energy?**

Sue McMillin, president of With Time to Spare, Washington, D.C., has demonstrated to thousands that being organized adds time to their schedule, space to their environment, and peace of mind to their daily living. Nationally and internationally, Miss McMillin has helped organizations declutter their offices. She has worked with many governmental agencies including the Department of the Navy, the Department of Agriculture, the Internal Revenue Service, and the Environmental Protection Agency.

— 96 —

Write a Book

Before you begin to write, determine the extent of your editorial project. Do you want to leave posterity a record of your life? Do you want to entertain with comedy, chronicle history, inspire with fiction, write a how-to-do-it book, or set forth a collection of epigrams, maxims, poems, and aphorisms? Once your goal is determined, immerse yourself in books with similar goals and observe what worked and what didn't. An outline of your book will help you immensely at the start. Then consider these questions.

1. **What are my tools?**

   Great writing can be accomplished with pad and pencil, but you can help yourself greatly by learning to type. Use only clean dark black ribbon on typewriter or computer printer, only 8½-x-11-inch white paper stock, and only pica type (not fancy, glitzy italic fonts that are difficult for an editor to read). Always double space your material. Do not attempt to bind the manuscript in any way. Send the numbered pages loose in an envelope or a box.

2. **How do I find a publisher?**

   Before spending weeks, months, and even years writing your book, sell it first by presenting a proposal to a publisher. Writers of fiction are excused from the query because often they have to write the entire story before a publisher can understand the book. They must realize that many publishers buy only one in five thousand unsolicited manuscripts they receive. For an article, you usually need only a one-page letter presenting the topic about which you want to write. For a nonfiction book, you need more: a statement showing the scope and purpose of the book, a table of contents including several sentences after each suggested chapter title telling the editor the thrust and theme of that chapter, and a brief paragraph revealing your profession, your education, and your experience.

3. How am I paid?

A publisher will issue a contract to a writer with a good salable idea. The contract shows the percentage of royalties (10 to 15 percent of retail and higher for writers with a track record) and who holds the copyright. The publisher might issue an advance of several thousand dollars if he or she eagerly wants the book, but beginning writers should not expect an advance. The contract sets forth rules of subsidiary rights, pegs a deadline for the finished manuscript, and indicates date of release. You will be asked to read the proofs to help the copy editor catch all errors and verify footnotes.

4. Should I hire a collaborator?

If you lack technical knowledge about writing, you might want to ask a writer to assist you in the preparation of the manuscript. You can (1) pay a writer or (2) share the proceeds from sales. Writers can be egocentric and undiplomatic, so be careful. Read what that writer has written and see if you like the style.

5. How do I carry out my research?

Research provides precise facts—weights, measures, numbers, costs, procedures, quotes, and accurate facts related to the people, places, and things in your book. They are extremely important. False, inaccurate information can lead to embarrassment and worse—lawsuits. Good research gives your writing authority and helps to establish you as a careful writer. Become a good reader, haunt libraries, talk to knowledgeable people, write letters, purchase cassette tapes, and ask friends to be alert for information on your subjects.

6. How do I copyright what I write?

Copyright means an author's ownership of the work and the right to control and profit by its printing, reproduction, or use in any other medium. To register your material, write to Register of Copyrights, Library of Congress, Washington, D.C. 20557. Mention that you are requesting forms to fill out to copyright a book manuscript. The cost will be $10. Since January 1, 1978, the law provides a term lasting the life of the author plus fifty years after the author's death.

7. Can I use copyrighted material in my book?

Yes, provided you give credit. Quote up to, say, one hundred words and give credit. But if you use much beyond that, it's a good idea to give credit *and* write to the publisher of the material and request permission. It is usually readily granted. Not giving credit to material written by someone else is immoral, illegal, and unprofessional. Using the writing of other authors can enhance your work. Just give credit to writer and publisher.

8. What is fair use?

Copyright laws allow the limited use of others' works for research, teaching, news reporting, criticism, and similar purposes. This permission is called fair use, but the laws never define that term. Instead, they list factors to consider, including the purpose and character of the use (e.g., for-profit vs. teaching), the nature of the work (e.g., a science text vs. a poem), the amount and substantiality of the use, and its effect on the market for the work.

9. What is work made for hire?

The creator of a piece of writing generally owns the copyright. There is an exception, however, for a work made for hire. The party who commissions and pays for the work, rather than the actual creator, owns the copyright.

10. How do I develop a pleasing style?

You might not be able to write like Charles Dickens or present your material like James A. Michener, but you can add reader appeal in several ways. First, be clear without being condescending. Second, use appropriate vocabulary. Get a thesaurus and/or a dictionary of synonyms and antonyms to add spice to your sentences. Third, spend less time watching television and more time associating with literate, articulate people. Don't be embarrassed to ask the meaning of new words. Fourth, avoid long, complicated sentences. Fifth, keep paragraphs well focused, conveying a major unit of the subject matter. Sixth, be lean on punctuation.

— OTHER QUESTIONS TO CONSIDER —

11. What new information do I have to offer?
12. Could I be a ghost writer?
13. What writer should I emulate?
14. How do I illustrate my book?
15. How do I promote my book?
16. Should I use a literary agent?
17. How long should my book be?
18. Should I grant permission to use my work?
19. Can I use portions of my book in articles?
20. Can I deduct my expenses for income tax purposes?

Norman B. Rohrer has been a professional writer since 1953. He has written twenty-three books and more than one thousand articles and news features. He is founder of the Christian Writers Guild. He has conducted "Write to Be Read" workshops on three continents and was for fourteen years executive secretary of the Evangelical Press Association.

Volunteering

Choose Where to Volunteer

Expressing your enduring passions and talent through working as a volunteer can be a rewarding complement to your full-time vocation. If you really know yourself and you choose self-consistent roles, you will be motivated, effective, and fulfilled in your work, and likely to stay with your jobs long-term.

1. **Are there some organizations that would let me sample a variety of volunteer roles over a period of several weeks?**
   If you want to see if a hat or coat fits, try it on. Through several hours of work in each of four or five roles, you can get some idea about what would be the best fit.

2. **How much of my time and energy can I give without compromising other important areas of my life?**
   A life of wholeness or integrity includes balanced expression in each of life's major areas—spiritual, relational, sexual, vocational, recreational, and physical. Investing yourself in volunteer work need not annihilate other important areas of expression.

3. **Why do I want to do volunteer work?**
   What really moves you to want to do volunteer work, and how can the best of your motives be harnessed in serving others? Are you motivated by a desire to affect the lives of others or to see results? Do you need adventure or challenge? Do you feel a need for acceptance and approval? Do you need recognition, prestige, respect, or fame? Are you seeking a feeling of belonging? Are you fulfilling a requirement of a parent or your church or school? None of these are inherently wrong, but even the apparently lowly roles have

meaning when they are done, in part, as an expression of love for and gratitude to God.

4. **Which of my talents and interests are not being expressed in my full-time occupation?**
   No occupation can provide opportunity for adequate expression of all your abilities and interests. Volunteer work, if committed to thoughtfully, can be a refreshing complement and contrast to your full-time work.

5. **How, when, and where have I already contributed significantly to the lives of others?**
   What compliments or other feedback have you gotten from others that would suggest you've made a difference in their lives? How would their lives be different if you hadn't been around? What you affirm in yourself through your answers to these questions may be a guide to future service.

6. **Is there anything in my background that would stand in the way of effectively participating in volunteer work?**
   Sometimes people are encumbered by fear or hurt from the past that needs to be resolved before they can freely give to others. Some are motivated out of guilt, and although they may serve well, they can't really be free to enjoy what they are doing and often become burdened with anger. By getting closure or resolution of issues past, one can be in a much stronger position to reach out to others. At the same time, helping others in certain roles may give a person additional leverage for breaking free from the past. For example, people who have been victims may tend to try to "rescue" other victims and do more than their part on others' behalf. The helping persons could serve in a role that does not include counseling other victims until closure in their own lives has been accomplished.

7. **Is there anything about me that would promote my getting into a volunteer role that I'm not suited for?**
   If you have difficulty saying no to people, you may tend to make choices on the basis of what would please others rather than on the basis of who you are—your talents, interests, and motivational themes (values and beliefs that you would like to affect your life). It wouldn't hurt to have a

trusted friend or two with whom you consult before saying yes to requests for help, or at least to say, "I'll sleep on it before making a decision." Occasionally, people looking for warm bodies to join their cause, though well-meaning, are just a tad on the manipulative side.

8. **Can I make a change in my life or schedule that will free up some time I can give to others?**
   Before you think of things that you can eliminate from your schedule, consider adding a couple. For example, if they are not already a part of your life, set aside time each day to pray and to read from and reflect on the Bible, and to get exercise (aerobic exercise and strength training). Interestingly, people who regularly set aside unhurried time for these expressions seem to find _more_ time and energy for things.

9. **What is the biggest waste of time in my weekly schedule?**
   Maybe there is a time-consuming thing in your life that is like the (recently proved untrue) word about chicken soup: "It won't do you any good, but it won't do you any harm, either." Is there some chicken soup activity that you could cut back on or jettison to free up time for reaching out to others?

10. **What is my _greatest_ personal resource, and how can that best be expressed in relating to the needs of the community?**
    Volunteer work is at its best when it does not compromise other important areas of life, is not merely what is left over after we've spent most of our time and energy on meeting our own needs, and is a self-consistent expression of the talents and enduring passions that God has instilled in us.

— OTHER QUESTIONS TO CONSIDER —

11. **Has one particular need in others been on my heart a long time?**

12. **Of the tasks and jobs I have experienced, which have been the most interesting to me?**

13. **What abilities or aptitudes have I demonstrated over the years?**

14. Do I have a hidden talent that could be revealed through trying something new?

15. Which community service organizations and churches in my area could use my help?

16. What are the needs of people in my community?

17. How have I benefited from others giving themselves to me?

18. What are the three most meaningful experiences in my life?

19. If, at the end of my life, I could look back and say that I had made a lasting difference in the world, what would I want my contribution to be?

20. Are there some needs within arm's reach that I can relate to?

Bill White, Ph.D., develops resources and programs for bringing committed people into contact with community service organizations that depend on the availability of qualified volunteers. Helping people find the best way to express their abilities and passions has been a major emphasis in his roles as teacher, trainer, and consultant over the past twenty-five years. He resides in Pittsburgh, Pennsylvania.

— 98 —

Visit a Prisoner

The following questions have been adapted from How to Establish a Jail and Prison Ministry *by Duane Pederson (Nashville: Thomas Nelson Publishers, 1979).* Ministry in Action: Jail and Prison—A Basic Training Guide, *printed in 1991, incorporates Duane's book with additional material, published by the Assemblies of God Chaplaincy Department.*

1. What are my motives in wanting to visit prisoners?

Ask yourself these questions:

- Do I have a strong desire and willingness to love the unloved and often the unlovely?
- Can I honestly accept people who are different from me in background and culture?
- Do I have prejudices against prisoners, and if so, can I deal with them?
- Am I willing to continue to visit, even in the face of rejection, if I believe prisoners are being helped?
- Do I truly believe the inner direction of a person's life can change—even a habitual criminal or drug addict?
- Am I on an ego trip, seeking self-satisfaction or the praise of people, or are my efforts dedicated to the betterment of the prisoners?
- Am I ready to commit myself for a year or more to a one- or two-hour weekly visit or other time constraint?

2. Why should I be concerned about prisoners?

Prisoners need to know someone cares. All too often, families of prisoners ignore or forsake them when they are incarcerated, thus perhaps paving the way for a basically good person who made some wrong choices to become a hardened criminal. And even hardened criminals may respond positively to genuine concern and caring. Relatively few people become involved in prison visitation; thus, an extremely critical need is unfulfilled.

3. Am I compassionate enough to see past the crime into the heart?

Nonjudgmental love and compassion can break through barriers nothing else can touch. However, for the safety of society, incarceration is necessary. Under like circumstances—rejection or abuse by parents, lack of education, a miserable childhood, previous time in jail—would we have done better?

4. What steps may I take to prepare myself for jail and prison visitation?

Talk with others involved in prison visitation. Attend prison seminars and enroll in courses dealing with people skills and interpersonal communications.

5. **Where may I find information and training programs for volunteers?**

Information on current seminars may be available at your local library or public information office. Community colleges and night schools offer helpful courses. The easiest way to get started is to work with an experienced person as a member of a team.

6. **How can I relate to prisoners?**

Be natural. Introduce yourself by your first name only as a friend. Avoid titles. Recognize the value of a positive rather than a negative approach, especially to prisoners already saturated with negatives. Look for areas of common interest. You may feel uneasy at first, but focus on your purpose in being there—look for good in each person.

7. **What types of responses may I expect from inmates?**

Many will respond positively when approached with understanding and genuine concern. Trust is usually established, however, only after you have consistently shown that your life and continuing concern for them match your words. Even then, many may talk very little. Some will even curse you and want nothing to do with you at all. Some will try to con you into doing little favors or test you by harassing you for a while; you lose their respect if you do the favors, and the entire relationship if you get uptight. Some may feign friendship to gain favors, such as early release. The volunteer needs to observe the inmate over a period of time and move on to others if no positive responses are evident.

8. **What are the first things to consider in starting this type of visitation?**

You must keep in mind at all times that by going to a penal institution, you are in "somebody else's house." It is imperative you know and adhere strictly to all rules; security is crucial. Confer with the staff before doing anything, and do nothing without approval; they need your help, not additional problems! Inflexible rules include taking nothing in or out of the facility, not even a letter or stamp, without the institution's express approval. Do not assume anything, however trifling it may seem.

9. **What types of people are confined, and why?**
Men, women, and children are in the various types of institutions. A million may be confined in the U.S. at any one time, and several million pass through jails in the course of a year. Most are in prison for robbery, burglary, murder, and drug offenses. Many children are abused or rejected by parents and on the streets; they are often put in detention centers because no other place is found for them, even many who have committed no crime. For large numbers of people in trouble, few alternatives to imprisonment exist in our nation, which has the highest ratio of inmates to total citizens of any democratic country.

10. **What is the difference between a prison and a jail?**
Prison inmates have been tried and convicted of crimes; those in jail may be awaiting trial. The jail population is much more transient, and few jails have facilities for counseling or rehabilitation. A prison is under the jurisdiction of either federal or state government, but the jail holds people accused under federal, state, county, and/or city laws. A jail holds inmates from two days to a year. Conditions are usually worse than prisons, with more crowding, virtually no privacy, blaring noise, and enforced boredom—a volunteer must be flexible and adjust to these difficult conditions.

— OTHER QUESTIONS TO CONSIDER —

11. **Have I considered the effect on my emotions in dealing with sensitive issues, such as a prisoner's confession to me?**

12. **What opportunities exist at other confinement institutions?**

13. **How can I especially help the prisoner improve self-image?**

14. **Am I willing to help released inmates adjust to life in the world again?**

15. **Am I, as a volunteer, willing to view the staff as the leaders?**

16. **Have I considered preventive work with young people on the street to encourage a positive life-style?**

17. Have I considered what I can do on the "outside" to help those within and, if permitted, their families?

18. Have I determined the local need for prison volunteers?

19. Have I come to terms with the reality that I face more risk *outside* the prison than inside?

20. Is my heart at peace with my decision to engage in prison visitation?

Duane Pederson has ministered for twenty-eight years, volunteering in prisons, jails, and juvenile halls, along with an active ministry among gang members, ex-convicts, runaways, and the homeless. Duane is an ordained priest in the Eastern Orthodox Church. He resides in Hollywood, California.

— 99 —

Work with High Schoolers

It has been said that the fever of young people keeps the world at its normal temperature. Young people, in particular high schoolers, are some of the most strategic individuals we can work with. They are worth our investment of time, and many organizations and programs will give you the opportunity to volunteer your time and talents to work with young people. The following twenty questions will help you choose the best place to volunteer.

1. **What goals has the organization set in the work with young people for the next twelve months?**
   By looking at an organization's goals, you will be able to discern how well the leaders plan ahead and if they are able

to set goals consistent with their purposes. Goals will help you determine what may be expected of you as a volunteer.

2. **What skills do I need to work with young people in this program?**
Above everything else, working with young people requires authenticity and transparency. Kids respond to honest personalities. However, ask what specific skills may be needed for this role and whether this role fits your strengths and desires.

3. **Have I discussed this volunteer role with my immediate family?**
Working with young people takes time at unique hours of the day (e.g., evenings and weekends). Has your immediate family given you its blessing and released you time-wise to fulfill this role? As a family, you need to be committed together to young people.

4. **What training will this organization provide for me to fulfill my role?**
Every organization should provide training in the overall philosophy of work that it is carrying out and specific training that will help you in your role. Ask when the training takes place and how much time it will involve.

5. **What is the minimum length of time that this organization is asking me to commit for this particular volunteer role?**
How long will this organization need your help? Also, will there be a time within two to six months after you begin your role to review how things are going and to make sure both sides are satisfied with the relationship?

6. **How often will I be able to interact with the person I report to?**
You need a good working relationship with someone who can give you direction and counsel and would be readily available to talk with. Without such a person, you could begin to feel quite isolated.

7. **What type of budget will I have available to fulfill my role?**
There may be expenses involved with your role, such as providing materials for students. Find out in advance how all

financial responsibilities in your work will be handled, what money is available, etc. Talk through some of the expenses you may have with your supervisor. Determine what financial responsibilities you need to assume.

8. Is this team my kind of people?
Team up with people you feel relatively comfortable with. Do you share the same interests and values? Could particular people on this team be good friends?

9. What is this organization's reputation in the community?
What is its credibility in the community? How is it viewed from your perspective? Will you receive the support from the community that you need if you are volunteering with this group?

10. Can I work with this organization, even though there are some things I may not agree with or like?
It is not likely that you can find any organization that you will agree with 100 percent or find that you like everything about. However, the needs of young people are more important than the perfect working environment. Select the group that you feel most comfortable with, then through your influence, perhaps you can bring positive change over a period of time to weak areas of the organization.

— OTHER QUESTIONS TO CONSIDER —

11. What are the vision and the purpose of this high-school organization?

12. What does this organization believe doctrinally or morally and ethically?

13. What are this organization's distinctive principles and philosophy in working with young people?

14. What positions are available for volunteer help?

15. Why am I needed?

16. What role am I to fulfill?

17. How many hours are required weekly to fulfill the responsibilities of this role?

18. What is this organization's commitment to prayer (if it is a Christian organization or ministry)?

19. What is the "feel" of the staff team of this organization?

20. What was my first impression of this youth organization or program?

Chuck Klein is the national director of Student Venture, the high-school outreach of Campus Crusade for Christ, located in San Diego, California. Since 1969, Chuck has been working with high-school students, intensively involved in their lives.

Index of Key Words

Bobb Biehl is the president of Masterplanning Group International, a consulting firm founded in 1976 that specializes in personal and organizational development.

Since 1976 Biehl's team has consulted with over a hundred clients. Approximately one third are large and growing churches, one third are not-for-profit organizations, and one third are for-profit corporations.

Masterplanning Group makes available over thirty-five proven resources (books, tapes, workbooks) as well as associates who can make on-site consultations.

Bobb Biehl, *President*
Masterplanning Group International
Box 6128
Laguna Niguel, California 92607

1-800-443-1976